CREATIVE KNITTING

For my grandmother
Kato Yamashiro
a beloved inspiration

Kaori O'Connor
CREATIVE KNITTING

BLOOMSBURY

First published in Great Britain 1987
Copyright © 1987 by Kaori O'Connor

Bloomsbury Publishing Ltd, 4 Bloomsbury Place, London WC1A 2QA

British Library Cataloguing in Publication Data
O'Connor, Kaori
Creative knitting.
1. Knitting – Patterns
I. Title
746.43′2041   TT820

ISBN 0-7475-0096-7

Designed by Julian Holland
Phototypeset by Rowland Phototypesetting Ltd, Bury St Edmunds, Suffolk
Printed in Italy

Contents

Introduction

I had a horrifying insight into what it must be like to suffer from dyslexia the first time I had to read a knitting pattern. This happened when I was working on *Vogue* in London, when it would occasionally fall to my unhappy lot to check that the typed instructions for the magazine's knitting features matched the printed instructions sent back from the typesetters. This involved one person reading the printed sheets aloud, while a second person read from the typed original. Though we chorused 'K2, P2, sl.1, K1, psso' and so on with great gusto, neither of us had any idea of what we were saying or whether the pattern was correct, as neither of us could knit. These episodes always left me with splitting headaches and a profound mistrust of knitting. I frequently thought of the devilish Madame Defarge, the most infamous knitter in English literature, whose knitting contained a secret code that sent Sydney Carton and many others to the guillotine in *A Tale of Two Cities*. Charles Dickens, I reflected, had got knitting absolutely right.

All this changed overnight when one of the men in a stationer's around the corner from Vogue House turned up wearing the most splendid sweater I had ever seen – a riot of diamond bands, Trees of Life, lozenges and crosses – in a rainbow of exhilarating colours. What heaven! It was, of course, a hand-knitted Fair Isle. Not in his first youth and rather embarrassed by my enthusiasm, all the poor man was willing or able to volunteer about this delicious creation was that it had been knitted for him by his mother, 'after the War'. It was difficult to believe that this wonderful thing had anything to do with the knitting patterns I had been grappling with upstairs. Strictly speaking it didn't, since this was before the great Fair Isle revival, and tortuously textured knits – Arans in particular – were then all the rage. When I discovered that Fair Isles like the one I had seen were nowhere to be found ready-made at any price, I was presented with the first good reason I'd ever had to take an interest in knitting.

I haunted the thrift shops, rifling through trays of old knitting patterns. I waded through jumble sales in search of old jumpers and knitting books, begged old patterns off friends, and generally succumbed to a positive mania for Fair Isle knitting. I must have overdone it, because today it takes a really exceptional Fair Isle – like *Belvedere* – to arouse even the slightest flicker of interest in me. The only legacy of my Fair Isle period is my enduring passion for Shetland 2-ply wool, which is the yarn for which colour knitting might have been invented. Light and supple, marvellously warm for its weight, it takes to colour like a fish to water, comes in a wonderful range of shades, and is very hardwearing, yet soft enough to be a joy to knit with. Best of all, it holds its shape beautifully – both after it has been knitted up, and while it is being knitted; so much so that if you find you have to undo a few rows – an all-too-common occurrence in colour knitting – the loops stand up beautifully, and you very rarely drop a stitch.

As my taste for Fair Isles flagged, my enthusiasm for Shetland yarn led me to find out what I could about colour knitting in other parts of the world, and at other periods in history. What I discovered is that handknitting and the ideal royal bride have one striking thing in common; both have a great future, and not much of a past. At least, in the case of handknitting, not much of a past that can be documented with any certainty. The oldest surviving examples of knitting, now in the collection of Yale University, are three woollen fragments dated to AD 256, which were found at Dura-Europos in present-day Syria. The use to which the textiles were put has not been determined, but two of the fragments are worked in a K3 P2 rib with horizontal stripes of colour, while the third is worked in an elaborate design, indicating that by the third century AD knitting was already a highly developed art in that part of the world. Beyond that, absolutely nothing is known about very early knitting, but the prevailing theory is that what we call *colour knitting* – stranded colour knitting in stocking stitch or crossed stocking stitch – originated in the East, probably in Eastern Central Asia, where it was developed as a means of making sturdy stockings that would more accurately be described as 'knitted boots'. From there the technique was carried westwards by land and sea through the Middle East and the Arabian peninsula to Coptic Egypt, North Africa and finally to Western Europe. At exactly what stage the technique was adapted to fibres other than wool and garments other than boots or stockings is unknown, but intricate colour knitting in silk was well established in Arabia by the seventh century AD, a full thousand years before silk colour knitting reached its height in Europe in the early eighteenth century. As for the arrival of colour knitting on our own fair shores, you may believe, as I do not, that it is a legacy of the Spanish Armada. As there is not a shred of proof either way, it seems best to leave the past to reveal itself in its own time and concentrate on enjoying colour knitting in the present. For the world is full of wonderful patterns, just begging to be knitted up and enjoyed.

In knitting, as with all things, variety is the spice of life, and I am always amazed at how little we tend to know about knitting in other countries. A little intrepid investigation along these lines will add immeasurably to the holiday enjoyment of the ardent knitter. On my travels, I always make it a point to seek out the clicking of knitting needles – and sometimes not even needles, as in Chichicastenango and San Francisco El Alto in the highlands of Guatemala, where I watched the Indians using lengths of straightened-out coathanger wire to knit patterns that took on an incandescent brightness in the cold, clear air. Hungary is another rich field for discovery. Apart from gipsy violins and sublime food, Hungary boasts many bookshops where lavishly illustrated books on folk art, crafts and knitting are offered at extremely affordable prices. In the knitting books language is less of a problem than one might think, as the Hungarians follow the old Continental practice of showing texture stitches on visual graphs using symbols, rather than writing the pattern out laboriously as we do. Hungarian handknitting is mainly of the textured sort, using stitches the likes of which I've never seen in Britain. One of them was so lovely that I managed to overcome my deep-rooted dislike of texture long enough to use it in a design. This is the ribbon border in *Tweedie*, a delicate cluster and lattice stitch that looks just as nice without the ribbon threaded through it. The Hungarians also have a wonderful repertoire of cross-stitch embroidery patterns, both in the traditional scarlet, black or dark blue on white and in naturalistic colours, and these have been a very fruitful source for many of my designs.

The most interesting of my journeys to date from a knitting point of view began in Trebizond in a snowstorm and ended in the Grand Bazaar of Aleppo – straight out of the Arabian Nights, and assuredly the finest bazaar in the world. I had come up the Black Sea to Trebizond on the Turkish Maritime Line's *S.S Izmir*, and climbed the steep hills behind the port to seek out the great palace towers, rising in ruined splendour against a darkening sky. Any romantic worthy of the name would have lingered long, as I did, watching for a flicker of light in the high, empty windows and listening for the echoes of another age in the whistling wind. But all thoughts of lost Byzantium were swept away when, on the way back to the ship, I glanced into a shop window and saw two curious objects that looked somewhat like short boots made of carpet, but seemed on closer inspection to have been knitted by hand. My first Turkish socks! The shop of course was closed, and the three days it took to sail back to Istanbul were spent in a thrash of anxiety. Would I ever find another pair? In the end I acquired more than twenty pairs along a route that began in Istanbul itself, in the shanty villages at Rumeli Hisar Ustu overlooking the Bosphorus, where women from the Sivas region have formed a knitting commune, and in the home of Professor Kenan Ozbel, Turkey's leading expert on village arts, part of whose vast collection of Turkish handknitted socks is displayed in the Alay Kiosk of Topkapi Palace.

From there I struck out for Anatolia, the heartland of Turkey, where stockings are still knitted to traditional designs. Language differences present no barriers if you are willing to look foolish. Armed with my one word of Turkish – *urgu* or stockings – pointing to my feet and gesticulating wildly, I made my way east through Antalya, Adana, Konya and Antakya, the ancient Antioch, gathering stockings along the way and doubtlessly providing vast amusement to everyone but my long-suffering travelling companion. As I was to discover, every region – and indeed, every village – has its own stocking patterns with different designs for men and women, for the married and the single, for women of different ages, for everyday wear and for special occasions. Less fitted than Western socks, and worked on five needles instead of on four, Turkish stockings have a wonderful richness of colour and pattern. Long strands of yarn in different shades hang over the knitter's shoulders and down her back, and she passes each strand from one shoulder to another as she knits along the row. Every inch of the stockings are beautifully patterned, even the soles. In this collection, *Trebizond*, *Parsley*, *Izmir* and *Whirling Dervish* are based on Turkish stocking patterns.

I left Turkey and went on through northern Syria to the city of Aleppo, dominated by the magnificent citadel of Saladin, in the shadow of which nestles the Grand Bazaar. The bazaar is a puzzle of souks within souks, joined by a maze of lanes that seem to have neither end nor beginning, and down which hurtle heavily-laden donkeys ridden by high-spirited young boys. Crowds press and surge on every side, sometimes parting to let through a sheik from the desert followed by a bevy of wives in brightly embroidered black dresses, or a group of merchants in long robes, wide striped sashes and high turbans that would not have looked out of place at the court of Haroun al-Raschid. In the souk of the carpet sellers I was greatly taken with a fine Turkish kelim, and saved myself both the price and the problems of transportation by copying the main motifs and colour scheme, which I have used in my *Turkish Kelim* design. I cannot think of a better sort of travel souvenir, nor can I recommend too highly that you take advantage of every opportunity that comes your way to enrich your repertoire of colour knitting patterns.

In colour knitting, I am dedicated to the proposition that simplicity is all. To me, the idea is to achieve the maximum effect with the minimum of effort on the knitter's part – which boils down to using no more than two colours of yarn on any row. Not for me the maddening business of fumbling about with little balls of yarn that have to be twisted around each other every time the pattern changes colour. This tortuous technique – called *intarsia* or motif knitting – has always seemed to me ideally suited only to an octopus trained to juggle and knit at the same time, and although I am well aware that there are those who have managed to master the method, there are very many more who invariably find that it all tends to end in holes, puckers and tears. I like knitting to be enjoyable and relaxing and, to my way of thinking, when a pattern becomes too complicated, the game ceases to be worth the candle. For this reason, only one design in this collection – *Persian Garden* – requires more than two colours per line. All the others require two colours only, stranded across the back in the traditional way.

Simplicity is also the reason that I like to work with repeat patterns – patterns that repeat horizontally across the sweater from seam to seam. In knitting terms, repeat work is easier on the eyes and on the powers of concentration, and from a design point of view repeat patterns are easy to work up into a number of sizes. As I see it, non-repeat patterns – like *intarsia* knitting – tend to introduce needless complications that are very rarely justified. In this collection, only the front panels of the *Transylvania* coat are non-repeat patterns. My favourite repeat number of stitches is 12 – large enough to make an interesting pattern, small enough to fit on to different shapes – which has the added advantage that all 12-stitch repeat patterns can be swapped around from slipover to sweater to waistcoat to cardigan very easily.

I like the discipline of working to two colours and to repeats – the challenge is to see them not as limitations, but as a framework within which to explore different design possibilities. Because the pattern repeats horizontally, I like to introduce as much vertical variety as possible, and I particularly enjoy working on designs like *Sweetheart Sampler* and *Kensington Dandy*, where the pattern is different all the way up from hip to shoulder. When the same patterns do recur vertically, as in *Tzigane* and *Paisley Stripe*, I think it's important to add variety by changing the colours. To me, nothing could be less amusing than knitting the same few rows over and over again, in exactly the same colours – although for those who like minimalist knitting I've included one design – *Parsley* – that does just that.

As I said in *Creative Dressing*, good design is based on a combination of shape, colour, pattern and texture. In knitwear, shape is not quite the open book it is when designing with fabric, because there are some things that yarn just will not do – like stand up straight, or stand out stiffly. Or, if it does, it doesn't do so for long. In practice, shape in knitwear is largely a matter of length, width and necklines. For me, the best shapes will always be simple, subtle and classic. While it is true that classic knitwear shapes have not changed for many years, neither has the shape of the human body. It seems to me nitwitted to turn one's back on shapes that retain their popularity precisely because they work, and work well. Wearability and practicality should *never* be sacrificed to mere novelty.

I am not a fan of very shaped sweaters. You can build an hourglass shape into a sweater, but it will only look good on hourglass-shaped people, of whom there are not many about. Nor am I a great believer in trying to adapt the latest fashion shapes to handknitwear. Usually, they are quite unsuitable and in any case, by the time you've knitted the design the look is out, and your knit is *passé*. Colour knitting is not quick to do, but it is meant to give pleasure for a long time to come, and for this simple, classic shapes cannot be bettered. By simple I do *not* mean 'easy' in the sense of those short boxy tops with shoulders cast off on a single row and stubby sleeves that are not properly set in. A sweater that is *too* easy to knit is impossibly hard to wear with any semblance of style, and I have yet to see one that did not make its hapless wearer look thick around the middle and stoop shouldered besides.

Where length is concerned I like sweaters to be long in the body rather than short, because a long line is much kinder to the figure. As for necklines, I have never forgotten what royal designer Hardy Amies pointed out while showing me one of his menswear collections when I was writing the *Fashion Guides*. On that occasion, all his sleeveless slipovers had crew necklines because, he said, they were more flattering than any other, and a good way of keeping an open necked shirt from going too far. He was speaking of slipovers in plain knitting, but the truth of his remarks holds good for patterned knits too, and for women's blouses as well as men's shirts. To design or knit a nice colourful pattern, then to chop a great wedge out of the front with a V-neckline, strikes me as being the knitting equivalent of shooting yourself in the foot. Rollnecks are a positive hazard to hairdos, makeup and pierced earrings, and as for turtlenecks, they are all too aptly named.

Colour is one of the great joys of life, and although I use only two colours per line, I like to use as many different colours as I can in a design as a whole. Of all the natural senses, colour is the one that is most underrated. You often hear of 'an ear for music', a 'sense of rhythm' or 'an eye for line' – but very rarely do you hear of 'a feeling for colour'. I am convinced that we all see colours differently, and although we may not be fully aware of it, we all have very personal palettes of colours we like, and colours we loathe. For myself, I like working with bright, clear, *definite* colours – from that point of view, doing *Lantern Festival* was sheer delight – and I prefer contrast effects to close harmonies. Pastels make me feel twitchy, and the colours I dislike above all others are those earnest, muddy shades that look like they've been stewed in a vat of tea.

Pattern is my favourite part of design, and I can stare at patterns for hours on end. I work in a room with bare white walls and a plain dark brown carpet, so nothing will distract me except for my Raoul Dufy portrait of Helena Rubinstein and my Yves Saint Laurent ballet drawing. I prefer naturalistic and pictorial patterns to abstract and purely geometrical ones, although in practice the line between them is not a firm one, since the same pattern can look either naturalistic or geometric depending on the colourings you use and the motifs you place around it. What I like best about patterns is that they have a life of their own – an inborn vitality and movement – and although you enhance the movement with colour, it is in the pattern itself that the movement really begins. Without pattern to give it direction, colour is like someone who is all dressed up with nowhere to go.

Balance is an important part of the patterns I like – I prefer symmetrical motifs to asymmetrical ones, and closely spaced designs to patterns with a lot of plain background. Above all, I like pattern to be placed evenly and consistently over the garment as a whole. As I see it, it is better to have an absolutely plain sweater or no sweater at all than to have one with a patterned front but plain back and sleeves, or a sweater with different patterns on the front and on the back.

I always find myself drawn to flower patterns and this is probably because in Hawaii, where I grew up, flowers are in season all the year round. There, we do not cut flowers for the house but wear them as *leis* or garlands, or let them remain in the garden to weave their fragrant spell for as long as possible. I still prefer my flowers in gardens rather than in vases, and, because I think of flowers as something to wear as well as to look at, a flower-covered sweater gives me much more enjoyment than armfuls of cut orchids or lilies. I particularly like wearing flower sweaters during the long grey months of winter, and only wish there were some way of knitting flower scents into my designs.

I love carpets too, the richer and rarer the better, for the finest have a king's ransom of pattern and colour packed into every square inch. Carpets that are too intricate to adapt to knitting invariably compensate by suggesting interesting colour schemes, while for pure pattern there are plenty of knotted carpets of the simpler kind as well as flat-woven *kelims* and *dhurries*. Fabrics – particularly woven ones – are another splendid source of patterns, as are tapestries, quilts, wallpapers, mosaics and ceramics. Embroidery

11

patterns and embroideries are full of inspiration, but I don't think embroidery itself has any place in knitting. Struggling to embroider a supple, stretchy piece of knitted fabric cannot be anyone's idea of fun, and to me an effect that can't be knitted in isn't worth having.

I have a particular fondness for what I call storyline sweaters – designs that tell a story, like *Blue Willow*, or designs built around a particular theme, like *Christmas Cracker*. But all designs have a history, because there is really nothing new under the sun – just new ways of looking at familiar things. That is why I like to tell the story behind each design – it adds to the interest and, I think, makes the knitting more enjoyable.

Pattern and colour bring out the best in each other, and are a perfect team to which texture is, in my opinion, the third wheel, the fly in the ointment, the cuckoo in the nest and the snake in the grass. Texture is the aspect of knitting for which I have the least affinity and affection, and this is only partly because written texture instructions set my teeth on edge. Between them pattern and colour create a convincing illusion of depth that is flattened the minute you add texture. Texture plays havoc with tension, which is a knitter's nightmare at the best of times, and texture also adds bulk, which is not a desirable quality. To me, stocking stitch is the most pleasing of stitches, and there are very few texture stitches that look well with it, particularly openwork ones. If texture must be used, I think it is most satisfactory when it is a variation of stocking stitch, as in *Flora*. Nor do I like to introduce texture by mixing different sorts of yarn – flat yarns with fluffy ones, or matte yarns with shiny ones. They wear and clean at different rates, and have a thuggish tendency to fight among themselves.

Getting down to yarn and needles, I assume – as I did in *Creative Dressing* – that you already know how to knit. If you do not, there are plenty of excellent and inexpensive books that will soon teach you everything you need to know to start colour knitting. All you require is to know how do a knit stitch and a purl stitch, how to cast on and cast off, how to increase and how to decrease – knitting at its most basic. Carrying the second colour of yarn across the back and catching it in soon becomes second nature. Indeed, you are spoiled for choice as far as first-rate how-to-knit books go. The problem, I have always found, is not learning to knit but finding interesting and unusual things to knit once you know how, which is why I did this collection. So you provide the know-how – and I'll supply the knits. I hope you enjoy them – happy knitting!

Notes for knitters

1 All the designs in this collection are knitted using the *Fair Isle technique*, which consists of working a stocking stitch fabric (alternate rows of knit stitches and purl stitches) in two colours of yarn, the second colour when not in use being carried across the back of the work. When carrying the second colour across the back, catch it in at the back by looping it gently around the first colour of yarn every third or fourth stitch. The object of catching the second colour in at the back in this way is to avoid leaving long, easily breakable loops on the reverse side of the fabric. Do not pull the second colour too tightly along the back, or the front of the knitting will pucker.

2 When carrying the second colour of yarn across the back, carry it to the end of the row, even if it will not be needed again in the last repeat. Some knitters carry the second colour vertically up the back instead of to the end of the row, in an effort to save yarn. This is a false economy as it results in flimsy side seams that cannot support the weight of the knitting, thus ruining the entire garment.

3 In the pattern charts, each square represents 1 stitch of knitting. Unless otherwise stated, all odd-numbered rows are K (knit stitch) rows and should be read from right to left, and all even-numbered rows are P (purl stitch) rows, and should be read from left to right.

4 If you are not used to working from charts, these four lines from *Izmir* show how the system works. If they were written out as instructions instead of shown in chart form, this is how they would read:

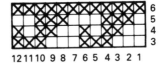

⊠ = French Blue   FB = French Blue
☐ = Light Natural   LN = Light Natural

Row 3: K * 3LN 3FB 3LN 3FB * rep from * to * 11(12:13:14) times.
Row 4: P * 1FB 1LN 2FB 2LN 1FB 1LN 2FB 2LN * rep from * to * 11(12:13:14) times.
Row 5: K * 1LN 3FB 3LN 3FB 2LN * rep from * to * 11(12:13:14) times.
Row 6: P * 12FB * rep from * to * 11(12:13:14) times.

5 The numbers that run up the sides of the pattern charts are the row numbers. The numbers that run along the bottom of the pattern charts are the stitch numbers; there are 12 stitches in the *Izmir* chart. These stitches make up a unit called a *repeat*, which is repeated horizontally across the row to make up the overall pattern for that row. For example, on *Izmir* you will have 132,

144, 156 or 168 stitches on your needle when you begin to work in pattern on row 1. You will work the 12-stitch repeat across 11, 12, 13 or 14 times (12 × 11 = 132, 12 × 12 = 144, 12 × 13 = 156, 12 × 14 = 168).

6 If you are working a K row and a repeat of 12 stitches, the stitches are worked in this order: 1–12. If you are working a P row and a repeat of 12 stitches, the stitches are worked in this order: 12–1. 3-stitch, 9-stitch, 24-stitch and all other repeats are worked in the same way.

7 Repeat knitting is very straightforward at the beginning of a sweater, when every K row begins on stitch 1 of a repeat, and every P row begins on the last stitch of a repeat, unless otherwise stated. But when shaping begins, everything changes, and you will have to *be sure to maintain continuity of pattern* – a phrase that is engraved upon my heart, as Queen Mary Tudor said that 'Calais' was engraved upon hers. This armhole shaping chart from *Heraldry* (12-stitch repeat) shows what maintaining continuity of pattern means. For size 2 (144 sts) the instructions say:
Rows 91–92: cast off 7 sts at beg of each row.
Rows 93–96: cast off 4 sts at beg of each row.
Rows 97–106: dec 1 st at beg of each row for 10 rows.
Rows 107–162: work in pattern without shaping.
This what the instructions for rows 91–111 look like:

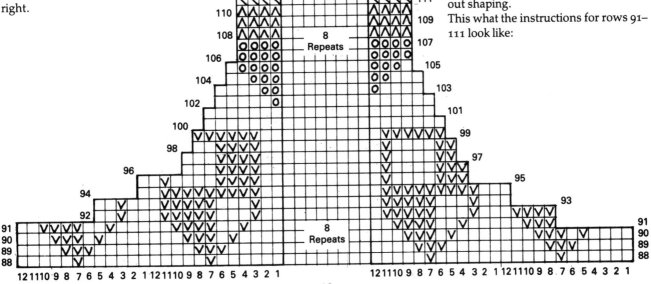

After armhole shaping is complete, K rows will begin on stitch 9, and P rows will begin on stitch 4. This is how you would proceed:

Row 107: work sts 9–12, then repeat sts 1–12 8 times, then work sts 1–4.

Row 108: work sts 4–1, then work sts 12–1 8 times, then work sts 12–9.

Continuity of pattern must be maintained in this way when you are decreasing for arm, neck and shoulder shapings.

8 Continuity of pattern must also be maintained when you are working the sleeves, but in that case you will be increasing rather than decreasing. This sleeve shaping chart from *Parsley* (12-stitch repeat) shows what maintaining continuity of pattern means when increasing. For size 2 (72 sts) the instructions say:

Rows 1–3: on K rows work sts 1–12 across 6 times, on P rows work sts 12–1 across 6 times.

Row 4: proceed in pattern, increasing 1 stitch at both ends of row 4 and every following 4th row until there are 102 sts on needle.

This is what the instructions for rows 1–22 look like:

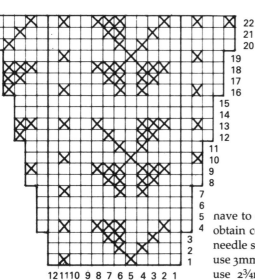

12 11 10 9 8 7 6 5 4 3 2 1

Repeat 6 times

Continuity of pattern must be maintained in this way when you are increasing on the sleeves or body.

9 *Tension:* It is essential, repeat *essential*, to get your tension right, for both

the stitches *and* the rows. A common error is to concentrate on the stitch count at the expense of the row count, which can result in such undesirable articles as the four-foot-long sleeve and the thigh-length slipover. Check tension *before* beginning work on the design by knitting a 4 inch (10 cm) patterned test square using the needle size and yarn type specified in the pattern. Proceed *only* if the row and stitch tension of your test square, measured over a 2-inch square in the middle of the test swatch, is the same as that given in the pattern. If it isn't, try again, using smaller needles if your first test swatch was too large, and larger needles if it was too small. Don't worry about changing needle sizes – what matters is getting the tension right. Do not start work on the design until you have mastered the tension.

10 All 1-colour rows must be worked on smaller needles than the 2-colour rows to keep the tension even. The object is to have the tension of 1-colour rows the same as for 2-colour rows. Usually 1 size smaller needle is sufficient; if you are using 3¼mm needles on the 2-colour rows, use 3mm needles on the 1-colour rows. If you find you

have to change 2-colour needle size to obtain correct tension, adjust 1-colour needle size as well; for example, if you use 3mm needles on the 2-colour rows, use 2¾mm needles on the 1-colour rows.

11 *Measurements and sizes:* most of the measurements in this collection are given as *actual measurements* – what the finished garment measures all round when it has been knitted to proper tension. Conventional sizing wisdom holds that you will probably want to

knit up a size that is two or three inches larger all round than your chest measurement. For example, if you have a 36 inch (91.5 cm) chest, the usual choice would be to knit up a size 3 (39 inch/99 cm) sweater. I go up one size in this way on the knits I wear myself, but as fit is very much a matter of personal taste, I leave it to you to match up your actual measurements with those of the design you choose.

12 When only one set of figures is given in the pattern, it applies to all sizes. When more than one set of figures is given, the figures for the larger sizes are in brackets.

13 All the designs in this collection are knitted in Shetland 2-ply jumper weight wool (4-ply equivalent). The numbers that are given in the patterns next to the yarn colour names are the stock numbers for the different shades in the range of Shetland yarns I use. It is recommended, but not essential, that you use the same yarn when knitting up the designs. Many of the 4-ply wool, cotton and synthetic yarns on the market will be suitable for substitution, but you *must* make sure that the yarn you choose will knit up to the tension specified in the pattern. Not all 4-plys knit up the same, so when substituting yarns always do a test swatch *before* buying large quantities.

14 *Yarn quantities 1:* 1 oz (25 gr) is the minimum quantity in which yarn can be purchased. When the patterns specify that 1 oz of a colour is required, it does not mean that the entire ounce will be used.

15 *Yarn quantities 2:* switching shapes and patterns around, as described in 'Ringing the changes', will alter the amount of yarn required. Yarn quantities are approximate as they are based on average requirements.

16 *Yarn quantities 3:* substituting yarns may alter the amount of yarn required.

17 In Vertical Stripe ribbing, the second colour of yarn is carried along one side of the work only. This side becomes the back of the work when you begin to knit in pattern on the body of the sweater.

Ringing the changes

Sixteen of the designs in this collection are 12-stitch repeats which have been knitted up into eight shapes; round neck cardigan (*Cottage Garden*), round neck sweater (*Gingham*)), collared sweater (*Harvest Home*), collared cardigan (*Tweedie*), straight waistcoat (*Christmas Cracker*), pointed waistcoat (*Paisley Stripe*), slipover (*Izmir*) and square neck sweater (*Parsley*). If, as often happens, you like a 12-stitch pattern that has been used for a waistcoat or slipover, but would prefer it knitted up as a cardigan or sweater, you can change the patterns and shapes around – there are 105 possible variations – in the following way:

1 Lengthen or shorten the chart of the pattern you like so that it is the same body length – or number of rows – as the new shape you have chosen. Extra rows of pattern are made up by repeating a motif from the chart or by adding a motif of your own.
2 If you are adding sleeves, make up a separate sleeve chart of 8 or 22 rows (see below). For pointed waistcoats, make up charts for rows 1–31/32.
3 Knit up the lengthened or shortened pattern chart, and sleeve and point charts where necessary, using the instructions for the new shape you have chosen.

Body lengths for shapes

Pointed waistcoat = 162 rows long. Collared cardigan and straight waistcoat = 187 rows long. Round neck cardigan = 186 rows long. Collared sweater and square neck sweater = 173 rows long. Round neck sweater and slipover = 172 rows long.

Sleeve lengths

Sleeves do not start on the same row of pattern as the body of the cardigan or sweater. To make the pattern on the body and sleeves line up properly, the following number of extra rows of pattern have to be added at the beginning of the sleeves, after the ribbing has been worked. Extra rows of pattern are made up by repeating a motif from the chart or adding a motif of your own.

> cardigan = 8 extra rows (row 9 of cardigan sleeve is the same as row 1 of cardigan body).
> sweater = 22 extra rows (row 23 of sweater sleeve is the same as row 1 of sweater body).

EXAMPLES

Straight waistcoat into round neck sweater (Christmas Cracker)

1 Shorten chart CC1; new last row is 172.
2 Make up a 22-row sleeve chart consisting of rows 155–176 of chart CC1.
3 Knit up shortened chart CC1 and new sleeve chart following instructions for *Gingham* sweater.

Pointed waistcoat into round neck cardigan (Paisley Stripe)

1 Lengthen chart PS1 by adding 24 rows; repeat rows 55–78 of chart PS1 after completing row 162.
2 Make up 8-row sleeve chart consisting of rows 101–108 of chart PS1,
3 Knit up lengthened chart PS1 and new sleeve chart following instructions for *Cottage Garden* cardigan.

Round neck sweater into pointed waistcoat (Turkish Kelim)

1 Shorten chart TK1; new last row is 162.
2 Make up point charts for rows 1–31 and 1–32 for your size.
3 Knit up shortened chart TK1 and new point charts following instructions for *Paisley Stripe* waistcoat.

REFINEMENTS

In some cases, you may want to modify the spacing and colours on the pattern charts to achieve the best results. For example:

Slipover into round neck cardigan (Heraldry)

1 Lengthen chart HR1 by 14 rows. If you complete row 172 of chart HR1 then start again at row 1 of chart, there will be 6 plain rows between the shields instead of the usual 2. To avoid this, complete row 169 of chart, then start again on row 2 of chart HR1 and continue until you have completed row 18. When working rows 4–18 of chart for the second time, vary the design by changing the colours – substitute Crimson for Purple and Charcoal Black for Crimson.
2 Make up a sleeve chart. Normally you would do an 8-row sleeve chart; in this case it would result in a 3-line space between the first two shields on the sleeve. To avoid this, make the sleeve chart 9 rows long and begin working from chart HR1 on row 2. Use rows 49–57 for sleeve chart, substituting French Blue for Crimson and Charcoal Black for Saffron Yellow.
3 Knit up lengthened chart HR1 and new sleeve chart following instructions for *Cottage Garden* cardigan.

Pointed waistcoat into slipover (Kensington Dandy)

1 Lengthen chart KD1 to a total of 172 rows; complete row 160, then repeat rows 17–28 of chart KD1, substituting Pale Lilac for Purple and Turquoise Blue for Bright Mauve on rows 21–27.
2 Knit up lengthened chart KD1 following instructions for *Izmir* slipover.

A SPECIAL CASE

Every rule needs an exception, and in this collection it's *Sweetheart Sampler*. This is the only design in which the shape and 12-stitch pattern cannot be switched around as described. If you want to put a 12-stitch pattern on to a square neck shape, use the instructions for the *Parsley* sweater. If you want to use the *Sweetheart Sampler* pattern on other shapes, proceed as follows.

Square neck sweater into round neck sweater (Sweetheart Sampler)

1 Cross out all end stitches on pattern charts S1 and S4, cross out stitch X on pattern charts S2 and S3.
2 Shorten chart S1; new last row is 172.
3 Make up a 22-row sleeve chart using rows 119–140 of chart S1, and substituting French Blue for Crimson on rows 138–140.
4 Knit up shortened chart S1, new sleeve chart and charts S2 and S3 following instructions for *Gingham* sweater *but* instructions for rows 88–94 on Front and Back should be as follows. *On P rows, size 1*; work sts 132–1 across. *Size 2*; work sts Q–M, then work sts 133–1, then work sts L–G. *Size 3*; work sts W–M, then work sts 133–1, then work sts L–A. *On K rows, size 1*; works sts 1–132 across. *Size 2*; work sts G–L, then work sts 1–133, then work sts M–Q. *Size 3*; work sts A–L, then work sts 1–133, then work sts M–W. *For all sizes*; when working rows 88–94 on the sleeves, work from chart S4.

Square neck sweater into round neck cardigan (Sweetheart Sampler)

1 Cross out all end stitches on pattern charts S1 and S4, cross out stitch X on pattern chart S2.
2 Lengthen chart S1 to make up a total of 186 rows; complete row 170, then begin at row 1, and continue until you have completed row 16.
3 Make up an 8-row sleeve chart consisting of rows 15–19, then rows 168–170.
4 Knit up lengthened chart S1 and new sleeve chart following instructions for *Cottage Garden* cardigan. For sleeves and left and right fronts, use chart S4 on rows 88–94. For back on rows 88–94, use chart S2 following instructions given above for round neck sweater, or use chart S4.

Abbreviations and Americanisms

alt = alternate; beg = beginning; cm = centimetres; dec = decrease; foll = following; inc = increase; in = inch(es); K = knit; K2tog = knit 2 stitches together; ML = make 1 stitch by picking up horizontal loop lying before next stitch and working into the back of it; nil = o; patt = pattern; psso = pass slipped stitch over; P = purl; rem = remaining; rep = repeat; right side row = K stitch row; SL.1 = slip one; st(s) = stitch(es); st.st = stocking stitch (1 row knit, 1 row purl); tog = together; YO = yarn over (make one).

For American knitters: American knitting needle sizes are given in the patterns. The American equivalent of 4-ply yarn is sport yarn. In American knitting terminology, cast off = bind off, stocking stitch = stockinette stitch, and tension = gauge.

The Collection

1
Belvedere

THIS SLIPOVER is very like the one that first attracted me to colour knitting, and it is something of a wolf in sheep's clothing, for it is not at all the Armada-vintage Fair Isle it seems to be, and demonstrates that Fair Isle type patterns should not be treated with undue veneration, for they are neither as old nor as immutably fixed as we are often led to believe.

However long they may have been there, patterned knits from the Shetland Islands were first reported only in the 1850s, when they consisted of simple lozenge-and-cross (or OXO) designs worked on to scarves, hats and gloves. The range of colours was extremely limited, consisting of natural and a few home-dyed shades – mainly red ochre, mustard and dark blue – but striking effects were achieved by changing both the background and foreground colours every few rows. It was not until the beginning of this century, when knitted jerseys became popular for sport and leisure wear, that Fair Isle patterns began to be used on fashion sweaters. Development then proceeded rapidly, stimulated by the growing availability of commercially dyed yarns, the addition of new patterns to the knitters' repertoire, and the huge popular demand created when the Prince of Wales – later Edward VIII and Duke of Windsor – took up Fair Isle sweaters in the 1920s. Patterned sweaters continued to be the height of leisure fashion through the 1930s, changing all the time. Traditional OXO motifs were combined with Art Deco zigzags and dashes, diamond bands and Argyll patterns were introduced, and the old practice of changing the background colour was abandoned in favour of using a single background colour throughout – usually fawn or beige. Although the choice of colours was much improved, the shades remained muted, and the emphasis was on close colour harmonies rather than on contrasts. The exigencies and shortages of World War II stopped the patterned sweater in its tracks, and when it resurfaced in the 1950s it had undergone a dramatic transformation. The flamboyant large star or snowflake motif (chart B4) – not used before the War – had been added to the pattern repertoire, and yarns had left the subdued colour palette of the past behind and broken out in a range of clear, confident commercial shades that owed nothing to nature.

The sweater on which this design is based was knitted in the 1950s, and is a superb example of imaginative Fair Isle knitting at its best. It uses patterns from three stages of the Fair Isle's development – Thirties diamond bands (chart B1), earlier Tree of Life motifs (chart B2) and Fifties stars. It returned to the traditional practice of changing both the foreground and background shades, combines close colour harmonies with sharp contrasts, and uses twenty colours of yarn to achieve effects undreamed of in Fair Isle's early days. It is, in my opinion, a *tour de force* as an example of the way the old and the new should be combined. Authenticity is fine for museum pieces, but designs must move with the times if they are to be considered part of the living art of fashion.

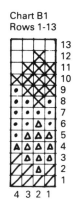

Chart B1
Rows 1-13

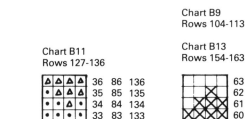

Chart B11
Rows 127-136

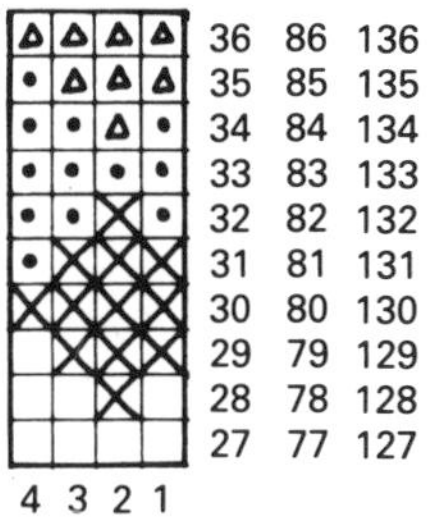

Chart B5
Rows 54-63

Chart B9
Rows 104-113

Chart B13
Rows 154-163

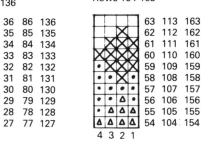

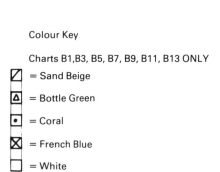

Colour Key

Charts B1,B3, B5, B7, B9, B11, B13 ONLY

☑ = Sand Beige

△ = Bottle Green

• = Coral

☒ = French Blue

☐ = White

Chart B4
Rows 37-53

Chart B8
Rows 87-103

Chart B12
Rows 137-153

Size: 2 only

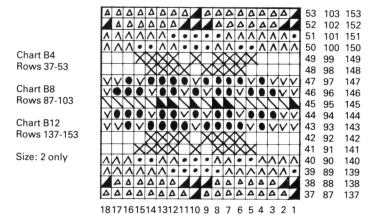

Colour Key

Charts B4, B4A, B12, B12A ONLY

△ = Bottle Green

◤ = Pale Yellow

• = Lemon Yellow

Λ = Purple

☒ = Flamingo

☐ = Navy Blue

◉ = Saffron Yellow

V = Lovat Green

◣ = Crimson

◩ = White

Colour Key

Charts B8 and B8A ONLY

△ = Bottle Green

◤ = Pale Yellow

• = Flamingo

Λ = Navy Blue

☒ = Lemon Yellow

☐ = Purple

◉ = Pale Grey

V = Sapphire Blue

◣ = Crimson

◩ = White

19

Chart B4A
Rows 37-53

Chart B8A
Rows 87-103

Chart B12A
Rows 137-153

Sizes 1,3 and 4 ONLY

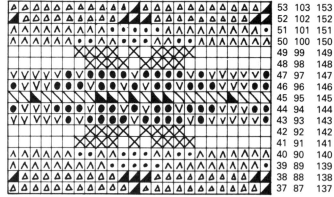

	53	103	153
	52	102	152
	51	101	151
	50	100	150
	49	99	149
	48	98	148
	47	97	147
	46	96	146
	45	95	145
	44	94	144
	43	93	143
	42	92	142
	41	91	141
	40	90	140
	39	89	139
	38	88	138
	37	87	137

24 23 22 21 20 19 18 17 16 15 14 13 12 11 10 9 8 7 6 5 4 3 2 1

Colour Key as for charts B4, B8, B12

Chart B2
Rows 14-26

Chart B10
Rows 114-126

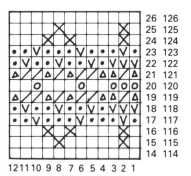

	26	126
	25	125
	24	124
	23	123
	22	122
	21	121
	20	120
	19	119
	18	118
	17	117
	16	116
	15	115
	14	114

12 11 10 9 8 7 6 5 4 3 2 1

Chart B6
Rows 64-76

Chart B14
Rows 164-172

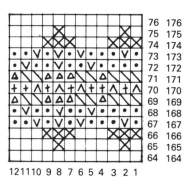

	76	176
	75	175
	74	174
	73	173
	72	172
	71	171
	70	170
	69	169
	68	168
	67	167
	66	166
	65	165
	64	164

12 11 10 9 8 7 6 5 4 3 2 1

Colour Key

Charts B2, B6, B10, B14 ONLY

☐ = White

⊠ = Sapphire Blue

Ⅴ = Bottle Green

• = Lemon Yellow

◿ = Pale Pink

△ = Bright Mauve on chart B2, B6, B14, Turquoise Blue on chart B10

◕ = Turquoise Blue on Chart B2, Bright Mauve on chart B10

◺ = Pale Aqua Blue

✚ = Pale Peach on chart B6, Saffron Yellow on chart B14

◸ = Purple

20

21

BELVEDERE SLIPOVER

YARN COLOURS AND NUMBERS	QUANTITIES REQUIRED IN OUNCES (1 oz = 28 g)			
	Size 1	Size 2	Size 3	Size 4
Sand Beige F C 43	1	2	3	3
Bottle Green 34	1	2	2	2
Coral 38	1	1	1	1
French Blue 16	1	1	1	1
Natural White 1a	1	2	2	2
Sapphire Blue F C 48	1	1	2	2
Lemon Yellow 46	1	1	1	1
Bright Mauve 44	1	1	1	1
Pale Pink 101	1	1	1	1
Turquoise Blue 48	1	1	1	1
Pale Yellow 96	1	1	1	1
Purple 20	1	1	2	2
Flamingo F C 7	1	1	1	1
Navy Blue 21	1	1	1	1
Saffron Yellow 90	1	1	1	1
Lovat Green 29	1	1	1	1
Crimson 55	1	1	1	1
Pale Aqua Blue 75	1	1	1	1
Pale Peach 207	1	1	1	1
Pale Grey 203	1	1	1	1

NEEDLES One pair each size 2¾ mm (No. 12 British, No. 1 American), 3 mm (No. 11 British, No. 2 American) and 3¼ mm (No. 10 British, No. 3 American) needles, and a stitch holder.

TENSION 16 sts and 16 rows to 2 in (5 cm) on 3¼ mm needles over Fair Isle pattern. For K2P2 ribbing: 9 sts and 9 rows to 1 in (2.5 cm) on 2¾ mm needles. Change needle size if necessary to obtain correct tension.

SIZES 4 sizes. Size 1 = 33 in (84 cm), size 2 = 36 in (91.5 cm), size 3 = 39 in (99 cm), size 4 = 42 in (106.5 cm), actual measurements.

ABBREVIATIONS See page 16. Colours: SB = Sand Beige.

NOTES FOR KNITTERS See page 13.

SPECIAL INSTRUCTIONS FOR THIS DESIGN Since only small amounts of certain colours are required for this slipover, you may wish to simplify the colour scheme in the interests of economy.

BACK

With 2¾ mm needles and SB yarn, cast on 120(132:140:152) sts and work in K2P2 rib for 2½ in (6.5 cm).

Next row: (increase row) K across, inc 12(12:16:16) sts evenly over the row giving 132(144:156:168) sts.

Next row: P across.

Using 3 mm needles on all 1-colour rows and 3¼ mm needles on all 2-colour rows, begin to work in pattern starting with row 1 of chart B1. On K rows work sts 1–4 across 33(36:39:42) times, on P rows work sts 4–1 across 33(36:39:42) times: 132(144:156:168) sts. Proceed to chart B2 and work as follows; on P rows work sts 12–1 across 11(12:13:14) times, on K rows work sts 1–12 across 11(12:13:14) times. Work chart B3 as for chart B1, then proceed to chart B4 or chart B4A and work as follows. **Size 2 only:** on K rows work sts 1–18 of chart B4 across 8 times, on P rows work sts 18–1 of chart B4 across 8 times: 144 sts. **Size 4 only:** on K rows work sts 1–24 of chart B4A across 7 times, on P rows work sts 24–1 across 7 times: 168 sts. **Sizes 1 and 3 only:** on K rows work sts 1–24 of chart B4A across 5(6) times then work sts 1–12, on P rows work sts 12–1 then work sts 24–1 across 5(6) times: 132(156) sts. **For all sizes:** work straight in pattern, working similar charts as given until you have completed row 90 (chart B8 or chart B8A). *Be sure to maintain continuity of pattern for remainder of work on Back.*

Armhole Shaping

Rows 91–92: cast off 5(7:9:11) sts at beg of each row: 122(130:138:146) sts rem.

Rows 93–96: cast off 4 sts at beg of each row: 106(114:122:130) sts rem.

Rows 97–106: dec 1 st at beg of each row for 10 rows: 96(104:112:120) sts rem.

Rows 107–162: work in pattern without shaping.

Shoulder Shaping

Rows 163–168: cast off 4(5:6:7) sts at beg of each row: 72(74:76:78) sts rem.

Rows 169–170: cast off 3(4:4:5) sts at beg of each row: 66(66:68:68) sts rem.

Rows 171–172: cast off 3(3:4:4) sts at beg of each row, work in pattern to end (60 sts rem).

Back Neck

Change to 2¾ mm needles and SB yarn and work the 60 sts for Back Neck in K2P2 rib for 9 rows. Cast off neatly in rib.

FRONT

Size 2 only: work as for Back until you have completed row 142 (Chart B12).

Size 4 only: work as for Back until you have completed row 142 (Chart B12A).

Sizes 1 and 3 only: work as for Back until you have completed chart B3, then work chart B4A in the following sequence. On K rows work sts 13–24, then work sts 1–24 across 5(6) times, on P rows work sts 24–1 across 5(6) times then work sts 24–13: 132(156) sts. Repeat this sequence on similar charts. Otherwise work as for Back until you have completed row 142 (Chart B12A).

For all sizes: *be sure to maintain continuity of pattern throughout.*

Divide for Neck

Row 143: work in pattern across 33(37:41:45) sts, turn, leave rem 63(67:71:75) sts on a spare needle or stitch holder and work on first group of sts as follows.

Left Front

Rows 144–158: dec 1 st at neck edge on every row: 18(22:26:30) sts rem.

Rows 159–162: work in pattern without shaping.

Shoulder Shaping

Row 163: cast off 4(5:6:7) sts at beg of row: 14(17:20:23) sts rem.

Row 164: work in pattern without shaping.

Row 165: as row 163: 10(12:14:16) sts rem.

Row 166: as row 164.

Row 167: as row 163: 6(7:8:9) sts rem.

Row 168: as row 164.

Row 169: cast off 3(4:4:5) sts at beg of row: 3(3:4:4) sts rem.

Row 170: as row 164.

Row 171: cast off rem sts.

Right Front

Slip 30 sts for Front Neck on to a stitch holder. Rejoin yarn to second group of 33(37:41:45) sts and work in pattern across row 143. Now work as for Left Front, reversing all shapings and ending by casting off rem sts on row 172.

FRONT NECKBAND

With 2¾ mm needles, SB yarn and right side of work facing, pick up and K 27 sts down left side of neck, 30 sts from centre front neck and 27 sts up right side of neck: 84 sts. Work in K2P2 rib for 9 rows. Cast off neatly in rib.

ARMBANDS

Gently press all pieces with a warm iron and damp cloth. Join shoulder seams, including neck ribbing. With 2¾ mm needles, SB yarn and right side of work facing, pick up and K 148(152:156:160) sts around armhole. Work in K2P2 rib for 9 rows. Cast off loosely in rib. Repeat for other side.

TO MAKE UP

Join side seams.

2
Sweetheart Sampler

SWEETHEART SAMPLER is based on nineteenth-century cross-stitch picture samplers, those pretty pieces of needlework that translate so well into knitting. Cross-stitch picture samplers originated in Germany in the eighteenth century, and had spread to the rest of Europe and to America by the nineteenth. Many of the cross-stitch motifs were adapted from earlier peasant embroideries that were worked on an unbleached linen ground in red, blue or black cross-stitch, or in combinations of red with blue and red with black. The eighteenth-century innovation was to work the motifs in naturalistic colours, giving them a two-dimensional look. Typical German motifs included ribbon borders, flowering and fruit-bearing trees either free-standing or growing in pots, and vases full of flowers.

Passages from scripture and moral rhymes were popular choices for the lines of text that dominate the centre of most samplers, but occasionally the text was romantic, as in this verse from an American sampler of 1808:

> When this you see
> Remember me
> Though many miles apart.
> When I do see you once again
> It will ease my troubled heart.

It was customary to include the name of the embroideress, her age and the date the sampler was finished. In many cases, when the young ladies later reached mature years, they carefully unpicked the stitches that gave their age away.

Sweetheart Sampler uses the Fair Isle knitting technique, but makes a refreshing change from geometric Fair Isle patterns. The repeated bands of small X's in red and blue recall the peasant cross-stitch designs from which the colourful patterns derive, and the flattering neckline is reminiscent of the sampler's square shape. The romantic rhyming couplet WHEN THIS YOU SEE, REMEMBER ME has been arranged so that REMEMBER ME runs across the back – after all, your exits should be as memorable as your entrances. But if you prefer not to be quite so provocative, the instructions tell you how to replace the letters with the large X motifs worked on the sleeves.

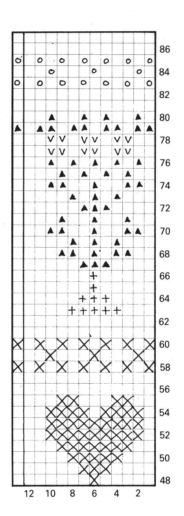

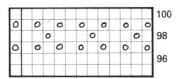

See Charts S2, S3 and S4

Chart S1
182 rows

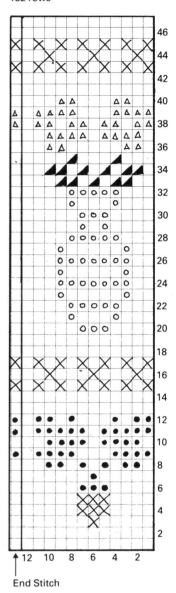

↑ 12 10 8 6 4 2

End Stitch

Colour Key

☐ = Light Natural	▲ = Lovat Green
✕ = Crimson	V = Saffron Yellow
O = Azure Blue	∧ = Watermelon Red
◣ = Leaf Green	◤ = Periwinkle Blue
△ = Bright Mauve	▼ = Fuchsia Pink
+ = Moorit Brown	● = Viridian Green

26

End Chart S1

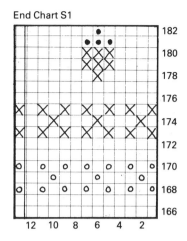

Chart S2: Back

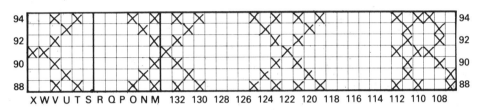

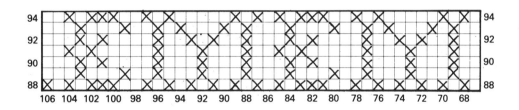

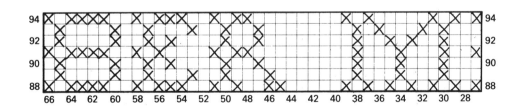

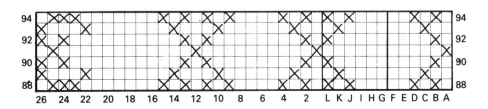

Chart S3: Front

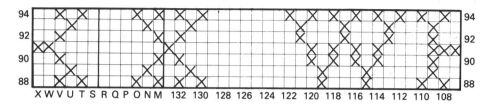

94 — 94
92 — 92
90 — 90
88 — 88

X W V U T S R Q P O N M 132 130 128 126 124 122 120 118 116 114 112 110 108

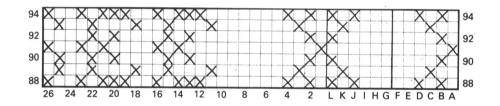

94 — 94
92 — 92
90 — 90
88 — 88

106 104 102 100 98 96 94 92 90 88 86 84 82 80 78 76 74 72 70 68

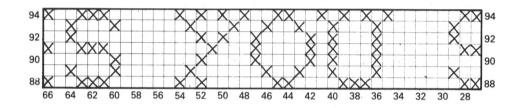

94 — 94
92 — 92
90 — 90
88 — 88

66 64 62 60 58 56 54 52 50 48 46 44 42 40 38 36 34 32 30 28

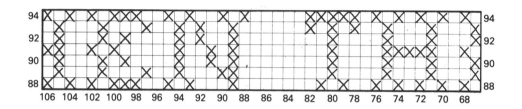

94 — 94
92 — 92
90 — 90
88 — 88

26 24 22 20 18 16 14 12 10 8 6 4 2 L K J I H G F E D C B A

Chart S4

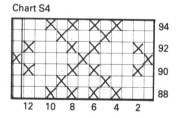

94
92
90
88

12 10 8 6 4 2

28

SWEETHEART SAMPLER SWEATER

YARN COLOURS AND NUMBERS	QUANTITIES REQUIRED IN OUNCES (1 oz = 28.3 g)		
	Size 1	Size 2	Size 3
Light Natural 202	8	9	9
Crimson 55	2	2	2
Azure Blue 17	1	1	2
Leaf Green 25	1	1	1
Bright Mauve 44	1	1	1
Moorit Brown	1	1	1
Lovat Green 29	1	1	1
Saffron Yellow 90	1	1	1
Watermelon Red F C 33	1	1	1
Periwinkle Blue F C 37	1	1	1
Fuchsia Pink 52	1	1	1
Viridian Green 65	1	1	1

NEEDLES One pair each size 2¾ mm (No. 12 British, No. 1 American), 3 mm (No. 11 British, No. 2 American) and 3¼ mm (No. 10 British, No. 3 American) needles, and a stitch holder.

TENSION 16 sts and 18 rows to 2 in (5 cm) on 3¼ mm needles over Fair Isle pattern. For K1P1 ribbing: 10 sts and 11 rows to 1 in (2.5 cm) on 2¾ mm needles. Change needle size if necessary to obtain correct tension.

SIZES 3 sizes. Size 1 = 33 in (84 cm), size 2 = 36 in (91.5 cm), size 3 = 39 in (99 cm), actual measurements.

ABBREVIATIONS See page 16. *Colours:* N = Light Natural.

NOTES FOR KNITTERS see page 13.

SPECIAL INSTRUCTIONS FOR THIS DESIGN (1) In this design, the cast-on stitches are not an exact multiple of the repeat. In charts S1 and S4, each row has 1 extra stitch in it. This extra stitch is called the *end stitch*, and it has been drawn on to the pattern charts. On the Back and Front, it is worked once in each row. It is the last stitch on all K rows and the first stitch on each P row, when working from charts S1 and S4. (If working from charts S2 and S3, rows 88–94 do not have an end stitch.) On the sleeves, the end stitch is worked *twice* on each row. (2) If you want to replace the letters on Back and Front with large X motifs, work rows 88–94 from chart S4 as follows. Work the 12-stitch repeat across 11(12:13) times, beginning with an end stitch on all P rows and finishing with an end stitch on all K rows. Continue until you have completed row 94, then return to chart S1. (3) Use 3 mm needles on all 1-colour rows.

BACK

**With 2¾ mm needles and N yarn, cast on 133(145:157) sts and work in K1P1 rib for 3 in (7.5 cm). Using 3 mm needles for all 1-colour rows and 3¼ mm needles for all 2-colour rows, begin to work in st.st, starting at row 1 of chart S1.

Rows 1 and 2: work the 12 st repeat across 11(12:13) times, finishing with an end st on each K row and starting with an end st on each P row.

Row 3: work in pattern until you have completed row 87 of chart S1.** Now start to work from chart S2.

Size 1: row 88: work sts 133–1 across.

Size 2: row 88; work sts R-M, then work sts 133–1, then work sts L-G.

Size 3: row 88; work sts X-M, then work sts 133–1, then work sts L-A.

Size 1: row 98: work sts 1–133 across.

Size 2: row 89; work sts G-L, then work sts 1–133, then work sts M-R.

Size 3: row 89; work sts A-L, then work sts 1–133, then work sts M-X.

Continue in this way for all sizes until you have completed row 94, then return to chart S1 and complete rows 95–104.

Armhole Shaping

Keeping correct in pattern, cast off 4 sts at the beg of the next 2 rows. Then dec 1 st at both ends of next and every alt row until 103(115:127) sts remain. Work straight until you have completed patt row 176.

Shoulder Shaping

Keeping correct in pattern, cast off 10(12:12) sts at beg of next 4 rows. Then cast off 11(11:15) sts at beg of next 2 rows: 41(45:49) sts. Change to 2¾ mm needles and N yarn and work 9 rows in K1P1 rib. Cast off neatly in rib.

FRONT

Work as for Back from ** to **. Then work pattern rows 88–94 as for Back, but using chart S3. Return to chart S1 and continue in pattern starting with row 95. Continue to work as for Back until armhole shaping is complete, and you have completed row 128 of chart S1.

Divide for Neck

Row 129: work in pattern across 31(35:39) sts, turn and leave remaining sts on a stitch holder. Proceed on first sts for left side and work in patt until you have completed row 176 of chart S1.

Shoulder Shaping

Keeping correct in pattern cast off 10(12:12) sts at beg of next and following alt row. Work 1 row. Cast off rem 11(11:15) sts. Now place centre 41(45:49) sts on a stitch holder, rejoin yarn to neck edge of remaining sts and complete right side of front to match the left, reversing all shaping.

SLEEVES

Pattern sequence: Sizes 1 and 2, start with row 125 of chart S1. Work until you have completed row 140, then begin at row 1 of chart S1 again. **Size 3:** with 3 mm needles, work 4 rows st.st in N. Change to 3¼ mm needles, work rows 121–140 from chart S1, then begin at row 1 of chart S1 again.

With 2¾ mm needles and N yarn, cast on 72 (76:76) sts and work in K1P1 rib for 2¾ in (7 cm).

Size 1: inc 1 st at both ends of last rib row (74 sts).

Sizes 2 and 3: rib 6, * inc into next st, rib 6, rep from * to last 7 sts, inc into next st, rib 6 (86 sts).

All sizes: using 3mm needles for all 1-colour rows and 3¼mm needles for all 2-colour rows, P1 row in N. Now work in st.st and pattern, using the sequence above, and beginning and ending each pattern row with an end stitch. Work the 12 st repeat across 6(7:7) times, **at the same time** shaping the sleeve as follows. Keeping correct in pattern, inc 1 st at both ends of the 5th and every following 4th row until there are 82(94:94) sts, then inc 1 st at both ends of every 6th (9th:9th) row until there are 100(112:112) sts. Work rows 88–94 from chart S4, then return to chart S1, and work straight until you have completed row 104 of chart S1.

Shape Sleeve Head

Cast off 4 sts at beg of next 2 rows, then dec 1 st at beg of each row for 52(40:40) rows. Then dec 1st at both ends of each row for 6(18:18) rows. Cast off remaining 28 sts.

Work second sleeve to match.

FRONT NECKBAND

With 2¾ mm needles and N yarn and with right side of work facing, pick up and knit 49 sts down left front edge, then using the same needle work the centre 41(45:49) sts as follows: K5 ML K5 ML, K2(K4:K6), ML K5 ML K7 ML K5 ML, K2 (K4:K6), ML K5 ML K5. Then pick up and knit 49 sts up right front edge 147(151:155) sts.

Row 1: (wrong side) (K1 P1) 23 times, K2tog, P1, K2tog, (P1 K1) alternately 22(24:26) times, P1, K2tog, P1, K2tog then (P1 K1) alternately 23 times.

Row 2: rib, allowing for decrease sts.

Row 3: rib 45 sts, K2tog, P1, K2tog, rib 43(47:51), K2tog, P1, K2tog, rib 45.

Row 4: rib.

Work 5 more rows, decreasing in this way on front corners on every wrong side row. Cast off neatly in rib.

TO MAKE UP

Carefully press all pieces with a damp cloth and a warm iron, omitting the ribbing. Join shoulder seams, including the ribbing, sew sleeves into position along armhole edge, then join side and sleeve seams.

3 and 4
Cottage Garden

RED AND white checked gingham is the jolliest fabric under the sun, and always makes me think of things I like – French cafés, pots of home-made jam, wicker picnic hampers, cheery cottage kitchens and gardens in the country full of old-fashioned flowers. It was the last two of these – the view of one from the other – that led to *Cottage Garden*. The flowers were all climbers that had draped themselves in great swags along the garden wall, looking their prettiest with the early morning sun behind them, seen through a window framed with gingham curtains. It was one of those natural pictures that take you by surprise, shake you by the shoulders and demand to be made up into a design. As patterns, checks and flowers have absolutely nothing in common, and this is one of those illogical designs that really oughtn't to work, but does – probably because the combination brings so many pleasant things to mind. I liked the pattern so much that I made it up into both a sweater and a cardigan.

COTTAGE GARDEN CHART CG1

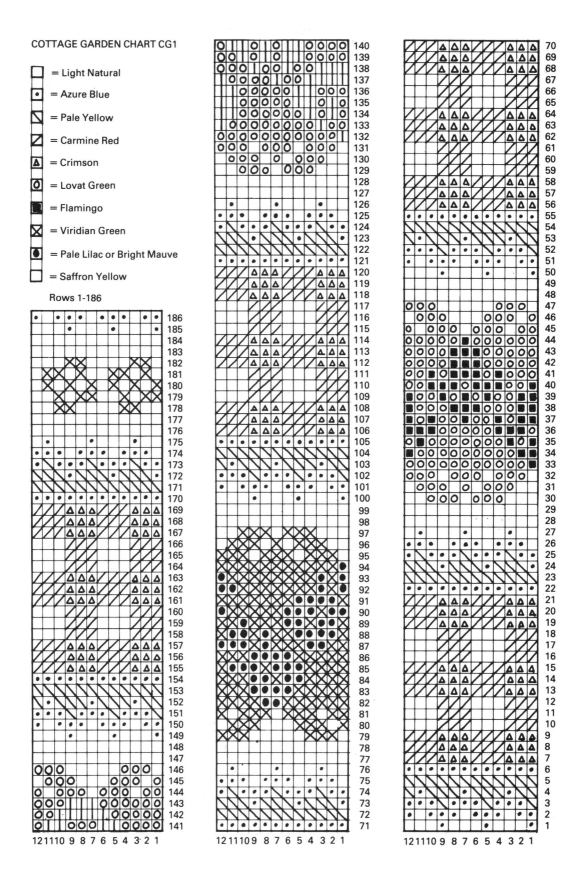

☐ = Light Natural

◨ = Azure Blue

◩ = Pale Yellow

◪ = Carmine Red

◭ = Crimson

◐ = Lovat Green

◼ = Flamingo

◙ = Viridian Green

◖ = Pale Lilac or Bright Mauve

☐ = Saffron Yellow

Rows 1-186

COTTAGE GARDEN SWEATER

YARN COLOURS AND NUMBERS	QUANTITIES REQUIRED IN OUNCES (1 oz = 28.3 g)			
	Size 1	Size 2	Size 3	Size 4
Light Natural 202	3	3	4	4
Crimson 55	1	1	2	2
Carmine Red 72	2	3	3	4
Azure Blue 17	1	2	2	2
Pale Yellow 96	1	1	1	2
Lovat Green 29	1	2	2	2
Flamingo FC7	1	1	1	1
Viridian Green 65	1	1	1	2
Bright Mauve 44	1	1	1	1
Saffron Yellow 90	1	1	1	1

NEEDLES One pair each size 2¾ mm (No. 12 British, No. 1 American), 3 mm (No. 11 British, No. 2 American) and 3¼ mm (No. 10 British, No. 3 American) needles, and a stitch holder.

TENSION 16 sts and 16 rows to 2 in (5 cm) on 3¼ mm needles over Fair Isle pattern. For K1P1 ribbing: 10 sts and 11 rows to 1 in (2.5 cm) on 2¾ mm needles. Change needle size if necessary to obtain correct tension.

SIZES 4 sizes. Size 1 = 33 in (84 cm), size 2 = 36 in (91.5 cm), size 3 = 39 in (99 cm), size 4 = 42 in (106.5 cm), actual measurements.

ABBREVIATIONS See page 16. *Colours:* CR = Carmine Red, LN = Light Natural.

NOTES FOR KNITTERS See page 13.

SPECIAL INSTRUCTIONS FOR THIS DESIGN If you want to use a K2P2 rib instead of a K1P1 rib, work as follows. **BACK and FRONT:** cast on 120(132:140:152) sts. **Increase row:** inc 12(12:16:16) evenly over the row. **SLEEVES:** cast on 52(60:68:72) sts. **Increase row:** inc 8(12:16:24) sts evenly over the row. **NECK RIBBING:** pick up 84 sts around front neck.

BACK

With 2¾ mm needles and CR yarn, cast on 118(130:140:152) sts and work 3 rows in K1P1 rib. **Rows 4–6:** rib in LN. **Rows 7–9:** rib in CR. **Rows 10–12:** rib in LN. **Rows 13–15:** rib in CR. **Rows 16–18:** rib in LN. **Rows 19–21:** rib in CR. **Rows 22–24:** rib in LN. **Rows 25–27:** rib in CR.
Next row: (increase row) in LN, K across, inc 14(14:16:16) sts evenly over the row: 132(144:156:168) sts.
Next row: P across in LN.
Using 3 mm needles on all 1-colour rows and 3¼ mm needles on all 2-colour rows, begin to work in pattern starting with row 1 of chart CG1. On K rows work sts 1–12 across 11(12:13:14) times, on P rows work sts 12–1 across 11(12:13:14) times. Work straight in pattern until you have completed row 98 of chart. *Be sure to maintain continuity of pattern for remainder of work on Back.*

Armhole Shaping

Rows 99–100: cast off 5(7:9:11) sts at beg of each row: 122(130:138:146) sts rem.
Rows 101–114: dec 1 st at beg of each row: 108(116:124:132) sts rem.

Rows 115–118: work in pattern without shaping.
Rows 119–120: dec 1 st at beg of each row: 106(114:122:130) sts rem.
Rows 121–124: work in pattern without shaping.
Rows 125–126: dec 1 st at beg of each row: 104(112:120:128) sts rem.
Rows 127–138: work in pattern without shaping.
Rows 139–140: inc into first st of each row: 106(114:122:130) sts.
Rows 141–148: work in pattern without shaping.
Rows 149–150: inc into first st of each

row: 108(116:124:132) sts.

Rows 151–158: work in pattern without shaping.

Rows 159–160: inc into first st of each row: 110(118:126:134) sts.

Rows 161–162: work in pattern without shaping.

Shoulder Shaping

Rows 163–170: cast off 5(6:7:8) sts at beg of each row: 70 sts rem.

Rows 171–172: cast off 5 sts at beg of each row, work in pattern to end: 60 sts rem.

Back Neck

With 2¾ mm needles and CR yarn, work the 60 sts for back neck in K1P1 rib for 9 rows; 3 rows CR, 3 rows LN, 3 rows CR. Cast off neatly in rib on the 10th row in CR.

FRONT

Work as for Back until you have completed row 142 of chart CG1: 106(114:122:130) sts rem. *Be sure to maintain continuity of pattern throughout.*

Divide for Neck

Row 143: work in pattern across 38(42:46:50) sts, turn, and leave rem 68(72:76:80) sts on spare needle or stitch holder and work on first group of sts as follows.

Left Front

Rows 144–148: dec 1 st at neck edge on every row: 33(37:41:45) sts rem.

Row 149: inc 1 st at beg of row, work across in pattern to last 2 sts, dec 1 st at neck edge: 33(37:41:45) sts rem.

Rows 150–156: dec 1 st at neck edge on every row: 26(30:34:38) sts rem.

Rows 157–158: work in pattern without shaping.

Row 159: inc 1 st at beg of row, work across in pattern to last 2 sts, dec 1 st at neck edge: 26(30:34:38) sts rem.

Row 160: dec 1 st at neck edge, work in pattern across row: 25(29:33:37) sts rem. Now keep neck edge straight for remainder of work.

Rows 161–162: work in pattern without shaping.

Shoulder Shaping

Row 163: cast off 5(6:7:8) sts, work in pattern to end: 20(23:26:29) sts rem.

Row 164: work in pattern without shaping.

Row 165: as row 163: 15(17:19:21) sts rem.

Row 166: work in pattern without shaping.

Row 167: as row 163: 10(11:12:13) sts rem.

Row 168: work in pattern without shaping.

Row 169: as row 163: 5 sts rem.

Row 170: work in pattern without shaping.

Row 171: cast off rem 5 sts.

Right Front

Slip 30 sts for Front Neck on to spare needle or stitch holder, then rejoin yarn to rem 38(42:46:50) sts and work in pattern across row 143. Now work as for Left Front, reversing all shapings and ending by casting off rem 5 sts on row 172.

SLEEVES

With 2¾ mm needles and CR yarn cast on 54(60:66:72) sts and work in striped K1P1 rib for 27 rows as given for Front and Back.

Next row: (increase row) in LN, K across, inc 6(12:18:24) sts evenly over the row: 60(72:84:96) sts.

Next row: P across in LN.

Next row: K across in LN.

Using 3 mm needles on all 1-colour rows and 3¼ mm needles on all 2-colour rows begin to work in pattern starting with **row 164** of chart CG1. *Be sure to maintain continuity of pattern throughout.*

Row 164: work sts 12–1 across 5(6:7:8) times.

Row 165: work sts 12–1 across 5(6:7:8) times.

Row 166: inc 1 st at both ends of row: 62(74:86:98) sts.

Rows 167–169: work in pattern without shaping.

Row 170: as row 166: 64(76:88:100) sts.

Rows 171–173: work in pattern without shaping.

Row 174: as row 166: 66(78:90:102) sts.

Rows 175–177: work in pattern without shaping.

Row 178: as row 166: 68(80:92:104) sts.

Rows 179–181: work in pattern without shaping.

Row 182: as row 166: 70(82:94:106) sts.

Rows 183–184: work in pattern without shaping.

Now return to **row 1** of chart CG1 and continue to work in pattern, inc 1 st at both ends of row 2 and every following 4th row until there are 90(102:114:126) sts on needle. (Row 38 of chart will now have been worked.)

Rows 39–44: work in pattern without shaping.

Rows 45–94: inc 1 st at both ends of row 45 and every following 7th row until there are 106(118:130:142) sts on needle. (Row 94 of chart will now have been worked.)

Rows 95–97: work in pattern without shaping.

Row 98: inc 1 st at both ends of row: 108(120:132:144) sts.

Rows 99–100: work in pattern without shaping.

Shape Sleeve Head

Rows 101–104: cast off 1(3:5:7) sts at beg of each row: 104(108:112:116) sts.

Rows 105–114: cast off 2 sts at beg of each row: 84(88:92:96) sts rem.

Rows 115–116: dec 1 st at beg of each row: 82(86:90:94) sts rem.

Rows 117–118: cast off 2 sts at beg of each row: 78(82:86:90) sts rem.

Rows 119–122: dec 1 st at beg of each row: 74(78:82:86) sts rem.

Rows 123–126: cast off 2 sts at beg of each row: 66(70:74:78) sts rem.

Rows 127–128: dec 1 st at beg of each row: 64(68:72:76) sts rem.

Rows 128–142: cast off 2 sts at beg of each row: 36(40:44:48) sts rem.

Rows 143–144: cast off 5 sts at beg of each row: 26(30:34:38) sts rem.

Rows 145–147: cast off 3(4:5:6) sts at beg of each row: 17(18:19:20) sts rem.

Row 148: cast off rem sts.

Work second sleeve to match.

NECKBAND

With 2¾ mm needles, CR yarn and right side of work facing, pick up 28 sts down left side of neck, 30 sts from centre front neck and 28 sts up right side of neck: 86 sts. Work in K1P1 rib for 9 rows; 3 rows CR, 3 rows LN, 3 rows CR. Cast off neatly in rib on the 10th row in CR.

TO MAKE UP

Gently press all pieces using a warm iron and damp cloth. Join shoulder seams including neck ribbing. Sew sleeves into place along armhole edge then join side and sleeve seams.

COTTAGE GARDEN CARDIGAN

YARN COLOURS AND NUMBERS	QUANTITIES REQUIRED IN OUNCES (1 oz = 28.3 g)			
	Size 1	Size 2	Size 3	Size 4
Light Natural 202	4	4	5	5
Crimson 55	1	2	2	2
Carmine Red 72	2	2	3	3
Azure Blue 17	1	2	2	2
Pale Yellow 96	1	1	1	2
Lovat Green 29	1	2	2	2
Flamingo FC7	1	1	1	1
Viridian Green 65	1	1	1	2
Pale Lilac 49	1	1	1	1
Saffron Yellow 90	1	1	1	1

NEEDLES One pair each size 2¾ mm (No. 12 British, No. 1 American), 3 mm (No. 11 British, No. 2 American) and 3¼ mm (No. 10 British, No. 3 American) needles, and a stitch holder. *Also:* 8 buttons.

TENSION 16 sts and 16 rows to 2 in (5 cm) on 3¼ mm needles over Fair Isle pattern. For K1P1 ribbing: 10 sts and 11 rows to 1 in (2.5 cm) on 2¾ mm needles. Change needle size if necessary to obtain correct tension.

SIZES 4 sizes. Size 1 = 33 in (84 cm), size 2 = 36 in (91.5 cm), size 3 = 39 in (99 cm), size 4 = 42 in (106.5 cm), actual measurements.

ABBREVIATIONS See page 16. *Colours:* LN = Light Natural.

NOTES FOR KNITTERS See page 13.

SPECIAL INSTRUCTIONS FOR THIS DESIGN If you want to use a K2P2 rib instead of a K1P1 rib, work as follows. **BACK:** cast on 120(132:140: 152) sts. **Increase row:** inc 12(12:16: 16) sts evenly over the row: 132(144: 156:168) sts. **FRONTS:** cast on 60(64:68:72) sts. **Increase row:** inc 6(8:10:12) sts evenly over the row: 66(72:78:84) sts. **SLEEVES:** cast on 52(60:68:72) sts. **Increase row:** increase 8(12:16:24) sts evenly over the row: 60(72:84:96) sts. **NECK RIBBING:** pick up 144 sts, work in K2P2 rib. **BUTTON and BUTTONHOLE BAND:** work in K1P1 rib.

BACK

With 2¾ mm needles and LN yarn, cast on 118(130:140:152) sts and work in K1P1 rib for 2½ in (6.5 cm).

Next row: (increase row) K across, inc 14(14:16:16) sts evenly over the row: 132(144:156:168) sts.

Next row: P across.

Using 3 mm needles on all 1-colour rows and 3¼ mm needles on all 2-colour rows, begin to work in pattern from chart CG1, starting with row 1. On K rows, work sts 1–12 across 11(12:13:14) times, on P rows work sts 12–1 across 11(12:13:14) times. Work straight in pattern until you have completed pattern row 112 of chart CG1. *Be sure to maintain continuity of pattern for remainder of work on Back.*

Armhole Shaping

Rows 113–114: cast off 5(7:9:11) sts at beg of each row: 122(130:138:146) sts rem.

Rows 115–128: dec 1 st at beg of row: 108(116:124:132) sts rem.

Rows 129–132: work in pattern without shaping.

Rows 133–134: dec 1 st at beg of each row: 106(114:122:130) sts rem.

Rows 135–138: work in pattern without shaping.

Rows 139–140: dec 1 st at beg of each row: 104(112:120:128) sts rem.

Rows 141–152: work in pattern without shaping.

Rows 153–154: inc into first st of each row: 106(114:122:130) sts.

Rows 155–162: work in pattern without shaping.

Rows 163–164: inc into first st of each row: 108(116:124:132) sts.

Rows 165–172: work in pattern without shaping.

Rows 173–174: inc into first st of each row: 110(118:126:134) sts.

Rows 175–176: work in pattern without shaping.

Shoulder Shaping

Rows 177–184: cast off 5(6:7:8) sts at beg of each row: 70 sts rem.

Rows 185–186: cast off 5 sts at beg of each row, work in pattern to end: 60 sts rem.

Leave rem 60 sts on a stitch holder.

LEFT FRONT

With 2¾ mm needles and LN yarn, cast on 60(66:70:76) sts and work in K1P1 rib for 2½ in (6.5 cm).

Next row (increase row): K across, inc 6(6:8:8) sts evenly over the row: 66(72:78:84) sts.

Next row: P across.

Using 3 mm needles on all 1-colour rows and 3¼ mm needles on all 2-colour rows, begin to work in pattern starting with row 1 of chart CG1 *in the following sequence*. **For sizes 1 and 3 only:** on K rows work sts 1–12 across 5(6) times, then work sts 1–6. On P rows work sts 6–1, then work sts 12–1 5(6) times. **For sizes 2 and 4 only:** on K rows work sts 1–12 across 6(7) times, on P rows work sts 12–1 across 6(7) times. *For all sizes:* work straight in pattern until you have completed pattern row 112 of chart CG1. *Be sure to maintain continuity of pattern for remainder of work on Left Front.*

Armhole Shaping

Row 113: cast off 5(7:9:11) sts at beg of row: 61(65:69:73) sts rem.

Row 114: work in pattern without shaping.

Rows 115–127: Keeping front edge straight, dec 1 st at armhole edge on row 115 and every alternate row: 54(58:62:66) sts rem.

Rows 128–132: work in pattern without shaping.

Row 133: dec 1 st at beg of row, work in pattern to end: 53(57:61:65) sts rem.

Rows 134–138: work in pattern without shaping.

Row 139: dec 1 st at beg of row, work in pattern to end: 52(56:60:64) sts rem.

Rows 140–152: work in pattern without shaping.

Row 153: inc into first st, work in pattern to end: 53(57:61:65) sts.

Rows 154–157: work in pattern without shaping.

Neck Shaping

Row 158: cast off 15 sts at neck edge, work in pattern to end: 38(42:46:50) sts rem.

Row 159: work in pattern without shaping.

Row 160: cast off 2 sts at beg of row, work in pattern to end: 36(40:44:48) sts rem.

Row 161: work in pattern without shaping.

Row 162: cast off 2 sts, work in pattern to end: 34(38:42:46) sts rem.

Row 163: inc into first st (armhole edge), work in pattern to end: 35(39:43:47) sts.

Rows 164–170: keeping armhole edge straight, dec 2 sts at neck edge on row 164 and every alternate row 3 more times: 27(31:35:39) sts rem.

Rows 171–172: work in pattern without shaping.

Row 173: inc into first st, work in pattern to end: 28(32:36:40) sts.

Row 174: dec 1 st (neck edge), work in pattern to end: 27(31:35:39) sts rem.

Rows 175–176: work in pattern without shaping.

Shoulder Shaping

Row 177: cast off 5(6:7:8) sts, work in pattern to end: 22(25:28:31) sts rem.

Row 178: dec 1 st, work in pattern to end: 21(24:27:30) sts rem.

Row 179: as row 177: 16(18:20:22) sts rem.

Row 180: work in pattern without shaping.

Row 181: as row 177: 11(12:13:14) sts rem.

Row 182: dec 1 st, work in pattern to end: 10(11:12:13) sts rem.

Row 183: as row 177: 5 sts rem.

Row 184: work in pattern without shaping.

Row 185: cast off rem 5 sts.

RIGHT FRONT

Pattern sequence as follows. **For sizes 1 and 3 only:** on K rows work sts 7–12, then work sts 1–12 across 5(6) times. On P rows work sts 12–1 across 5(6) times, then work sts 12–7. **For sizes 2 and 4 only:** on K rows work sts 1–12 across 6(7) times, on P rows work sts 12–1 across 6(7) times. **For all sizes:** work as for Left Front, reversing all shapings, beginning neck shaping on row 159, and ending by casting off remaining 5 sts on row 186.

SLEEVES

With 2¾ mm needles and LN yarn, cast on 54(60:66:72) sts and work in K1P1 rib for 2½ in (6.5 cm).

Next row: (increase row) K across, inc 6(12:18:24) sts evenly over the row: 60(72:84:96) sts.

Next row: P across.

Using 3 mm needles on all 1-colour rows and 3¼ mm needles on all 2-colour rows, begin to work in pattern starting with **row 177** of chart CG1. Be sure to maintain continuity of pattern throughout.

Row 177: work sts 1–12 across 5(6:7:8) times.

Row 178: work sts 12–1 across 5(6:7:8) times.

Row 179: as row 177.

Row 180: inc 1 st at both ends of row: 62(74:86:98) sts.

Rows 181–183: work in pattern without shaping.

Row 184: as row 180: 64(76:88:100) sts. Now return to **row 1** of chart and continue to work in pattern, inc 1 st at both ends of row 4 of chart, and every following 4th row, until there are 90(102:114:126) sts on needle (row 52 of chart CG1 will now have been worked).

Rows 53–58: work in pattern without shaping.

Rows 59–109: inc 1 st at both ends of row 59 and every following 7th row until there are 106(118:130:142) sts on needle (row 108).

Rows 109–111: work in pattern without shaping.

Row 112: inc 1 st at both ends of row: 108(120:132:144) sts.

Rows 113–114: work in pattern without shaping.

Shape Sleeve Head

Rows 115–118: cast off 1(3:5:7) sts at beg of each row: 104(108:112:116) sts rem.

Rows 119–128: cast off 2 sts at beg of each row: 84(88:92:96) sts rem.

Rows 129–130: dec 1 st at beg of each row: 82(86:90:94) sts rem.

Rows 131–132: cast off 2 sts at beg of each row: 78(82:86:90) sts rem.

Rows 133–136: dec 1 st at beg of each row: 74(78:82:86) sts rem.

Rows 137–140: cast off 2 sts at beg of each row: 66(70:74:78) sts rem.

Rows 141–142: dec 1 st at beg of each row: 64(68:72:76) sts rem.

Rows 143–156: cast off 2 sts at beg of each row: 36(40:44:48) sts rem.

Rows 157–158: cast off 5 sts at beg of each row: 26(30:34:38) sts rem.

Rows 159–161: cast off 3(4:5:6) sts at beg of each row.

Row 162: cast off rem 17(18:19:20) sts. Work second sleeve to match.

NECKBAND

Gently press all pieces using a warm iron and damp cloth. Join shoulder seams. *For all sizes:* with 2¾ mm needles, LN yarn and right side of work facing, pick up 42 sts evenly around right front neck edge, 60 sts across back neck and 42 sts evenly around left front neck edge (144 sts on needle). Work 9 rows in K1P1 rib. Cast off neatly in rib on the 10th row.

FRONT BANDS

Button band: with 2¾ mm needles and LN yarn, cast on 10 sts and work in K1P1 rib until band, when slightly stretched, measures the same as the front edge. Cast off in rib. Mark position for buttons, the first ½ in (1.5 cm) from beginning, the last ½ in (1.5 cm) from top of the band, the other six spaced evenly between. **Buttonhole band:** work as for button band for ½ in (1.5 cm) then work buttonhole as follows.

Next row: rib 4 sts, cast off 2 sts, rib 4 sts.

Next row: rib 4 sts, cast on 2 sts, rib 4 sts.

Continue to work as for button band, working buttonholes opposite button markers. Cast off in rib.

TO MAKE UP

Sew in sleeves. Join underarm and side seams. Sew front borders to front edges, easing to fit. Sew on buttons opposite buttonholes.

5
Chow Chow

CHOW CHOW is based on antique Chinese carpets, those rare and fine collector's pieces prized for their subtle colourings and serene patterns. While Persian and Caucasian rugs are distinguished by their use of many strongly contrasting colours, Chinese carpets used very few colours – mainly blue, reddish brown, white and yellow. However, each of these colours was broken up into many different shades, and it is the use of several shades of a single colour placed next to each other that gives Chinese carpets their unique glowing quality. A similarly restrained spirit pervades the Chinese use of pattern. The carpets of the Near East are noted for their intense and complicated patterns, but the Chinese preferred simpler motifs scattered over a plain background. As in other aspects of Chinese art, the motifs had a symbolic meaning, and auspicious symbols were purposely woven into the carpets to bring good fortune to their owners. I have chosen a number of these lucky patterns for *Chow Chow*, and this is what they mean. The *shou* character, rows 12–30, signifies long life. The *pearl* border, rows 49–56, is the emblem of perfection. The *knot of destiny*, rows 59–71, symbolizes Fate and its turnings. The motif representing four stylized bats flying in towards a central medallion, rows 100–114, is the sign for happiness and luck, for in China the bat is the most fortunate of creatures. Finally, the stylized *peony* flower, rows 143–152, symbolizes well being.

CHOW CHOW
Chart CC1
210 rows

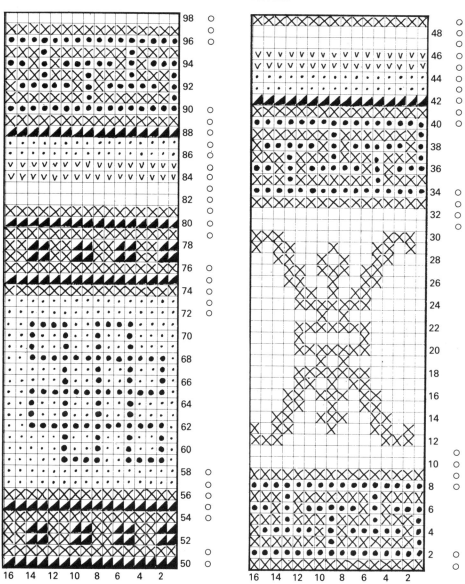

Colour Key

☐ = Russet   Ⅴ = Copper

☒ = Navy Blue   • = Ginger

⬤ = French Blue   ◤ = Mustard Yellow

Note: all rows marked on the right hand margin of
the chart with an ○ must be worked on 3mm needles.

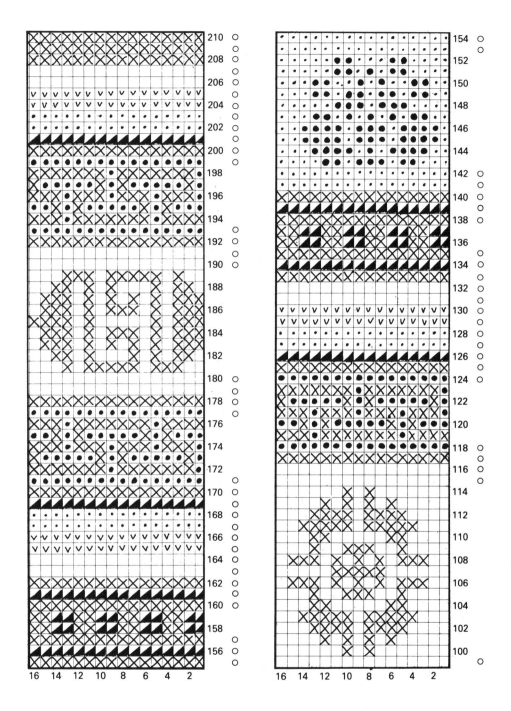

CHOW CHOW CARDIGAN

YARN COLOURS AND NUMBERS	QUANTITIES REQUIRED IN OUNCES (1 oz = 28.3 g)					
	Size 1	Size 2	Size 3	Size 4	Size 5	Size 6
Navy Blue 21	4	5	5	5	5	5
French Blue 16	3	3	3	3	3	3
Russet 45	4	4	4	4	5	5
Copper 31	1	1	1	1	1	1
Ginger 32	2	2	3	3	3	3
Mustard Yellow 28	1	1	1	2	2	2

NEEDLES One pair each size 2¾ mm (No. 12 British, No. 1 American), 3 mm (No. 11 British, No. 2 American) and 3¼ mm (No. 10 British, No. 3 American) needles. *Also:* 6 buttons.

TENSION 16 sts and 18 rows to 2 in (5 cm) over Fair Isle pattern on 3¼ mm needles. For K1P1 ribbing: 10 sts and 11 rows to 1 in (2.5 cms) on 2¾ mm needles. Change needle size if necessary to obtain correct tension.

SIZES 6 sizes. Size 1 = 32 in (81.5 cm), size 2 = 34 in (86.5 cm), size 3 = 36 in (91.5 cm), size 4 = 38 in (96.5 cm), size 5 = 40 in (101.5 cm), size 6 = 42 in (106.5 cm), actual measurements.

ABBREVIATIONS See page 16. *Colours:* NB = Navy Blue, FB = French Blue, R = Russet, C = Copper, G = Ginger, M = Mustard Yellow.

NOTES FOR KNITTERS See page 13.

BACK

With 2¾ mm needles and R yarn, cast on 128(136:144:152:160:168) sts and work in K1P1 rib for 28 rows as follows: 10 rows in R, 7 rows in C, 7 rows in G, 4 rows in M. Change to 3mm needles and NB yarn and K1 row. Change to FB yarn and P 1 row. Change to 3¼ mm needles and proceed to work in st.st. and pattern, starting at row 3 of Chart CC1.

Size 1: Row 3; work sts 1–16 across 8 times (128 sts).
Row 4: work sts 16–1 across 8 times.
Size 2: Row 3; work sts 13–16, then sts 1–16 (8 times), then sts 1–4 (136 sts)
Row 4: work sts 4–1, then sts 16–1 (8 times), then sts 16–13.
Size 3: Row 3; work sts 1–16 across 9 times (144 sts).
Row 4: work sts 16–1 across 9 times.
Size 4: Row 3; work sts 13–16, then sts 1–16 (9 times), then sts 1–4 (152 sts).
Row 4: work sts 4–1, then sts 16–1 (9 times), then sts 16–13.
Size 5: Row 3; work sts 1–16 across 10 times (160 sts).
Row 4: work sts 16–1 across 10 times.
Size 6: Row 3; work sts 13–16, then sts 1–16 (10 times), then sts 1–4 (168 sts).
Row 4: work sts 4–1, then sts 16–1 (10 times), then sts 16–13.
For all sizes, continue to work from chart in this way until you have completed pattern row 100(108:108:116:116:120).

Armhole Shaping

Row 101(109:109:117:117:121): Keeping correct in pattern, cast off 8(8:9:9:10:10) sts at beg of row.
Row 102(110:110:118:118:122): cast off 8(8:9:9:10:10:) sts at beg of row.
Now dec 1 st at each end of next 6(6:7:7:8:8) rows: 100(108:112:120:124:132) sts.
Continue straight for 64(66:68:70:72:74) rows.

Shoulder Shaping

Keeping correct in pattern, cast off 10(10:11:12:12:12) sts at beg of next 2 rows.
Cast off 10(11:12:12:12:13) sts at beg of next 2 rows.
Cast off 10(11:11:12:12:13) sts at beg of next 2 rows, then cast off remaining 40(44:44:48:52:56) sts.

LEFT FRONT

With 2¾ mm needles and R yarn, cast on 64(68:72:76:80:84) sts and work in K1P1 rib as for Back. Change to 3 mm needles and NB yarn and K1 row. Change to FB yarn and P1 row Change to 3¼ mm needles and proceed to work in st.st and pattern starting with row 3 of chart CC1 as follows:
Size 1: Row 3; work sts 1–16 across 4 times (64 sts).
Row 4: work sts 16–1 across 4 times.
Size 2: Row 3; work sts 5–16, then sts 1–16 (3 times), then sts 1–8 (68 sts).
Row 4: work sts 8–1, then sts 16–1 (3 times), then sts 16–5.
Size 3: Row 3; work sts 1–16 across 4 times, then sts 1–8 (72 sts).
Row 4: work sts 8–1, then sts 16–1 (4 times).
Size 4: Row 3; work sts 5–16, then sts 1–16 (4 times) (76 sts).
Row 4: work sts 16–1 (4 times), then sts 16–5.
Size 5: Row 3; work sts 1–16 (5 times) (80 sts).
Row 4: work sts 16–1 (5 times).
Size 6: Row 3; work sts 5–16, then sts 1–16 (4 times), then sts 1–8 (84 sts).
Row 4: work sts 8–1, then sts 16–1 (4 times), then sts 16–5.
For all sizes: work in pattern from chart until you have completed pattern row 92(100:100:108:108:112).

To Shape Neck and Armhole

Keeping correct in pattern, dec 1 st at neck edge on next and every following 3rd row 10(14:14:16:16:20) times, and then every 4th row. **At the same time**, when 100(108:108:116:116:120) pattern rows have been completed, shape armhole as follows.

Cast off 8(9:9:10:10:11) sts at beg of next row.

Dec 1 st at armhole edge of next 6(7:7:8:8:9) rows.

Now keep armhole edge straight and dec as explained at neck edge until 30(32:34:36:36:38) sts remain.

Work straight as for Back, to shoulder shaping.

Shoulder Shaping

Cast off 10(10:11:12:12:12) sts at beg of next row.

Work 1 row.

Cast off 10(11:12:12:12:13) sts at beg of row.

Work 1 row.

Cast off remaining 10(11:11:12:12:13) sts.

RIGHT FRONT

With 2¾ mm needles and R yarn, cast on and work in K1P1 rib as for Left Front. Change to 3 mm needles and NB yarn and K1 row. Change to FB yarn and P1 row. Change to 3¼ mm needles and proceed to work in st.st and pattern starting with row 3 of chart CC1 as follows:

Size 1: Row 3; work sts 1–16 (4 times) (64 sts).

Row 4: work sts 16–1 (4 times).

Size 2: Row 3; work sts 9–16, then sts 1–16 (3 times), then sts 1–12 (68 sts).

Row 4: work sts 12–1, then sts 16–1 (3 times), then sts 16–9.

Size 3: Row 3; work sts 9–16, then sts 1–16 (4 times) (72 sts).

Row 4: work sts 16–1 (4 times), then sts 16–9.

Size 4: Row 3; work sts 1–16 (4 times), then sts 1–12 (76 sts).

Row 4: work sts 12–1, then sts 16–1 (4 times).

Size 5: Row 3; work sts 1–16 (5 times) (80 sts).

Row 4: work sts 16–1 (5 times).

Size 6: Row 3; work sts 9–16, then sts 1–16 (4 times), then sts 1–12 (84 sts).

Row 4: work sts 12–1, then sts 16–1 (4 times), then sts 16–9.

For all sizes: following this stitch se-

quence, work to match the Left Front, reversing all shapings.

SLEEVES

With 2¾ mm needles and R yarn cast on 62(66:66:70:70:76) sts and work 28 rows in K1P1 rib. Change to st.st and work as follows;

Next row: (increase row) in R, K across, inc 10(14:14:18:18:20) sts evenly over the row: 72(80:80:88:88:96) sts.

Next row: P across in R. Change to 3 mm needles and work in st.st as follows: 3 rows in C, 3 rows in G, 2 rows in M, 1 row in NB, 1 row in FB. Now change to 3¼ mm needles and begin to work in pattern starting with row 3 of chart CC1.

Sizes 2, 3 and 6: Row 3; work sts 1–16 across 5(5:6) times: 80(80:96) sts.

Row 4: work sts 16–1 across 5(5:6) times.

Sizes 1, 4 and 5: Row 3; work sts 13–16, then sts 1–16 4(5:5) times, then sts 1–4: 72(88:88) sts.

Row 4: work sts 4–1, then sts 16–1 4(5:5) times, then sts 16–13.

For all sizes, keeping correct in pattern, inc 1 st at both ends of every 4th row until there are 116(124:124:132:132:140) sts.

Work straight until 100(108:108:116:116:120) rows of pattern have been completed.

Shape Sleeve Head

Cast off 8(9:9:10:10:12) sts at beg of next 2 rows. Dec 1 st at each end of next 6(7:7:8:8:9) rows. Now dec 1 st at each end of next and every alternate row until 48 sts remain.

Cast off 3 sts at beg of next 6 rows.

Cast off remaining 30 sts. Work second sleeve to match.

Now carefully press pieces with a warm iron and damp cloth, omitting the ribbing. Join shoulder seams, sew sleeves into position along armhole edge, then join side and sleeve seams.

BUTTONHOLE BORDER

With 2¾ mm needles and R yarn, cast on 12 sts and work 4 rows in K1P1 rib.

Row 5: (buttonhole row) rib 4, cast off 3, rib 5.

Row 6: rib 5, cast on 3, rib 4.

Rib 24(25:25:27:27:28) rows straight, then work rows 5 and 6. Continue in this way until 6 buttonholes have been worked. Continue straight until band, when slightly stretched, fits around front and back neck edges of cardigan. Cast off neatly in rib.

TO MAKE UP

Attach the buttonhole border with a fine slip stitch and press gently. Sew on buttons opposite buttonholes.

6
Kensington Dandy

THE SHORT sleeveless waistcoat with points came on the scene at the beginning of the nineteenth century, as men were giving up the well-cut but voluminous costume of the previous century for clothes that fit the figure closely. Worn with cutaway coats, tight long breeches or the newly modish trousers, fancy waistcoats in rich and colourful materials showed off the newly fashionable masculine waist to perfection, and turned every man into a dandy. King George IV, though not possessed of the ideal figure, was extremely fond of fancy waistcoats – he paticularly liked to wear one in purple velvet embroidered with golden monkeys – and at Court during his reign the waistcoats of the gentlemen often outshone the gowns of the ladies, both sexes dressing in such showy fabrics that they looked 'as rich as a bed of flowers'. Almost to the end of the century, fancy waistcoats continued to be the most decorative article in the wardrobe of the well-dressed man. The young Benjamin Disraeli loved to wear flowered waistcoats over lace shirts, Albert the Prince Consort was partial to sprigged vests, and some sharp dressers took things to such extremes 'that they wore two waistcoats at once, one peeping out from under the other'.

Near the end of Queen Victoria's reign the fancy waistcoat was all but swallowed up by the encroaching sobrieties of the three-piece suit, but it made a dramatic reappearance in the 1950s when men about town took it up as an antidote to the austerities of the post-War years. Brocade waistcoats came in for evenings, checked waistcoats were worn by day, and *Tailor and Cutter* magazine got quite hot under the collar about men who persisted in wearing their waistcoats with loud ties 'that seem to be more about the palette than the palate'. I have always found fancy waistcoats tremendously appealing and, as it seemed to me that men had had them to themselves for far too long, I designed this waistcoat for dandy ladies covered with flowers in all the colours you see in the flowerbeds at Kensington Gardens in springtime.

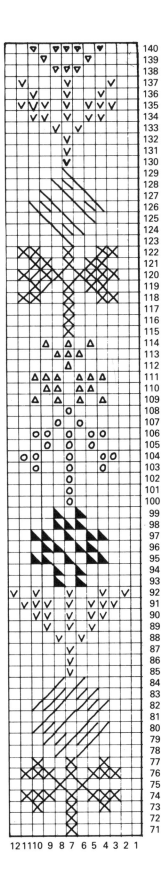
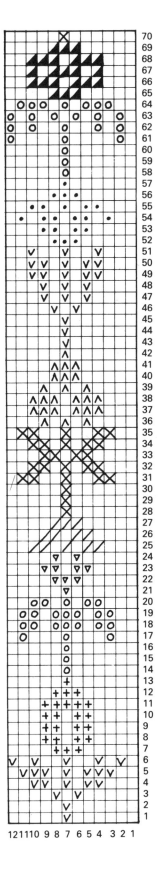

KENSINGTON DANDY

Chart KD1
Rows 1-162

�◣ = Carmine Red

◢△ = Turquoise Blue

◣ = Flamingo

◢ = Watermelon Red

⊡ = Pale Lilac

⋀ = Rose Pink

◿ = Bright Mauve ·

▽ = Purple

⊞ = Fuchsia Pink

⊙ = Leaf Green

⊠ = Viridian Green

⋁ = Lovat Green

☐ = Sand Beige

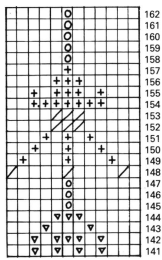

47

KENSINGTON DANDY
Chart KD2
Right Front
Rows 1-31
Sizes 1 and 3 only

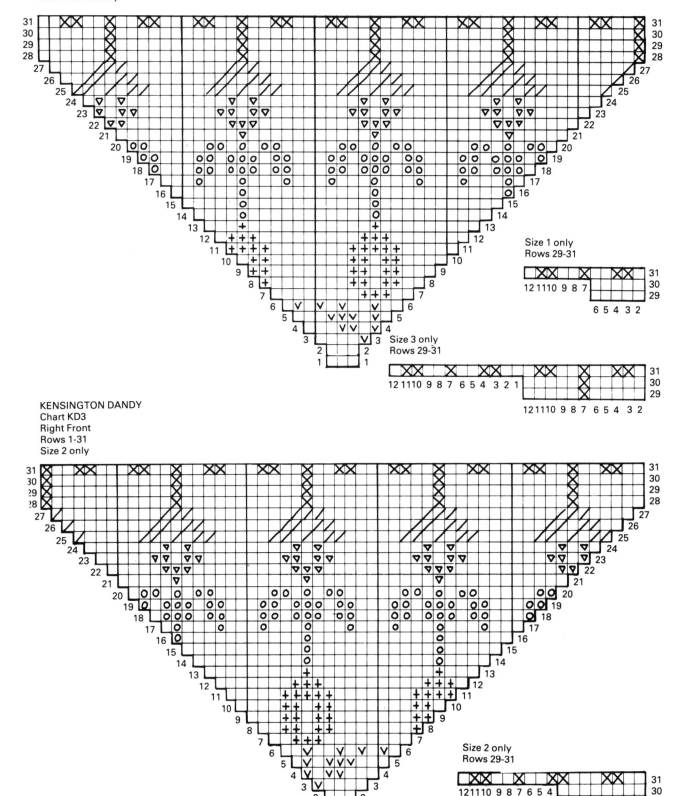

Size 1 only
Rows 29-31

Size 3 only
Rows 29-31

KENSINGTON DANDY
Chart KD3
Right Front
Rows 1-31
Size 2 only

Size 2 only
Rows 29-31

KENSINGTON DANDY
Chart KD4
Left Front
Rows 1-31
Sizes 1 and 3 only

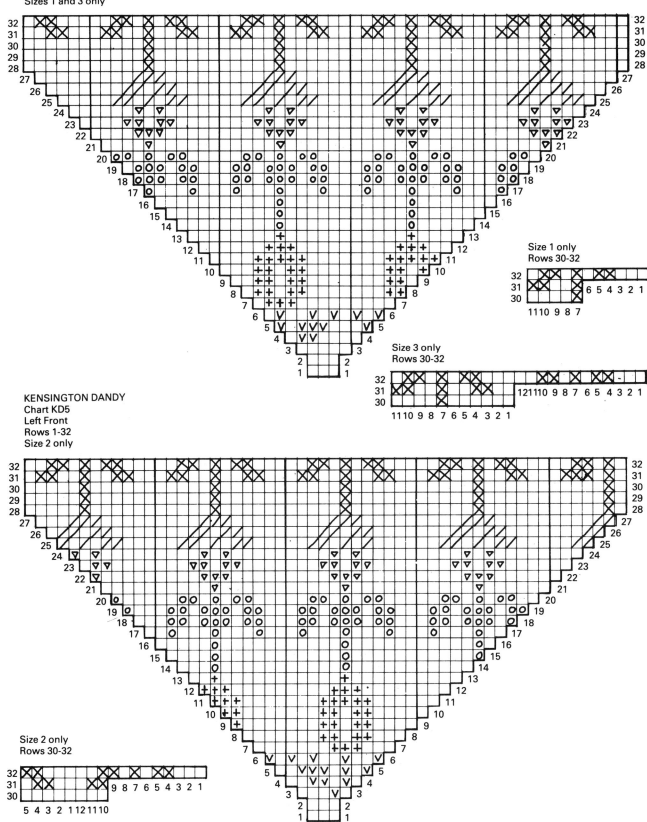

Size 1 only
Rows 30-32

Size 3 only
Rows 30-32

KENSINGTON DANDY
Chart KD5
Left Front
Rows 1-32
Size 2 only

Size 2 only
Rows 30-32

50

KENSINGTON DANDY POINTED WAISTCOAT

YARN COLOURS AND NUMBERS	QUANTITIES REQUIRED IN OUNCES (1 oz = 28.3 g)		
	Size 1	Size 2	Size 3
Sand Beige F C 43	3	4	4
Leaf Green 25	1	1	1
Viridian Green 65	1	1	1
Lovat Green 29	1	1	1
Purple 20	1	1	1
Bright Mauve 44	1	1	1
Fuchsia Pink 52	1	1	1
Rose Pink F C 22	1	1	1
Watermelon Red F C 33	1	1	1
Flamingo F C 7	1	1	1
Turquoise Blue 48	1	1	1
Pale Lilac 49	1	1	1
Carmine Red 72	1	1	1

NEEDLES One pair each size 2¾ mm (No. 12 British, No. 1 American), 3 mm (No. 11 British, No. 2 American) and 3¼ mm (No. 10 British, No. 3 American) needles. *Also:* 5 buttons.

TENSION 16 sts and 16 rows to 2 in (5 cm) on 3¼ mm needles over Fair Isle pattern. Change needle size if necessary to obtain correct tension.

SIZES 3 sizes. Size 1 = 33 in (84 cm), size 2 = 36 in (91.5 cm), size 3 = 39 in (99 cm), actual measurements.

ABBREVIATIONS See page 16. *Colours:* SB = Sand Beige, LL = Pale Lilac, FP = Fuchsia Pink, TQ = Turquoise Blue, RP = Rose Pink.

NOTES FOR KNITTERS See page 13.

SPECIAL INSTRUCTIONS FOR THIS DESIGN This waistcoat has been designed to be very short at the back, and is meant to sit above the back waist like a bolero. Knitted to correct tension, the back length from the centre back neck to the first row of pattern (not including neckband and bottom border) should measure approximately 16¼ in (41 cm). If you would like to increase the length, add 16 rows in the following way. Work as given for Back and Fronts, but do not begin armhole shaping until rows 109–110. Adjust all other shapings accordingly. Work to the end of row 160, then finish by repeating rows 17–35 of chart KD1, substituting Pale Lilac for Purple and Turquoise Blue for Bright Mauve on rows 21–27. I do not recommend that you increase the length any further, as the waistcoat points will then sit much too low at the front. A lengthened waistcoat will require six buttons.

BACK

With 2¾ mm needles and SB yarn, cast on 132(144:156) sts. Using 3 mm needles on all 1-colour rows and 3¼ mm needles on all 2-colour rows, begin to work in pattern starting with row 32 of chart KD1. Work sts 12–1 across 11(12:13) times.

Next row: work sts 1–12 across 11(12:13) times. Work straight in pattern until you have completed row 92 of chart KD1. *Be sure to maintain continuity of pattern for remainder of work on Back.*

Armhole Shaping

Rows 93–94: cast off 5(7:9) sts at beg of each row: 122(130:138) sts rem.

Rows 95–98: cast off 4 sts at beg of each row: 106(114:122) sts rem.

Rows 99–102: dec 1 st at both ends of each row: 98(106:114) sts rem.

Rows 103–158: work straight in pattern.

Shoulder Shaping

Rows 159–162: cast off 13(15:17) sts at beg of each row.

Row 163: cast off rem 46 sts.

RIGHT FRONT

With 2¾ mm needles and SB yarn, cast on 3 sts.

Next row: K 3 sts.

Next row: P 3 sts. Using 3 mm needles on all 1-colour rows and 3¼ mm needles on all 2-colour rows, work waistcoat point using chart KD2 for sizes 1 and 3 and chart KD3 for size 2. Begin on row 3 of chart for your size and inc 1 st at both ends of every row as shown. Work as shown until you have completed row 28 of chart for your size.

Row 29: work across 55 sts in pattern, then cast on 5(8:11) sts as shown.

Row 30: work across 60(63:66) sts in pattern.

Row 31: work across 60(63:66) sts in pattern, then cast on 6(9:12) sts as shown. There should now be 66(72:78) sts on needle.

Row 32: now change to chart KD1 and continue to work in pattern starting with row 32 of chart KD1 *in the following sequence.* **Sizes 1 and 3 only:** work sts 12–1 5(6) times, then work sts 12–7: 66(78) sts. **Size 2 only:** work sts 12–1 across 6 times (72 sts).

Row 33: Sizes 1 and 3 only; work sts 7–12, then work sts 1–12 5(6) times. **Size 2 only:** work sts 1–12 across 6 times.

Rows 34–93: work straight in pattern. *Be sure to maintain continuity of pattern for remainder of work on Right Front.*

Armhole and Neck Shaping

Row 94: cast off 5(7:9) sts at beg of row: 61(65:69) sts rem.

Row 95: dec 1 st at beg of row (neck edge), work across in pattern: 60(64:68) sts rem.

Row 96: cast off 4 sts at beg of row, work across in pattern: 56(60:64) sts rem.

Row 97: dec 1 st at beg of row (neck edge), work across in pattern: 55(59:63) sts rem.

Row 98: cast off 4 sts at beg of row, work across in pattern: 51(55:59) sts rem.

Row 99: dec 1 st at *both* ends of row: 49(53:57) sts rem.

Row 100: dec 1 st at beg of row: 48(52:56) sts rem.

Row 101: dec 1 st at *both* ends of row: 46(50:54) sts rem.

Row 102: dec 1 st at beg of row: 45(49:53) sts rem.

Rows 103–139: keep armhole edge straight for remainder of work and dec 1 st at neck edge on row 103 and every alt row until there are 26(30:34) sts on needle. (Row 139 of chart KD1 will now have been worked.)

Rows 140–159: work straight in pattern.

Shoulder Shaping

Row 160: cast off 13(15:17) sts at beg of row, work across in pattern.

Row 161: work across in pattern.

Row 162: cast off rem 13(15:17) sts.

LEFT FRONT

Rows 1–28: work waistcoat point using chart KD4 for sizes 1 and 3 and chart KD5 for size 2.

Row 29: work in pattern without shaping.

Row 30: work across 55 sts in pattern, then cast on 5(8:11) sts as shown.

Row 31: work across 60(63:66) sts in pattern.

Row 32: work across 60(63:66) sts in pattern, then cast on 6(9:12) sts as shown. There should now be 66(72:78) sts on needle.

Row 33: now change to chart KD1 and continue to work in pattern starting with row 33 of chart KD1 *in the following sequence.*

Sizes 1 and 3 only: work sts 1–12 5(6) times, then work sts 1–6: 66(78) sts.

Size 2 only: work sts 1–12 6 times: 72 sts.

Row 34: Sizes 1 and 3 only: work sts 6–1, then work sts 12–1 5(6) times.

Size 2 only: work sts 12–1 6 times.

Be sure to maintain continuity of pattern for remainder of work on Left Front. Now work as for Right Front, reversing all shapings and ending by casting off rem 13(15:17) sts on row 161.

ARMBANDS

Gently press all pieces with a warm iron and damp cloth. Join shoulder seams. With 2¾ mm needles, LL yarn and right side of work facing, pick up 138(142:146) sts around armhole edge. **Row 1:** P all sts in LL. **Rows 2–4:** K all sts in FP. **Row 5:** P all sts in TQ. **Row 6:** K all sts in TQ. **Row 7:** P all sts in RP. **Row 8:** in RP K across, inc 20 sts evenly over the row. **Row 9:** P all sts in RP. Cast off neatly. Repeat for other side.

LEFT BORDER AND NECKBAND

Join side seams. With 2¾ mm needles and SB yarn, cast on 11 sts.
Row 1: sl.1 K1 * P1 K1, rep from * to last st, K1.

Row 2: sl.1 * P1 K1, rep from * to end. Repeat rows 1 and 2 until border when slightly stretched fits along lower edge from left side seam to base of point, ending with a row 1. *Shape point as follows:* **1st row:** rib 2. **2nd row:** sl.1 K1. **3rd row:** rib 4, turn. **4th row:** sl.1, rib to end. **5th row:** rib 6, turn. **6th row:** sl.1, rib to end. **7th row:** rib 8, turn. **8th row:** sl.1, rib to end. **9th row:** rib 10, turn. **10th row:** sl.1, rib to end. Now continue in rib on all sts until border when slightly stretched fits along lower front point, up front edge and round to centre back of neck. Cast off in rib. Sew border into place. Mark position for 5 buttons; bottom button just above pattern row 28, top button just below pattern row 95, remaining buttons spaced evenly between.

RIGHT BORDER AND NECKBAND

Work as for Left Border, repeating rows 1 and 2 until border when slightly stretched fits along lower edge of back from left side seam to base of point of right front, ending with a row 2. Shape point as given for Left Border. Continue in rib, working buttonholes opposite button markers as follows. **1st row:** rib 4, cast off 3 sts, rib 4. **2nd row:** rib across, casting on 3 sts above those cast off on 1st row. Complete as for Left Border.

TO MAKE UP

Sew Right Border into place, joining borders at back of neck and left side seam. Sew on buttons opposite buttonholes. Finish by turning armbands through and sewing them down along inside edges of Back and Fronts.

7
Heraldry

W HEN I WAS up at Oxford, one of my favourite shops was a gentlemen's outfitters of the most old fashioned sort. This splendid establishment – sadly no longer with us – boasted more polished dark wood than a City boardroom, cupboards and cabinets capable of producing everything from spats to wing collars, and a staff half as old as time who were held in high esteem as the ultimate arbitrators in disputes concerning the fine points of maculine good taste. Everything they had was the last word in distinction – the jackets were flawless in cut and cloth, the cricket whites truly immaculate and the summer boaters and striped blazers as crisply cool as one could wish – but what appealed to me most were the painted shields of different schools and colleges that hung upon the walls. Bright and bold, simple yet marvellously inventive, they made me think of pageantry and valour, officers and gentlemen, and Laurence Olivier doing the St Crispian's Day speech from Shakespeare's *King Henry IV part II*, and it was a memory of that fine display that led to this design.

Like much else in England, systematic heraldry seems to have come in with the Normans, and was well established by the beginning of the thirteenth century. The earliest shields tended to be relatively plain, with the choice of design left to the bearer. Crosses were a common device, as were stripes, chevrons and naturalistic motifs that were often a pun on the family name – three apples, for example, being the emblem of the Applegarths. Shield designs became more elaborate with the passing of time and the adoption of the practice of quartering, and ultimately the shield itself became just one of the elements in the coat of arms that includes a crest, supporters and motto. To my way of thinking, the complex devices of later times, handsome though they are, look less well in knitting than the massed effect of simpler shields worked in the seven colours or tinctures used in English heraldry – yellow (or gold), white (or silver) for which Sand Beige substitutes in this design, black, purple, blue, red and green.

HERALDRY

Chart HR1
Rows 1-172

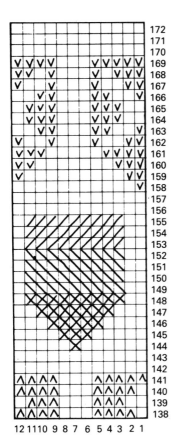

Λ = French Blue

Ⓞ = Charcoal Black

Ⅴ = Viridian Green

• = Crimson

☒ = Purple

◺ = Saffron Yellow

☐ = Sand Beige

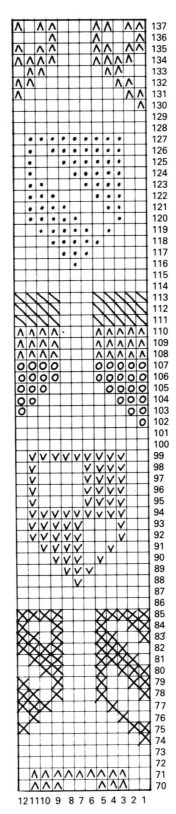

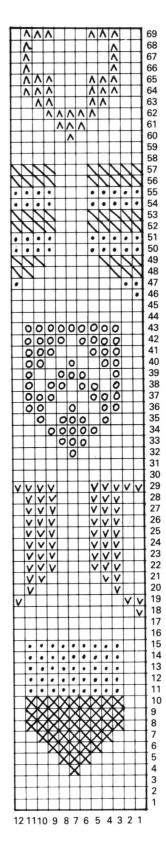

HERALDRY SLIPOVER

YARN COLOURS AND NUMBERS	QUANTITIES REQUIRED IN OUNCES (1 oz = 28.3 g)			
	Size 1	Size 2	Size 3	Size 4
Sand Beige FC43	4	5	5	6
Crimson 55	1	1	1	1
Purple 20	1	1	1	1
Viridian Green 65	1	1	1	1
Charcoal Black 81	1	1	1	1
French Blue 16	1	1	1	1
Saffron Yellow 90	1	1	1	1

NEEDLES One pair each size 2¾ mm (No. 12 British, No. 1 American), 3 mm (No. 11 British, No. 2 American) and 3¼ mm (No. 10 British, No. 3 American) needles, and a stitch holder.

TENSION 16 sts and 16 rows to 2 in (5 cm) on 3¼ mm needles over Fair Isle pattern. For K2P2 ribbing: 9 sts and 9 rows to 1 in (2.5 cm) on 2¾ mm needles. Change needle size if necessary to obtain correct tension.

SIZES 4 sizes. Size 1 = 33 in (84 cm), size 2 = 36 in (91.5 cm), size 3 = 39 in (99 cm), size 4 = 42 in (106.5 cm), actual measurements.

ABBREVIATIONS See page 16.
Colours: SB = Sand Beige.

NOTES FOR KNITTERS: See page 13.

BACK

With 2¾ mm needles and SB yarn, cast on 120(132:140:152) sts and work in K2P2 rib for 2½ in (6.5 cm).
Next row: (increase row) K across, inc 12(12:16:16) sts evenly over the row: 132(144:156:168) sts.
Next row: P across.
Using 3 mm needles on all 1-colour rows and 3¼ mm needles on all 2-colour rows, begin to work in pattern starting with row 1 of chart HR1. On K rows work sts 1–12 across 11(12:13:14) times, on P rows work sts 12–1 across 11(12:13:14) times. Work straight in pattern until you have completed pattern row 90 of chart HR1. *Be sure to maintain continuity of pattern for remainder of work on Back.*

Armhole Shaping

Rows 91–92: cast off 5(7:9:11) sts at beg of each row: 122(130:138:146) sts rem.
Rows 93–96: cast off 4 sts at beg of each row: 106(114:122:130) sts rem.
Rows 97–106: dec 1 st at beg of each row: 96(104:112:120) sts rem.
Rows 107–162: work in pattern without shaping.

Shoulder Shaping

Rows 163–168: cast off 4(5:6:7) sts at beg of each row: 72(74:76:78) sts rem.
Rows 169–170: cast off 3(4:4:5) sts at beg of each row: 66(66:68:68) sts rem.
Rows 171–172: cast off 3(3:3:4) sts at beg of each row, work in pattern to end: 60 sts rem.

Back Neck

Change to 2¾ mm needles and SB yarn and work the 60 sts for back neck in K2P2 rib for 9 rows. Cast off neatly in rib.

FRONT

Work as for Back until you have completed row 142 of chart HR1: 96(104:112:120) sts rem. *Be sure to maintain continuity of pattern throughout.*

Divide for Neck

Row 143: work in pattern across 33(37:41:45) sts, turn, leave rem 63(67:71:75) sts on a spare needle or stitch holder and work on first group of sts as follows.

Left Front

Rows 144–158: dec 1 st at neck edge on every row: 18(22:26:30) sts rem.
Rows 159–162: work in pattern without shaping.

Shoulder Shaping

Row 163: cast off 4(5:6:7) sts at beg of row: 14(17:20:23) sts rem.
Row 164: work in pattern without shaping.
Row 165: as row 163: 10(12:14:16) sts rem.
Row 166: as row 164.
Row 167: as row 163: 6(7:8:9) sts rem.
Row 168: as row 164.
Row 169: cast off 3(4:4:5) sts at beg of row: 3(3:4:4) sts rem.
Row 170: as row 164.
Row 171: cast off rem sts.

Right Front

Slip 30 sts for Front Neck on to a stitch holder. Rejoin yarn to second group of 33(37:41:45) sts and work in pattern across row 143. Now work as for Left Front, reversing all shapings and ending by casting off rem sts on row 172.

FRONT NECKBAND

With 2¾ mm needles, SB yarn and right side of work facing, pick up and K 27 sts down left side of neck, 30 sts from centre front neck and 27 sts up right side of neck: 84 sts. Work in K2P2 rib for 9 rows. Cast off neatly in rib.

ARMBANDS

Gently press all pieces with a warm iron and damp cloth. Join shoulder seams including neck ribbing. With 2¾ mm needles, SB yarn and right side of work facing, pick up and K148(152:156:160) sts around armhole. Work in K2P2 rib for 9 rows. Cast off loosely in rib. Repeat for other side.

TO MAKE UP

Join side seams.

8 and 9
Tweedie

TWO LOVE affairs lie behind *Tweedie* – the first is Sir Walter Scott's love for Scotland and, largely through his writings, the great passion for all things Caledonian that swept the world in the nineteenth century. By the 1820s tartan fabrics were as indispensable to the smart wardrobe as Scott's novels were to the well-dressed bookcase, but ironically Scott was one of the few who did not take up the plaid. Clan tartans belonged strictly to the Highlands and Scott, being a man of the Borders, had no tartan he could call his own. He decided to adopt a black and white check fabric that had long been woven on the Borders for the use of Border shepherds as his clan cloth, and when in 1826 he ordered a pair of trousers in 'shepherd's check', he set a new fashion in menswear that took society by storm.

Soon the shepherd's check had been modified into a host of fancy patterns such as Dogstooth and Gun Club that came to be known as District Checks. Basic black and white gave way to colourings copied from nature – pale greys, sands, heathers and bluebells – and the new softly shaded woollens were given the general name of 'tweeds'. Country pursuits, preferably on a Scottish estate, became very fashionable in the 1850s and tweeds were the favourite fabric for shooting, stalking, riding, walking and leisured larking in the gloaming. But, as in Scott's heyday, these lovely fabrics were still worn primarily by men.

Coco Chanel's love affair with the second Duke of Westminster led her to poach on this masculine preserve. After showering her with jewels and placing his two yachts at her disposal, the Duke swept the designer off to England to introduce her to country life at its best. Love and the beauty of the Scottish tweeds worn on the Duke's estate proved a powerful inspiration, and in 1925 Chanel brought out the first of her collections in the *style Anglais*. Her elegantly cut tweed suits – worn with plain toning sweaters or blouses – caused a sensation, and turned mannish country tweeds into feminine high fashion overnight.

Today fashion has moved on again, and the feeling is for something richer than plain sweaters, softer than tailored tweeds. So here is *Tweedie* – A collared sweater and cardigan knitted in District Check and speckled Birdseye tweed patterns, in misty country colours and fine Shetland wool, threaded with velvet ribbon. The end of the affair brought a sparkling riposte from Mlle Chanel – *'There have been many Duchesses of Westminster, there is only one Coco Chanel!'* But she never fell out of love with tweeds – and nor, I hope, will you.

Tweedie
Colour Key

- ⬜ = Sand Beige
- ⊞ = Heather Purple
- ▲ = Pale Grey
- △ = Sapphire Blue
- ◼ = Burnt Orange
- ▣ = Golden Plum
- ◣ = Tweed Brown
- ◮ = Charcoal Black
- ◆ = Grey Lovat
- S = Camel Tan
- ✳ = Light Natural

Chart A. 12 sts and 2 rows.

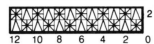

12 10 8 6 4 2 0

Chart B. 12 sts and 2 rows.

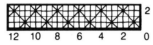

12 10 8 6 4 2 0

Chart C. 12 sts and 2 rows.

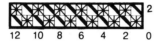

12 10 8 6 4 2 0

Chart D. 12 sts and 2 rows.

12 '0 8 6 4 2 0

Note: collar, ribbing, ribbon borders and edgings are worked in Sand Beige or Granite Grey.

TWEEDIE
Chart 1. 12 sts and 8 rows.

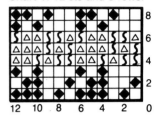

12 10 8 6 4 2 0

Chart 2. 12 sts and 8 rows.

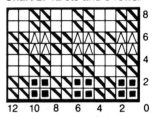

12 10 8 6 4 2 0

Chart 3. 12 sts and 8 rows.

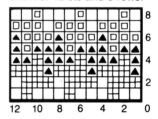

12 10 8 6 4 2 0

TWEEDIE SWEATER

YARN COLOURS AND NUMBERS	QUANTITIES REQUIRED IN OUNCES (1 oz = 28.3 g)			
	Size 1	Size 2	Size 3	Size 4
Sand Beige F C 43				
or				
Granite Grey 27	7	8	8	9
Sand Beige F C 43	2	2	2	2
Burnt Orange F C 38	1	1	1	1
Heather Purple 19	1	1	1	1
Golden Plum F C 10	1	1	1	1
Charcoal Black 81	1	1	1	1
Tweed Brown F C 46	2	2	2	2
Grey Lovat 30	2	2	3	3
Pale Grey 203	1	1	1	1
Sapphire Blue F C 48	1	1	1	1
Camel Tan F C 45	1	1	1	1
Light Natural 202	2	2	2	2

NEEDLES One pair each size 2¾ mm (No. 12 British, No. 1 American), 3 mm (No. 11 British, No. 2 American) and 3¼ mm (No. 10 British, No. 3 American) needles, plus set of 4 doublepointed 2¾ mm needles and 1 extra doublepointed 2¾ mm needle. *Also:* velvet ribbon for threading through sweater (optional), and velvet ribbon for threading through collar.

TENSION 9 sts and 8 rows to 1 in (2.5 cm) on 3¼ mm needles over Fair Isle pattern. For K1P1 ribbing: 10 sts and 11 rows to 1 in (2.5 cm) on 2¾ mm needles. Change needle size if necessary to obtain correct tension.

SIZES 4 sizes. Size 1 = 32 in (81 cm), size 2 = 35 in (88 cm), size 3 = 37½ in (95 cm), size 4 = 40 in (101.5 cm), actual measurements.

ABBREVIATIONS See page 16. *Colours:* B = Sand Beige, G = Granite Grey.

NOTES FOR KNITTERS See page 13.

SPECIAL INSTRUCTIONS FOR THIS DESIGN (1) The ribbon borders, collar and all ribbing are worked in B or G yarn. (2) The fabric of this sweater consists of wide bands of Fair Isle pattern (charts 1, 2 and 3) and narrow bands of Fair Isle pattern (charts A, B, C and D), worked alternately with ribbon borders. Each wide Fair Isle band is worked by repeating the 8 rows of charts 1, 2 or 3 twice (16 rows). Each narrow Fair Isle band is worked by repeating the 2 rows of charts A, B, C and D three times (6 rows). Each ribbon border is 8 rows wide. (3) When counting rows worked in total, ribbon border rows count as pattern rows.

BACK

With 2¾ mm needles and B or G yarn, cast on 136(144:152:160) sts and work in K1P1 rib for 2½ in (6.5 cm).
Size 1 next row: * K16, inc into next st, rep from * to end of row (144 sts).
Size 2 next row: * K11, inc into next st, rep from * to end of row (156 sts).
Size 3 next row: K4 * K8, inc into next st, rep from * to last 4 sts, K4 (168 sts).
Size 4 next row: * K7, inc into next st,

rep from * to end of row (180 sts).
For all sizes: next row: P across.
Using 3¼ mm needles on Fair Isle bands and 3 mm needles on ribbon borders, begin to work in pattern following the pattern sequence below, starting with row 1 of chart 1. On K rows repeat sts 1–12 of charts across row 12(13:14:15) times, 144(156:168:180) sts. On P rows repeat sts 12–1 across row. Continue in sequence until you have worked 98 pattern rows.

Pattern Sequence for Back and Front

1. Chart 1 twice (16 rows).
2. Ribbon Border (8 rows).
3. Chart A three times (6 rows).
4. Ribbon Border (8 rows).
5. Chart 2 twice (16 rows).
6. Ribbon Border (8 rows).
7. Chart B three times (6 rows).
8. Ribbon Border (8 rows).
9. Chart 3 twice (16 rows).
10. Ribbon Border (8 rows).
11. Chart C three times (6 rows).
12. Ribbon Border (8 rows).
13. Chart 2 twice (16 rows).
14. Ribbon Border (8 rows).
15. Chart D three times (6 rows).
16. Ribbon Border (8 rows).
17. Chart 1 twice (16 rows).
18. Ribbon Border (without holes: 4 rows).

Stitch Sequence for Ribbon Borders

Row 1: using 3 mm needles and B or G yarn, K across.
Row 2: P4 * P1 K3, rep from * to last 4 sts, P4, 34(37:40:43) reps in all: 144 (156:168:180) sts.
Row 3: K4 * P3 K1, rep from * to last 4 sts, K4.
Row 4: as row 2.
Row 5: K4 * YO P3 tog YO K1, rep from * to last 4 sts, K4.
Row 6: P4 * K2 P1 K1, rep from * to last 4 sts, P4.
Row 7: K4 * P1 K1 P2, rep from * to last 4 sts, K4.
Row 8: as row 6.

Armhole Shaping

Row 99: keeping continuity of pattern, cast off 7(9:11:13) sts at beg of next 2 rows, starting with row 7 of ribbon border, no. 10 in pattern sequence.

Now dec 1 st at beg of every row for 14 rows.

Rows 115–118: work without shaping.
Rows 119–120: dec 1 st at beg of next 2 rows: 114(122:130:138) sts.
Rows 121–124: work without shaping for 4 rows.
Rows 125–126: dec 1 st at beg of next 2 rows: 112 (120:128:136) sts.
Rows 127–138: work 12 rows without shaping.
Rows 139–140: inc into first st of next 2 rows: 114(122:130:138) sts.
Rows 141–148: work 8 rows without shaping.
Rows 149–150: inc into first st of next 2 rows: 116(124:132:140) sts.
Rows 151–158: work 8 rows without shaping.
Rows 159–160: inc into first st of next 2 rows.
Rows 161–162: work 2 rows without shaping: 118(126:134:142) sts.

Shoulder Shaping

Rows 163–170: cast off 5(6:7:8) sts at beg of next 8 rows: 78 sts.
Row 171: cast off 6 sts at beg of row.
Row 172: cast off 9 sts at beg of row.
Row 173: cast off 3 sts at beg of row.
Leave remaining 60 sts on a stitch holder.

FRONT

Work exactly as for Back until you have completed row 144.

Divide for Neck

Row 145: patt across 47(51:55:59) sts. Cast off the next 20 sts, leave the remaining 47(51:55:59) sts on a stitch holder. Working on first group of sts only, proceed as follows:

Left Front

Row 146: cast off 5 sts (neck edge), patt to end: 42(46:50:54) sts.
Row 147: patt without shaping.
Row 148: cast off 4 sts, patt to end: 38(42:46:50) sts.
Row 149: inc into first st (armhole edge), patt to end: 39(43:47:51) sts.
Rows 150–156: keeping armhole edge straight, dec 2 sts at neck edge on row 150 and every alternate row three more times: 31(35:39:43) sts.
Rows 157–158: patt without shaping.
Row 159: inc into first st, patt to end: 32(36:40:44) sts.

Row 160: dec 2 sts at neck edge, patt to end:
Rows 161–162: patt without shaping.

Shoulder Shaping

Row 163: cast off 5(6:7:8) sts, patt to end.
Row 164: dec 1 st, patt to end.
Row 165: as row 163.
Row 166: patt without shaping.
Row 167: as row 163.
Row 168: patt without shaping.
Row 169: as row 163.
Row 170: patt without shaping.
Row 171: cast off 6 sts, patt to end.
Row 172: patt without shaping.
Row 173: cast off remaining 3 sts.

Right Front

Rejoin yarn to remaining group of 47(51:55:59) sts at neck edge and work in pattern to correspond with left side, reversing all shapings.

SLEEVES

With 2¾ mm needles and B or G yarn, cast on 60(66:72:78) sts and work in K1 P1 rib for 2½ in (6.5 cm).
Size 1 next row: * K4, inc into next st, rep from * to end: 72 sts.
Size 2 next row: K6 * K2, inc into next st, rep from * to last 6 sts, K6: 84 sts.
Size 3 next row: * K2, inc into next st, rep from * to end: 96 sts.
Size 4 next row: K9 * K1, inc into next st, rep from * to last 9 sts, K9: 108 sts.
For all sizes: next row: P across.
Using 3 mm needles on ribbon borders and 3¼ mm needles on Fair Isle bands, begin to work in pattern in the following sequence:

Pattern Sequence for Sleeves

1. Ribbon Border (8 rows).
2. Chart D three times (6 rows).
3. Ribbon Border (8 rows).
4. Chart 1 twice (16 rows).
5. Ribbon Border (8 rows).
6. Chart A three times (6 rows).
7. Ribbon Border (8 rows).
8. Chart 2 twice (16 rows).
9. Ribbon Border (8 rows).
10. Chart B three times (6 rows).
11. Ribbon Border (8 rows).
12. Chart 3 twice (16 rows).
13. Ribbon Border (8 rows).
14. Chart C three times (6 rows).
15. Ribbon Border (8 rows).
16. Chart 2 twice (16 rows).
17. Ribbon Border (8 rows).

18. Chart D three times (6 rows).
19. Stocking stitch in B or G (4 rows).

For ribbon borders: work stitch sequence as given for Back, 16(19:22:25) reps in all: 72(84:96:108) sts.
For charts: work sts 1–12 across row 6(7:8:9) times on K rows, work sts 12–1 across on P rows.
Proceed in pattern, increasing 1 st at both ends of **row 4**, and every following 4th row until there are 102(114:126:138) sts on needle (**row 60**). When working ribbon borders, work increased sts as extra end sts until you have enough (4) sts to incorporate them into patt as a rep.
Rows 61–66: work without shaping.
Row 67: inc 1 st at both ends of row 67 and every following 7th row until there are 118(130:142:154) sts on needle (**row 116**).
Rows 117–119: patt without shaping.
Row 120: inc 1 st at both ends of row: 120(132:144:156) sts.
Rows 121–122: work without shaping.

Shape Sleeve Head

Rows 123–126: cast off 3(5:7:9) sts at beg of next 4 rows: 108(112:116:120) sts.
Rows 127–136: cast off 2 sts at beg of next 10 rows: 88(92:96:100) sts.
Rows 137–138: dec 1 st at beg of next 2 rows.
Rows 139–140: cast off 2 sts at beg of next 2 rows.
Rows 141–144: dec 1 st at beg of next 4 rows.
Rows 145–148: cast off 2 sts at beg of next 4 rows.
Rows 149–150: dec 1 st at beg of next 2 rows.
Rows 151–164: cast off 2 sts at beg of next 14 rows: 40(44:48:52) sts.
Rows 165–166: cast off 5 sts at beg of next 2 rows.
Rows 167–168: cast off 4(5:6:7) sts at beg of next 2 rows.
Row 169: cast off 4(5:6:7) sts at beg of row.
Cast off remaining 18(19:20:2) sts. Work second sleeve to match.

NECKBAND

Sew up the shoulder seams using back stitch. With B or G yarn and set of 4 plus 1 doublepointed 2¾ mm needles, pick up and K20 sts cross centre front neck on to 1st needle. Using B or G yarn and with right side of work facing, pick up and K33 sts up right side of front neck on to 2nd needle, 60 sts across back neck on to 3rd needle, and 33 sts down left side of front neck on to 4th needle. Turn work and proceed as follows:

Row 1: Working in K1P1 rib, rib 33 sts from 4th needle, 60 sts from 3rd needle, 33 sts from 2nd needle. Then rib 2 sts from centre front 20 sts (leaving 18 sts on double-pointed needle at centre front).

Row 2: (right side) rib sts from 2nd, 3rd and 4th needles, then rib 2 sts from centre front 18 sts (leaving 16 sts on doublepointed needle at centre front).

Continue to rib neckband in this way, taking 2 sts from centre front sts on doublepointed needle at the end of every row until you have worked 10 rows in all, when every st will have been taken up from the centre front. Cast off neatly in rib.

COLLAR

With 3 mm needles and B or G yarn, cast on 16 sts and P 1 row. Proceed to work in pattern as follows:

Row 1: (wrong side) K1 SL.1 K1 psso, YO twice, K2 tog P8, inc into next st, K2.

Row 2: K14 P1 K2.

Row 3: K1 SL.1 K1 psso, YO twice, K2 tog P9, inc into next st, K2.

Row 4: K12, turn, P9, inc into next st, K2.

Row 5: K16 P1 K2.

Row 6: K1 SL.1 K1 psso, YO twice, K2 tog P12 K2.

Row 7: K13, turn, P9, P2 tog K2.

Row 8: K15 P1 K2.

Row 9: K1 SL.1 K1 psso, YO twice K2 tog P9, P2 tog K2.

Row 10: K14 P1 K2.

Row 11: K1 SL.1 K1 psso, YO twice, K2 tog P8, P2 tog K2.

Row 12: K13 P1 K2.

Row 13: K1 SL.1 K1 psso, YO twice, K2 tog K11.

Row 14: K2 P8, turn, K10.

Row 15: K2 P8, turn, K10.

Row 16: K2 P9 K2 P1 K2.

These 16 rows form the collar pattern. Repeat them 10 times, then work rows 1–13. Cast off knitwise.

TO MAKE UP

Lightly press all pieces using a warm iron and damp cloth. Thread ribbon through ribbon borders, sewing in beginning and ending at the centre front of neck. Thread ribbon through holes, leaving ends long enough to tie in a bow at centre front.

neatly at ends. Sew in sleeves using back stitch. Sew up sleeve seams and side seams using back stitch. Oversew collar to neckband, placing the collar just inside the top of the rib neckband,

TWEEDIE CARDIGAN

YARN COLOURS AND NUMBERS	QUANTITIES REQUIRED IN OUNCES (1 oz = 28.3 g)			
	Size 1	Size 2	Size 3	Size 4
Sand Beige F C 43				
or				
Granite Grey 27	7	8	8	9
Sand Beige F C 43	2	2	2	2
Burnt Orange F C 38	1	1	1	1
Heather Purple 19	1	1	1	1
Golden Plum F C 10	1	1	1	1
Charcoal Black 81	1	1	1	1
Tweed Brown F C 46	2	2	2	2
Grey Lovat 30	2	2	3	3
Pale Grey 203	1	1	1	1
Sapphire Blue F C 48	1	1	1	1
Camel Tan F C 45	1	1	1	1
Light Natural 202	2	2	2	2

NEEDLES One pair each size 2¾ mm (No. 12 British, No. 1 American), 3 mm (No. 11 British, No. 2 American) and 3¼ mm (No. 10 British, No. 3 American) needles, plus set of 4 doublepointed 2¾ mm needles and 1 extra doublepointed 2¾ mm needle. *Also*: velvet ribbon for threading through cardigan (optional), and velvet ribbon for threading through collar.

TENSION 9 sts and 8 rows to 1 in (2.5 cm) on 3¼ mm needles over Fair Isle pattern. For K1P1 ribbing: 10 sts and 11 rows to 1 in (2.5 cm) on 2¾ mm needles. Change needle size if necessary to obtain correct tension.

SIZES 4 sizes. Size 1 = 32 in (81 cm), size 2 = 35 in (88 cm), size 3 = 37½ in (95 cm), size 4 = 40 in (101.5 cm) actual measurements.

ABBREVIATIONS See page 16. *Colours:* B = Sand Beige, G = Granite Grey.

NOTES FOR KNITTERS See page 13.

SPECIAL INSTRUCTIONS FOR THIS DESIGN (1) The ribbon borders, collar and all ribbing are worked in G or B yarn. (2) The fabric of this cardigan consists of wide bands of Fair Isle pattern (charts 1, 2, and 3) and narrow bands of Fair Isle pattern (charts A, B, C and D), worked alternately with ribbon borders. Each wide Fair Isle band is worked by repeating the 8 rows of charts 1, 2 or 3 twice (16 rows). Each narrow Fair Isle band is worked by repeating the 2 rows of Charts A, B, C or D three times (6 rows). Each ribbon border is 8 rows wide. (3) When counting rows worked in total, ribbon borders rows count as pattern rows.

BACK

With 2¾ mm needles and B or G yarn, cast on 136(144:152:160) sts and work in K1P1 rib for 2½ in (6.5 cm).
Size 1: next row;* K16, inc into next st, rep from * to end of row (144 sts).
Size 2: next row;* K11, inc into next st, rep from * to end of row (156 sts).
Size 3: next row; K4 * K8, inc into next st, rep from * to last 4 sts, K4 (168 sts).
Size 4: next row; * K7, inc into next st,

rep from * to end of row (180 sts).
For all sizes: next row; P across.
Using 3¼ mm needles on Fair Isle bands and 3 mm needles on ribbon borders, begin to work in pattern in the following sequence, starting with row 1 of chart D. On K rows repeat sts 1–12 of charts across row 12(13:14:15) times, 144(156:168:180) sts. On P rows repeat sts 12–1 across row. Continue in sequence until you have worked 112 pattern rows.

Pattern Sequence for Back and Front

Work as follows:
1. Chart D three times (6 rows).
2. Ribbon Border (8 rows).
3. Chart 1 twice (16 rows).
4. Ribbon Border (8 rows).
5. Chart A three times (6 rows).
6. Ribbon Border (8 rows).
7. Chart 2 twice (16 rows).
8. Ribbon Border (8 rows).
9. Chart B three times (6 rows).
10. Ribbon Border (8 rows).
11. Chart 3 twice (16 rows).
12. Ribbon Border (8 rows).
13. Chart C three times (6 rows).
14. Ribbon Border (8 rows).
15. Chart 2 twice (16 rows).
16. Ribbon Border (8 rows).
17. Chart D three times (6 rows).
18. Ribbon Border (8 rows).
19. Chart 1 twice (16 rows).
20. Ribbon Border (without holes: 4 rows).

Stitch Sequence for Ribbon Borders

Row 1: using 3 mm needles and B or G yarn, K across.
Row 2: P4 * P1 K3, rep from * to last 4 sts, P4, 34(37:40:43) reps in all: 144(156:168:180) sts.
Row 3: K4 * P3 K1, rep from * to last 4 sts, K4.
Row 4: as row 2.
Row 5: K4 * YO P3 tog YO K1, rep from * to last 4 sts, K4.
Row 6: P4 * K2 P1 K1, rep from * to last 4 sts, P4.
Row 7: K4 * P1 K1 P2, rep from * to last 4 sts, K4.
Row 8: as row 6.

Armhole Shaping

Row 113: keeping continuity of pattern, cast off 7(9:11:13) sts at beg of next 2 rows, starting with row 7 of ribbon border, no. 12 in pattern sequence. Now dec 1 st at beg of every row for 14 rows.

Rows 129–132: work without shaping.

Rows 133–134: dec 1 st at beg of next 2 rows: 114(122:130:138) sts.

Rows 135–138: work without shaping for 4 rows.

Rows 139–140: dec 1 st at beg of next 2 rows: 112(120:128:136) sts.

Rows 141–152: work 12 rows without shaping.

Rows 153–154: inc into first st of next 2 rows: 114(122:130:138) sts.

Rows 155–162: work 8 rows without shaping.

Rows 163–164: inc into first st of next 2 rows: 116(124:132:140) sts.

Rows 165–172: work 8 rows without shaping.

Rows 173–174: inc into first st of next 2 rows: 118(126:134:142) sts.

Rows 175–176: work 2 rows without shaping

Shoulder Shaping

Rows 177–184: cast off 5(6:7:8) sts at beg of next 8 rows: 78 sts.

Row 185: cast off 6 sts at beg of row.

Row 186: cast off 9 sts at beg of row.

Row 187: cast off 3 sts at beg of row. Leave remaining 60 sts on a stitch holder.

LEFT FRONT

With 2¾ mm needles and B or G yarn, cast on 68(72:76:80) sts and work in K1 P1 rib for 2½ (6.5 cm).

Size 1: next row; * K16, inc into next st, rep from * to end of row (72 sts).

Size 2: next row; * K11, inc into next st, rep from * to end of row (78 sts).

Size 3: next row; K2 * K8, inc into next st, rep from * to last 2 sts, K2 (84 sts).

Size 4: next row; * K7, inc into next st, rep from * to end of row (90 sts).

For all sizes: next row; P across.

Using 3¼ mm needles on Fair Isle bands and 3 mm needles on ribbon borders, proceed to work in pattern as follows:

Size 1: for all charts; on all K rows work sts 1–12 across 6 times, on all P rows work sts 12–1 across 6 times, 72 sts.

For ribbon borders: work stitch sequence as given, 16 reps in all.

Size 2: for all charts; on all K rows work sts 1–12 across 6 times, then work sts 1–6. On all P rows work sts 6–1, then sts 12–1 across 6 times, 78 sts.

For ribbon borders: work stitch sequence as given, but begin and end **rows 2, 4, 6 and 8** with P5. Begin and end **rows 3, 5 and 7** with K5. 17 reps in all.

Size 3: for all charts; on all K rows work sts 1–12 across 7 times, on all P rows work sts 12–1 across 7 times, 84 sts.

For ribbon borders: work stitch sequence as given, 19 reps in all.

Size 4: for all charts: on all K rows work sts 1–12 across 7 times, then work sts 1–6. On all P rows work sts 6–1, then sts 12–1 across 7 times, 90 sts.

For ribbon borders: work stitch sequence as given, but begin and end **rows 2, 4, 6 and 8** with P3, and begin and end **rows 3, 5 and 7** with K3. 21 repeats in all.

For all sizes: continue to work in this way until you have completed 112 pattern rows.

Armhole Shaping

Row 113: Keeping continuity of pattern, cast off 7(9:11:13) sts at beg of row: 65(69:73:77) sts.

Row 114: patt across without shaping. Now work 14 rows, keeping front edge straight and decreasing 1 st at armhole edge on every alternate row: 58 (62:66:70) sts.

Rows 129–132: patt across without shaping.

Row 133: dec 1 st, patt to end: 57(61: 65:69) sts.

Rows 134–138: patt without shaping.

Row 139: dec 1 st, patt to end: 56(60. 64:68) sts.

Rows 140–152: patt without shaping.

Row 153: inc into first st, patt to end: 57(61:65:69) sts.

Rows 154–158: patt without shaping.

Neck Shaping

Row 159: patt across 47(51:55:59) sts, slip remaining 10 sts on to a safety pin.

Row 160: cast off 5 sts (neck edge), patt to end:42(46:50:54) sts.

Row 161: patt without shaping.

Row 162: cast off 4 sts, patt to end: 38(42:46:50) sts.

Row 163: inc into first st (armhole edge), patt to end: 39(43:47:51) sts.

Rows 164–170: keeping armhole edge straight, dec 2 sts at neck edge on row 164, and every alternate row three

more times: 31(35:39:43) sts.

Rows 171–172: patt without shaping.

Row 173: inc into first st, patt to end.

Row 174: dec 2 sts (neck edge), patt to end.

Rows 175–176: patt without shaping.

Shoulder Shaping

Row 177: cast off 5(6:7:8) sts, patt to end.

Row 178: dec 1 st, patt to end.

Row 179: as row 177.

Row 180: patt without shaping.

Row 181: as row 177.

Row 182: patt without shaping.

Row 183: as row 177.

Row 184: patt without shaping.

Row 185: cast off 6 sts, patt to end.

Row 186: patt without shaping.

Row 187: cast off remaining 3 sts.

RIGHT FRONT

For sizes 1 and 3: work exactly as for Left Front, reversing all shapings. **For sizes 2 and 4: for all charts:** on all K rows work sts 7–12, then work sts 1–12 across 6(7) times: 78(90) sts. On all P rows, work sts 12–1 across 6(7) times, then work sts 12–7. Otherwise work exactly as for Left Front, reversing all shapings.

SLEEVES

With 2¾ mm needles and B or G yarn, cast on 60(66:72:78) sts and work in K1 P1 rib for 2½ in (6.5 cm).

Size 1: next row; * K4, inc into next st,

rep from * to end, 72 sts.

Size 2: next row; K6 * K2, inc into next st, rep from * to last 6 sts, K6, 84 sts.

Size 3: next row; * K2, inc into next st, rep from * to end, 96 sts.

Size 4: next row; K9 * K1, inc into next st, rep from * to last 9 sts, K9, 108 sts.

For all sizes: next row; P across.

Using 3 mm needles on ribbon borders and 3¼ mm needles on Fair Isle bands, begin to work in pattern in the following sequence:

Pattern Sequence for Sleeves

1. Ribbon Border (8 rows).
2. Chart D three times (6 rows).
3. Ribbon Border (8 rows).
4. Chart 1 twice (16 rows).
5. Ribbon Border (8 rows).
6. Chart A three times (6 rows).
7. Ribbon Border (8 rows).
8. Chart 2 twice (16 rows).
9. Ribbon Border (8 rows).
10. Chart B three times (6 rows).
11. Ribbon Border (8 rows).
12. Chart 3 twice (16 rows).
13. Ribbon Border (8 rows).
14. Chart C three times (6 rows).
15. Ribbon Border (8 rows).
16. Chart 2 twice (16 rows).
17. Ribbon Border (8 rows).
18. Chart D three times (6 rows).
19. Stocking stitch in B or G (4 rows).

For ribbon borders: work stitch sequence as given for Back, 16(19:22:25) reps in all: 72(84:96:108) sts. **For charts:** work sts 1–12 across row 6(7:8:9) times on K rows, work sts 12–1 across on P rows. Proceed in pattern, increasing 1 st at both ends of row 4, and every following 4th row until there are 102(114:126:138) sts on needle (**row 60**). When working ribbon borders, work increased sts as extra end sts until you have enough (4) sts to incorporate them into patt as a rep.

Row 61–66: work without shaping.

Row 67: inc 1 st at both ends of row 67 and every following 7th row until there are 118(130:142:154) sts on needle (row 116).

Rows 117–119: patt without shaping.

Row 120: inc 1 st at both ends of row: 120(132:144:156) sts.

Rows 121–122: work without shaping.

Shape Sleeve Head

Rows 123–126: cast off 3(5:7:9) sts at beg of next 4 rows: 108(112:116:120) sts.

Rows 127–136: cast off 2 sts at beg of next 10 rows: 88(92:96:100) sts.

Rows 137–138: dec 1 st at beg of next 2 rows.

Rows 139–140: cast off 2 sts at beg of next 2 rows.

Rows 141–144: dec 1 st at beg of next 4 rows.

Rows 145–148: cast off 2 sts at beg of next 4 rows.

Rows 149–150: dec 1 st at beg of next 2 rows.

Rows 151–164: cast off 2 sts at beg of next 14 rows: 40(44:48:52) sts.

Rows 165–166: cast off 5 sts at beg of next 2 rows.

Rows 167–168: cast off 4(5:6:7) sts at beg of next 2 rows.

Row 169: cast off 4(5:6:7) sts at beg of row.

Cast off remaining 18(19:20:21) sts. Work second sleeve to match.

FRONT BANDS

With 2¾ mm needles and B or G yarn, cast on 10 sts and work in K1P1 rib until work measures 22 in (56 cm). Leave sts on a spare needle or safety pin.

Buttonhole band: with 2¾ mm needles and B or G yarn, cast on 10 sts and work in K1P1 rib for ½ in (1.5 cm), then work a buttonhole as follows:

Next row: rib 4, cast off 2 sts, rib 4.

Next row: rib 4, cast on 2 sts, rib 4.

Work another buttonhole in the same way 1½ in (4 cm) from beginning, then work another one 2½ in (6.5 cm) from beginning. Now work a buttonhole every 2⅜ in (6 cm), for a total of 11 buttonholes. The last one will be ½ in (1.5 cm) from the top of the band.

NECKBAND

Join shoulder seams using back stitch. Put the sts from buttonhole band on to a double-pointed size 2¾ mm needle, cast off the first 5 sts, then slip the 10 sts from neck edge of right front on to needle (15 sts on needle). Using another 2¾ mm needle and B or G yarn, and with right side of work facing, pick up and K33 sts up right side of neck, 60 sts across back neck, and 33 sts down left side of neck (126 sts on needle). Then take the button band on a separate 2¾ mm needle, cast off the first 5 sts, and slip the 10 sts from the neck edge of the left front on to the needle (15 sts on needle) keeping the button band to the left. Turn work and proceed as follows:

Row 1: Leaving these 15 sts unknitted, work in K1P1 rib to end of row, then rib 3 sts from group of 15 on other needle (leaving 12). Turn work.

Row 2: rib to end of row, then rib 3 sts from group of 15 on next needle (leaving 12). Turn work.

Continue in this way, taking 3 sts from those at centre front of neck on either side, until you have worked 9 rows of rib. Cast off ribwise on the 10th row.

COLLAR

With 3 mm needles and B or G yarn, cast on 16 sts and P1 row. Proceed to work in pattern as follows:

Row 1: (wrong side) K1 SL.1 K1 psso, Y O twice, K2 tog P8, inc into next st, K2.

Row 2: K14 P1 K2.

Row 3: K1 SL.1 K1 psso, Y O twice, K2 tog P9, inc into next st, K2.

Row 4: K12, turn, P9, inc into next st, K2.

Row 5: K16 P1 K2.

Row 6: K1 SL.1 K1 psso, Y O twice, K2 tog P12 K2.

Row 7: K13, turn, P9, P2 tog K2.

Row 8: K15 P1 K2.

Row 9: K1 SL.1 K1 psso, Y O twice, K2 tog P9, P2 tog K2.

Row 10: K14 P1 K2.

Row 11: K1 SL.1 K1 psso, Y O twice, K2 tog P8, P2 tog K2.

Row 12: K13 P1 K2.

Row 13: K1 SL.1 K1 psso, Y O twice, K2 tog K11.

Row 14: K2 P8, turn, K10.

Row 15: K2 P8, turn, K10.

Row 16: K2 P9 K2 P1 K2.

These 16 rows from the collar pattern. Repeat them 10 times, then work rows 1–13. Cast off knitwise.

TO MAKE UP

Lightly press all pieces using a warm iron and a damp cloth. Slip stitch button and buttonhole borders to the fronts. Sew buttons into position opposite buttonholes. Thread ribbon through ribbon borders, finishing ends inside neatly. Sew in sleeves using back stitch. Back stitch sleeve and side seams. Oversew collar on to neckband, placing the collar just inside the top of the rib neckband, beginning and ending at the centre front of neck. Thread ribbon through holes, leaving ends long enough to tie in a bow when cardigan is buttoned up.

10

Izmir

THIS IS the kind of sea sweater I like – not a Guernsey or an Aran, but a jaunty slipover covered with waves and fishes worked in seashell shades. The patterns and colourings are taken from Turkish stockings native to Corum, an Anatolian city that lies on the main road from Ankara to the Black Sea port of Samsun. From the moment I first saw them, the patterns on *Izmir* reminded me irresistibly of the marine pictures on old Greek mosaics and vases, which show strange and familiar creatures of the depths sporting in sunlit seas. Human and animal figures do not appear on Turkish stockings or in Islamic art generally, due to the Islamic prohibition on realistic portraiture. Nearly all Turkish patterns are geometric, and, although some designs have names like 'Butterfly' and 'Scorpion', they have become so stylized that their origins are no longer apparent. *Izmir*'s lifelike marine motifs are so utterly unlike any other Turkish patterns that I found their presence in the Turkish knitting repertoire curious, odd – and fishy.

A possible explanation for this puzzling pattern presented itself in the kitchen, where I was poring over the superb *Complete Book of Turkish Cooking* by Ayla Esen Algar, an author who believes in enhancing a splendid cuisine with delicious dollops of history. In the chapter on fish cookery, I read that during the formative period of Turkish Islamic culture in Anatolia from the eleventh century AD onwards, the Turkish people borrowed heavily from the social and material culture of the Greeks who had preceded them there, and the large number of Greek loanwords for different varieties of fish in the modern Turkish language is taken as proof that it was from the Greeks that the early Turks learned about fish and fishing. A bit more research revealed that the port of Samsun, known in ancient times as Amisus, was founded by Ionian Greek settlers in the mid-eighth century BC, and that Amisus along with neighbouring Sinop was famed for the wonderful fisheries that were described by the geographer Strabo. If the Turks borrowed fish words and fishing techniques from the Greeks, why not these fish designs? History is full of red herrings and this may well be one of them, but I like to think that this is the explanation for a pattern that, despite its Turkish provenance, will always be Greek to me.

IZMIR

Chart IZ1
Rows 1-172

Colour Key

O	= Bright Mauve
·	= Rose Pink
◣	= Leaf Green
▲	= Pale Yellow
V	= Turquoise Blue
☐	= Light Natural
✕	= French Blue

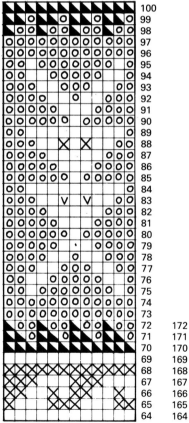

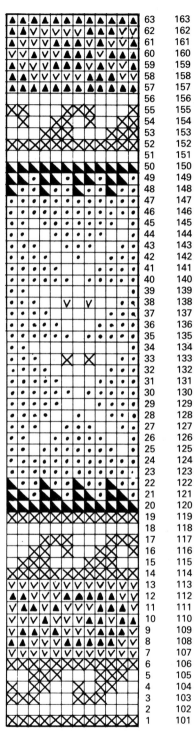

IZMIR SLIPOVER

YARN COLOURS AND NUMBERS	QUANTITIES REQUIRED IN OUNCES (1 oz = 28.3 g)			
	Size 1	Size 2	Size 3	Size 4
Light Natural 202	3	3	4	4
Bright Mauve 44	1	1	2	2
Rose Pink F C 22	1	2	2	3
Turquoise Blue 48	1	1	1	1
French Blue 16	1	1	1	1
Pale Yellow 96	1	1	1	1
Leaf Green 25	1	1	1	1

NEEDLES One pair each size 2¾ mm (No. 12 British, No. 1 American), 3 mm (No. 11 British, No. 2 American) and 3¼ mm (No. 10 British, No. 3 American) needles, and a stitch holder.

TENSION 16 sts and 16 rows to 2 in (5 cm) on 3¼ mm needles over Fair Isle pattern. For K2 P2 ribbing: 9 sts and 9 rows to 1 in (2.5 cm) on 2¾ mm needles. Change needle size if necessary to obtain correct tension.

SIZES 4 sizes. Size 1 = 33 in (84 cm), size 2 = 36 in (91.5 cm), size 3 = 39 in (99 cm), size 4 = 42 in (106.5 cm), actual measurements.

ABBREVIATIONS See page 16. *Colours:* LN = Light Natural.

NOTES FOR KNITTERS See page 13.

BACK
With 2¾ mm needles and LN yarn, cast on 120(132:140:152) sts and work in K2 P2 rib for 2½ in (6.5 cm).
Next row: (increase row) K across, inc 12(12:16:16) sts evenly over the row: 132(144:156:168) sts.
Next row: P across.
Using 3 mm needles on all 1-colour rows and 3¼ mm needles on all 2-colour rows, begin to work in pattern starting with row 1 of chart IZ1. On K rows work sts 1–12 across 11(12:13:14) times, on P rows work sts 12–1 across 11(12:13:14:15) times. Work straight in pattern until you have completed row 90 of chart IZ1. *Be sure to maintain continuity of pattern for remainder of work on Back.*

Armhole Shaping
Rows 91–92: cast off 5(7:9:11) sts at beg of each row: 122(130:138:146) sts rem.
Rows 93–96: cast off 4 sts at beg of each row: 106(114:122:130) sts rem.
Rows 97–106: dec 1 st at beg of each row for 10 rows: 96(104:112:120) sts rem.
Rows 107–162: work in pattern without shaping.

Shoulder Shaping
Rows 163–168: cast off 4(5:6:7) sts at beg of each row: 72(74:76:78) sts rem.
Rows 169–170: cast off 3(4:4:5) sts at beg of each row: 66(66:68:68) sts rem.
Rows 171–172: cast off 3(3:4:4) sts at beg of each row, work in pattern to end: 60 sts rem.

Back Neck
Change to 2¾ mm needles and LN yarn and work the 60 sts for back neck in K2P2 rib for 9 rows. Cast off neatly in rib.

FRONT
Work as for Back until you have completed row 142 of chart IZ1: 96(104:112:120) sts rem. *Be sure to maintain continuity of pattern throughout.*

Divide for Neck
Row 143: work in pattern across 33(37:41:45) sts, turn, leave rem 63(67:71:75) sts on a spare needle or stitch holder and work on first group of sts as follows.

Left Front
Rows 144–158: dec 1 st at neck edge on every row: 18(22:26:30) sts rem.
Rows 159–162: work in pattern without shaping.

Shoulder Shaping
Row 163: cast off 4(5:6:7) sts at beg of row: 14(17:20:23) sts rem.
Row 164: work in pattern without shaping.
Row 165: as row 163: 10(12:14:16) sts rem.
Row 166: as row 164.
Row 167: as row 163: 6(7:8:9) sts rem.
Row 168: as row 164.
Row 169: cast off 3(4:4:5) sts at beg of row: 3(3:4:4) sts rem.
Row 170: as row 164.
Row 171: cast off rem sts.

Right Front
Slip 30 sts for Front Neck on to a stitch holder. Rejoin yarn to second group of 33(37:41:45) sts and work in pattern across row 143. Now work as for Left Front, reversing all shapings and ending by casting off rem sts on row 172.

FRONT NECKBAND
With 2¾ mm needles, LN yarn and right side of work facing, pick up and K 27 sts down left side of neck, 30 sts from centre front neck and 27 sts up right side of neck: 84 sts. Work in K2P2 rib for 9 rows. Cast off neatly in rib.

ARMBANDS
Gently press all pieces with a warm iron and damp cloth. Join shoulder seams including neck ribbing. With 2¾ mm needles, LN yarn and right side of work facing, pick up and K 148(152:156:160) sts around armhole. Work in K2P2 rib for 9 rows. Cast off loosely in rib. Repeat for other side.

TO MAKE UP
Join side seams.

11
Parsley

THIS DESIGN, based on the flat-leafed oriental parsley, is one of the simplest motifs in the Turkish stocking pattern repertoire. While the more elaborate multi-coloured stockings combine several different bands of pattern, the parsley motif is almost always used on its own, carried in vertical rows up the stockings. As its dainty delicacy suggests, this is a pattern meant to be worn by women, and although it is sometimes worked in a pale yarn on a dark ground, it is usually knitted in dark or coloured yarn on a light background.

Texture stitches play a relatively small part in Turkish colour knitting, but when they are used they tend to appear on light stockings that carry a very simple colour pattern, like this one. Parsley pattern stockings are sometimes knitted with vertical rows of texture between the parsley sprigs, and although I do not think it is an essential part of the design, you can achieve the same effect here by doing reverse stitches – working a K stitch on a P row and a P stitch on a K row – on stitches 10 and 12 in every repeat and on every row, using the same colour as the background yarn.

PARSLEY

Chart PR1
Rows 1-173

Colour Key

☐ = Sand Beige

☒ = Viridin Green

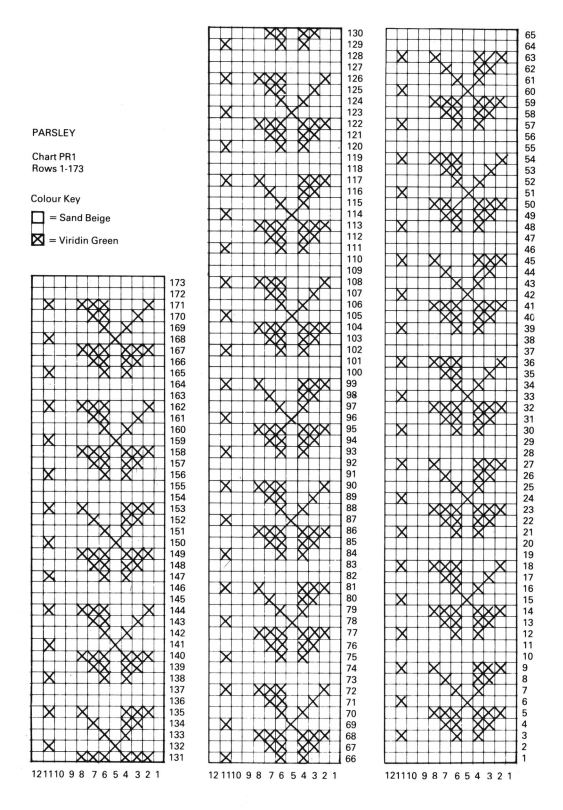

PARSLEY SWEATER

YARN COLOURS AND NUMBERS	QUANTITIES REQUIRED IN OUNCES (1 oz = 28.3 g)			
	Size 1	Size 2	Size 3	Size 4
Sand Beige FC43	8	8	9	9
Viridian Green 65	4	4	4	5

NEEDLES One pair each size 2¾ mm (No. 12 British, No. 1 American), 3 mm (No. 11 British, No. 2 American) and 3¼ mm (No. 10 British, No. 3 American) needles, and two stitch holders.

TENSION 16 sts and 16 rows to 2 in (5 cm) on 3¼ mm needles over Fair Isle pattern. For K1P1 ribbing: 10 sts and 11 rows to 1 in (2.5 cm) on 2¾ mm needles. Change needle size if necessary to obtain correct tension.

SIZES 4 sizes. Size 1 = 33 in (84 cm), size 2 = 36 in (91.5 cm), size 3 = 39 in (99 cm), size 4 = 42 in (106.5 cm), actual measurements.

ABBREVIATIONS See page 16. *Colours*: V G = Viridian Green, S B = Sand Beige.

NOTES FOR KNITTERS See page 13

BACK

With 2¾ mm needles and V G yarn cast on 118(130:140:152) sts and work in K1 P1 rib for 2 rows. Change to S B yarn and work 2 in (5 cm) in rib.

Next row: (increase row) in V G, K across, inc 14(14:16:16) sts evenly over the row: 132(144:156:168) sts.

Next row: P across in V G.

Using 3 mm needles on all 1-colour rows and 3¼ mm needles on all 2-colour rows, begin to work in pattern starting with row 1 of chart P R1. On K rows work sts 1–12 across 11(12:13:14) times, on P rows work sts 12–1 across 11(12:13:14) times. Work straight in pattern until you have completed row 98 of chart P R1. *Be sure to maintain continuity of pattern for remainder of work on Back.*

Armhole Shaping

Rows 99–100: cast off 5(7:9:11) sts at beg of each row: 122(130:138:146) sts rem.

Rows 101–114: dec 1 st at beg of each row: 108(116:124:132) sts rem.

Rows 115–118: work in pattern without shaping.

Rows 119–120: dec 1 st at beg of each row: 106(114:122:130) sts rem.

Rows 121–124: work in pattern without shaping.

Rows 125–126: dec 1 st at beg of row: 104(112:120:128) sts rem.

Rows 127–138: work in pattern without shaping.

Rows 139–140: inc into first st of each row: 106(114:122:130) sts.

Rows 141–148: work in pattern without shaping.

Rows 149–150: inc into first st of each row: 108(116:124:132) sts.

Rows 151–154: work in pattern without shaping.

Divide for Neck

Row 155: work across 25(29:33:37) sts, leave rem sts on spare needle or stitch holder and work on first group of sts as follows, keeping neck edge straight for remainder of work.

Right Back

Rows 156–158: work in pattern without shaping.

Row 159: inc into first st of row: 26(30:34:38) sts.

Rows 160–162: work in pattern without shaping.

Right Back Shoulder Shaping

Row 163: cast off 5(6:7:8) sts at beg of row: 21(24:27:30) sts rem.

Row 164: work in pattern without shaping.

Rows 165–169: cast off 4(5:6:7) sts at beg of row 165 and every alt row: 9 sts rem.

Row 170: work in pattern without shaping.

Row 171: cast off 6 sts at beg of row, work in pattern to end: 3 sts rem.

Row 172: work in pattern without shaping.

Row 173: cast off rem 3 sts.

Left Back

Slip 58 sts for centre neck on to a stitch holder, rejoin yarn to second group of 25(29:33:37) sts and work in pattern across row 155.

Work to match Right Back, reversing all shapings until row 171.

Row 171: work in pattern without shaping.

Row 172: cast off rem 9 sts.

FRONT

Work as for Back.

SLEEVES

With 2¾ mm needles and V G yarn cast on 54(60:66:72) sts and work in K1P1 rib for 2 rows. Change to S B yarn and work in rib for 2 in (5 cm).

Next row: (increase row) in V G, K across, inc 6(12:18:24) sts evenly over the row: 60(72:84:96) sts.

Next row: P across in V G.

Using 3 mm needles on all 1-colour rows and 3¼ mm needles on all 2-colour rows, begin to work in pattern starting with row 141 of chart P R1.

Row 141: work sts 1–12 across 5(6:7:8) times.

Row 142: work sts 12–1 across 5(6:7:8) times.

Row 143: as row 141.

Rows 144–160: inc 1 st at both ends of row 144 and every following 4th row until you have completed row 160: 70(82:94:106) sts.

Row 161–162: work in pattern without shaping.

Now return to row 1 of chart P R1 and continue to work in pattern, inc 1 st at both ends of row 2 and every following 4th row until there are 90(102:114:126) sts on needle. (Row 38 of chart will now have been worked.)

Rows 39–44: work in pattern without shaping.

Rows 45–94: inc 1 st at both ends of row 45 and every following 7th row until there are 106(118:130:142) sts on needle. (Row 94 of chart will now have been worked.)

Rows 95–97: work in pattern without shaping.

Row 98: inc 1 st at both ends of row: 108(120:132:144) sts.

Rows 99–100: work in pattern without shaping.

Shape Sleeve Head

Rows 101–104: cast off 1(3:5:7) sts at beg of each row: 104(108:112:116) sts.

Rows 105–114: cast off 2 sts at beg of each row: 84(88:92:96) sts rem.

Rows 115–116: dec 1 st at beg of each row: 82(86:90:94) sts rem.

Rows 117–118: cast off 2 sts at beg of each row: 78(82:86:90) sts rem.

Rows 119–122: dec 1 st at beg of each row: 74(78:82:86) sts rem.

Rows 123–126: cast off 2 sts at beg of each row: 66(70:74:78) sts rem.

Rows 127–128: dec 1 st at beg of each row: 64(68:72:76) sts rem.

Rows 129–142: cast off 2 sts at beg of each row: 36(40:44:48) sts rem.

Rows 143–144: cast off 5 sts at beg of each row: 26(30:34:38) sts rem.

Rows 145–147: cast off 3(4:5:6) sts at beg of each row: 17(18:19:20) sts rem.

Row 148: cast off remaining sts.

Work second sleeve in the same way.

BACK NECKBAND

For all sizes: join shoulder seams. With 2¾ mm needles and V G yarn and right side of Back facing, and working from right to left, pick up and K the last 6 sts down side of neck, the 58 sts across centre back and then the first 6 sts up side of neck (70 sts). Needle and sts should now be in position for working a P row.

Note: neckbands are not worked from shoulder seams in this design.

Next row: P the first 6 sts, now P28 sts across centre back, P2tog, then P the remaining 28 sts across centre back, then P the last 6 sts up side of neck: 69 sts rem.

Row 1: * K1 P1 * rep from * to last st, K1.

Row 2: change to S B yarn. Rib 4, work 2tog P1 work 2tog, rib 51, work 2tog P1 work 2tog, rib 4.

Row 3: work in rib allowing for decrease sts.

Row 4: rib 3, work 2tog P1 work 2tog, rib 49, work 2tog P1 work 2tog, rib 3.

Row 5: as row 3.

Row 6: rib 2, work 2tog P1 work, rib 47, work 2tog P1 work 2tog, rib 2.

Row 7: change to V G yarn, work as for row 3.

Row 8: rib 1, work 2tog P1 work 2tog, rib 45, work 2tog P1 work 2tog, rib 1. Cast off neatly in rib.

FRONT NECKBAND

With 2¾ mm needles and V G yarn and right side of Front facing, and working from right to left, pick up and K the remaining 30 sts down side of neck, the 58 sts across centre front and the remaining 30 sts up the other side of neck. Needle and sts should now be in position for working a P row.

Next row: P the first 30 sts, then P28 sts across centre front, P2tog, then P the remaining 28 sts across centre front, then the remaining 30 sts (117 sts).

Row 1: * K1 P1 * rep from * to last st, K1.

Row 2: change to S B yarn. Rib 28, work 2tog P1 work 2tog, rib 51, work 2tog P1 work 2tog, rib 28.

Row 3: work in rib, allowing for decrease sts.

Row 4: rib 27, work 2tog P1 work 2tog, rib 49, work 2tog P1 work 2tog, rib 27.

Row 5: as row 3.

Row 6: rib 26, work 2tog P1 work 2tog, rib 47, work 2tog P1 work 2tog, rib 26.

Row 7: change to V G yarn. Work as for row 3.

Row 8: rib 25, work 2tog P1 work 2tog, rib 45, work 2tog P1 work 2tog, rib 25. Cast off neatly in rib.

TO MAKE UP

Gently press all pieces with a warm iron and damp cloth. Join neckband seams. Sew sleeves into position along armhole edge, then join side and sleeve seams.

12
Whirling Dervish

I HAVE no idea what village the Turkish stockings on which this design is based originally came from, but I shall never forget the circumstances in which I acquired them. I had come to Konya in early January, when the winds from Siberia sweep across the high Anatolian plateau. The snow-covered streets were empty, shops shut and windows firmly shuttered against the piercing cold, but I was determined to see the great *Mevlana Tekke* – the shrine that honours Mevlana Celaleddin Rumi, founder of the Mevlevi order of dervishes. I stumbled along the icy roads, wincing with cold as snow seeped into my boots and the wind whipped at my clothing. Struggling to the door of the *tekke*, I was faced with an appalling choice – I must remove my shoes, as they were not permitted in the shrine, or forego my longed-for visit. Off came the shoes, and I padded in damp stockinged feet over a freezing marble floor, marvelling at the beauties around me, shivering and sneezing the while.

Chilled to the bone, I emerged to find that snow was falling. Losing all sense of direction, I lurched along on numb feet and, after many twistings and turnings, slipped on a patch of ice and pitched headlong into the only open shop in the street – the shop of a carpet seller. No grand establishment, this was a humble room with living quarters at the back and a storage loft above, reached by a rickety ladder. The kindly proprietor helped me towards the stove, plied me with welcome cups of fragrant hot tea and, seeing that I was not in a sound state, made only token efforts to sell me his carpets. Wishing to engage him in conversation to show my appreciation, I fell back on my sole word of Turkish – *urgu* or stocking. The face of my benefactor registered puzzlement, then disbelief, and finally the canny comprehension of a merchant who sees that a sale might, after all, be in prospect. Although I did not know it, old stockings are sometimes used as padding in bales of carpets and kelims. The proprietor scrambled up to the loft, rummaged among the bales, and began to throw down what he had found. Soon I was sitting in a shower of stockings – odd ones, pairs, coloured and plain. I left clutching a bundle of knitted booty, and did not feel the cold again that night, even when I fell into a snowbank. The vertical S motif (rows 17–20) in this design symbolizes riches and fertility, and I have used the striped pattern on the soles of the stockings for the ribbing.

WHIRLING DERVISH

Chart WD1
Rows 1-168

Colour Key

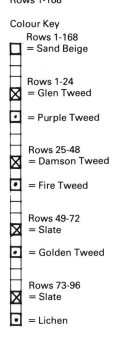

Rows 1-168
☐ = Sand Beige

Rows 1-24
☒ = Glen Tweed

⊡ = Purple Tweed

Rows 25-48
☒ = Damson Tweed

⊡ = Fire Tweed

Rows 49-72
☒ = Slate

⊡ = Golden Tweed

Rows 73-96
☒ = Slate

⊡ = Lichen

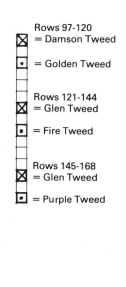

Rows 97-120
☒ = Damson Tweed

⊡ = Golden Tweed

Rows 121-144
☒ = Glen Tweed

⊡ = Fire Tweed

Rows 145-168
☒ = Glen Tweed

⊡ = Purple Tweed

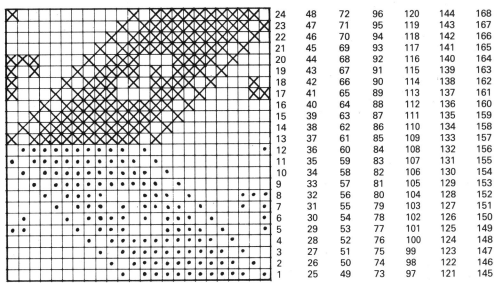

	24	48	72	96	120	144	168
	23	47	71	95	119	143	167
	22	46	70	94	118	142	166
	21	45	69	93	117	141	165
	20	44	68	92	116	140	164
	19	43	67	91	115	139	163
	18	42	66	90	114	138	162
	17	41	65	89	113	137	161
	16	40	64	88	112	136	160
	15	39	63	87	111	135	159
	14	38	62	86	110	134	158
	13	37	61	85	109	133	157
	12	36	60	84	108	132	156
	11	35	59	83	107	131	155
	10	34	58	82	106	130	154
	9	33	57	81	105	129	153
	8	32	56	80	104	128	152
	7	31	55	79	103	127	151
	6	30	54	78	102	126	150
	5	29	53	77	101	125	149
	4	28	52	76	100	124	148
	3	27	51	75	99	123	147
	2	26	50	74	98	122	146
	1	25	49	73	97	121	145

24 23 22 21 20 19 18 17 16 15 14 13 12 11 10 9 8 7 6 5 4 3 2 1

WHIRLING DERVISH SLIPOVER

YARN COLOURS AND NUMBERS	QUANTITIES REQUIRED IN OUNCES (1 oz = 28.3 g)			
	Size 1	Size 2	Size 3	Size 4
Sand Beige F C 33	2	3	3	3
Purple Tweed F C 56	1	1	1	2
Fire Tweed F C 55	1	1	2	2
Damson Tweed F C 54	1	1	1	1
Golden Tweed F C 57	1	1	1	2
Slate F C 53	1	1	2	2
Glen Tweed F C 58	1	1	1	2
Lichen F C 59	1	1	1	1

NEEDLES One pair each size 2¾ mm (No. 12 British, No. 1 American), 3 mm (No. 11 British, No. 2 American) and 3¼ mm (No. 10 British, No. 3 American) needles, and 2 stitch holders.

TENSION 16 sts and 16 rows to 2 in (5 cm) on 3¼ mm needles over Fair Isle pattern. For Vertical Stripe ribbing: 18 sts and 18 rows to 2 in (5 cm) on 2¾ mm needles. Change needle size if necessary to obtain correct tension.

SIZES 4 sizes. Size 1 = 33 in (84 cm), size 2 = 36 in (91.5 cm), size 3 = 39 in (99 cm), size 4 = 42 in (106.5 cm), actual measurements.

ABBREVIATIONS See page 16. *Colours:* P T = Purple Tweed, F T = Fire Tweed, D T = Damson Tweed, G T = Golden Tweed, S L = Slate, G L = Glen Tweed, L C = Lichen.

NOTES FOR KNITTERS See page 13.

SPECIAL INSTRUCTIONS FOR THIS DESIGN Vertical Stripe ribbing is less stretchy than regular K2 P2 ribbing. If you prefer a rib with lots of give, work regular K2 P2 ribbing in horizontal stripes using the colours given for Vertical Stripe ribbing.

BACK

With 2¾ mm needles and P T yarn, cast on 120(132:140:152) sts. Join in D T yarn and work in Vertical Stripe ribbing as follows.

Row 1: K2 PT, P2 DT, rep to last 2 sts, P2 DT.

Row 2: K2 DT, P2 PT, rep to last 2 sts, P2 PT.

Rows 3–4: as for rows 1 and 2.

Row 5: K2 PT, P2 GT, rep to last 2 sts, P2 GT.

Row 6: K2 GT, P2 PT to end.

Rows 7–8: as rows 5 and 6.

Row 9: K2 FT, P2 GT to end.

Row 10: K2 GT, P2 FT to end.

Rows 11–12: as rows 9 and 10.

Row 13: K2 FT, P2 SL to end.

Row 14: K2 SL, P2 FT to end.

Rows 15–16: as rows 13 and 14.

Row 17: K2 GL, P2 SL to end.

Row 18: K2 SL, P2 GL to end.

Rows 19–20: as rows 17 and 18.

Row 21: K2 GL, P2 LC to end.

Row 22: K2 LC, P2 GL to end.

Rows 23–24: as rows 21 and 22.

Row 25: (increase row) using 3 mm needles and GL yarn, K across, increasing 12(12:16:16) sts evenly over the row: 132(144:156:168) sts.

Next row: P across in PT.

Using 3 mm needles on all 1-colour rows and 3¼ mm needles on all 2-colour rows, begin to work in pattern starting with row 1 of chart W D 1 *in the following sequence.* **For sizes 2 and 4 only:** on K rows work sts 1–24 across 6(7) times, on P rows work sts 24–1 across 6(7) times. **For sizes 1 and 3 only:** on K rows work sts 1–24 across 5(6) times, then work sts 1–12. On P rows work sts 12–1, then work sts 24–1 across 5(6) times. Work straight in pattern until you have completed row 86 of chart W D 1. *Be sure to maintain continuity of pattern for remainder of work on Back.*

Armhole Shaping

Rows 87–88: cast off 5(7:9:11) sts at beg of each row: 122(130:138:146) sts rem.

Rows 89–92: cast off 4 sts at beg of each row: 106(114:122:130) sts rem.

Rows 93–102: dec 1 st at beg of each row for 10 rows: 96(104:112:120) sts rem.

Rows 103–158: work in pattern without shaping.

Shoulder Shaping

Rows 159–164: cast off 4(5:6:7) sts at beg of each row: 72(74:76:78) sts rem.

Rows 165–166: cast off 3(4:4:5) sts at beg of each row: 66(66:68:68) sts rem.

Rows 167–168: cast off 3(3:4:4) sts at beg of each row, work in pattern to end: 60 sts rem.

Leave rem 60 sts on spare needle or stitch holder.

FRONT

Work Vertical Stripe ribbing as for Back. **For sizes 2 and 4 only**: work as for Back until you have completed row 138 of chart WD1. **For sizes 1 and 3 only**: on K rows work sts 13–24, then work sts 1–24 across 5(6) times. On P rows, work sts 24–1 across 5(6) times, then work sts 24–13. Work as for Back until you have completed row 138 of chart WD1. *For all sizes: be sure to maintain continuity of pattern throughout.* There should be 96(104:112:120) sts on needle when row 138 has been worked.

Divide for Neck

Row 139: work in pattern across 33(37:41:45) sts, turn, leave rem 63(67:71:75) sts on a spare needle or stitch holder and work on first group of sts as follows.

Left Front

Rows 140–154: dec 1 st at neck edge on every row: 18(22:26:30) sts rem.
Rows 155–158: work in pattern without shaping.

Shoulder Shaping

Row 159: cast off 4(5:6:7) sts at beg of row: 14(17:20:23) sts rem.
Row 160: work in pattern without shaping.
Row 161: as row 159: 10(12:14:16) sts rem.
Row 162: as row 160.
Row 163: as row 159: 6(7:8:9) sts rem.
Row 164: as row 160.
Row 165: cast off 3(4:4:5) sts at beg of row: 3(3:4:4) sts rem.
Row 166: as row 160.
Row 167: cast off rem sts.

Right Front

Slip 30 sts for Front Neck on to a stitch holder. Rejoin yarn to second group of 33(37:41:45) sts and work in pattern across row 139. Now work as for Left Front, reversing all shapings and ending by casting off rem sts on row 168.

FRONT NECKBAND

With 2¾ mm needles and FT yarn and right side of work facing, pick up and K 27 sts down left side of neck, 30 sts from centre front neck and 27 sts up right side of neck: 84 sts. Work in Vertical Stripe ribbing as follows.
Row 1: K2 FT, P2 SL, to end.
Row 2: K2 SL, P2 FT, to end.
Rows 3–4: as rows 1 and 2.
Row 5: K2 FT, P2 GT, to end.
Row 6: K2 GT, P2 FT, to end.
Rows 7–8: as rows 5 and 6.
Row 9: K2 DT, P2 GT, to end.
Row 10: K2 GT, P2 DT, to end.
Cast off neatly in rib.

BACK NECK

With 2¾ mm needles, work the 60 sts at Back Neck to match Front Neckband.

ARMBANDS

Gently press all pieces using a warm iron and damp cloth. Join shoulder seams including neck ribbing. With 2¾ mm needles and FT yarn and right side of work facing, pick up and K 148(152:156:160) sts around armhole. Join in SL yarn and work 8 rows of Vertical Stripe ribbing as given for rows 1–8 of Front Neckband.
Row 9: K2 FT, P2 GT, to end.
Cast off neatly in rib. Repeat for other side.

TO MAKE UP

Join side seams.

13
Trebizond

SOME OF THE finest colour knitting in the world is to be found along the shores of the Black Sea, where from time immemorial traditional footwear has consisted of patterned knitted stockings worn with simple leather slippers. The triangle and diagonal stripe patterns in this design are motifs found on traditional stockings from the Caucasus and from Trebizond, that fabled city by the Black Sea that was once the capital of the last Byzantine Empire. Here the great caravan road from Tabriz ended, and from the thirteenth to the fifteenth centuries A D the city grew rich and powerful from the trade in silks and spices that came over the road from the East. Travellers and Crusaders brought back tales of the splendour of the palace in the high citadel that still dominates the shore. Its floors were all of white marble, Byzantine frescoes adorned the walls and the vaulted ceilings were emblazoned with stars of pure gold. The audience chamber was in a stately white marble pyramid, and here the ruling family of Trebizond pursued a delicate form of diplomacy that involved marrying their daughters to Muslim princes and their sons to princesses from Christian courts, in order to preserve a precarious political stability. The princesses of Trebizond were reknowned for their beauty, and it is tempting to think that dainty stockings of this very design may have been worn by a royal lady of those far-off times, as she sat in her palace by the sea wondering if she would find happiness in the seraglio that was to be her destiny.

Chart T1, 18 sts and 36 rows.

Trebizond Sweater Colour Key

☐ = Watermelon Red

⊡ = Pale Yellow

✳ = Light Natural

◪ = Purple

⬧ = Bright Mauve

◩ = Viridian Green

∨ = Leaf Green

◈ = Periwinkle Blue

⊞ = Heather Purple

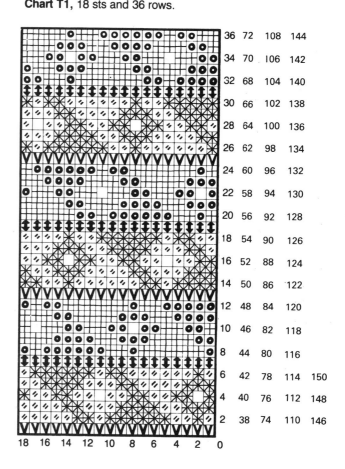

Chart T2, 9 sts and 144 rows.

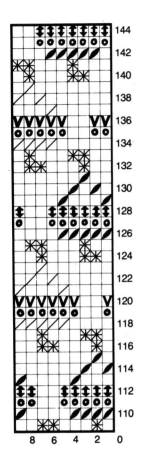

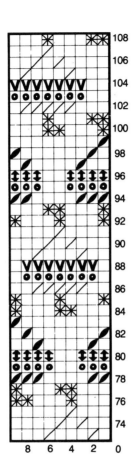

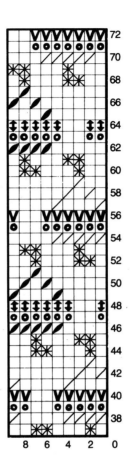

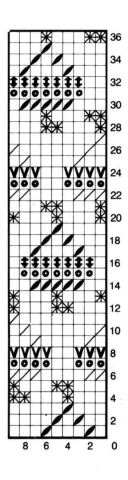

**Trebizond Sweater
Colour Key**

$\square$ = Watermelon Red

$\boxed{O}$ = Pale Yellow

$\maltese$ = Light Natural

$\blacksquare$ = Purple

$\blacklozenge$ = Bright Mauve

$\diagup$ = Viridian Green

$\mathbf{V}$ = Leaf Green

$\boxed{\bullet\bullet}$ = Periwinkle Blue

$\boxplus$ = Heather Purple

TREBIZOND SWEATER

YARN COLOURS AND NUMBERS	QUANTITIES REQUIRED IN OUNCES (1 oz = 28.3 g)			
	Size 1	Size 2	Size 3	Size 4
Watermelon Red FC 33	4	5	5	5
Leaf Green 25	2	2	2	2
Periwinkle Blue FC 37	2	2	2	2
Light Natural 202	2	3	3	3
Bright Mauve 44	1	1	2	2
Pale Yellow 96	2	2	3	3
Heather Purple 19	3	3	3	3
Viridian Green 65	1	1	1	1
Purple 20	1	1	1	1

SIZES 4 sizes. Size 1 = 34 in (86 cm), size 2 = 36 in (91.5 cm), size 3 = 38 in (97 cm) and size 4 = 40½ in (103 cm), actual measurements.

ABBREVIATIONS See page 15. *Colours:* HP = Heather Purple, WR = Watermelon Red.

NOTES FOR KNITTERS See page 13.

BACK
With 2¾ mm needles and HP yarn, cast on 126(132:138:144) sts and work in K1P1 rib in stripes of 2 rows HP, 2 rows WR. Continue in this way until work measures 2½ in (6.5 cm). Keeping continuity of colour stripe pattern, change to 3 mm needles and work as follows:
Size 1: K5 * K12, inc into next st, rep from * to last 4 sts, K4 (135 sts).
Size 2: * K10, inc into next st, rep from * to end (144 sts).
Size 3: K2 * K8, inc into next st, rep from * to last st, K1 (153 sts).
Size 4: * K7, inc into next st, rep from * to end (162 sts).
For all sizes: next row; P across.
Now begin to work in Fair Isle patt from Chart T1, starting with row 1.
Row 1: K across. Change to 3¼ mm needles and work as follows:
Size 1: row 2; work sts 9–1, then repeat sts 18–1 across 7 times (135 sts).
Row 3: repeat sts 1–18 across 7 times, then work sts 1–9.

Size 2: row 2; repeat sts 18–1 across 8 times (144 sts).
Row 3: repeat sts 1–18 across 8 times.
Size 3: row 2; work sts 9–1, then repeat sts 18–1 across 8 times (153 sts).
Row 3: repeat sts 1–18 across 8 times, then work sts 1–9.
Size 4: row 2; repeat sts 18–1 across 9 times (162 sts).
Row 3: repeat sts 1–18 across 9 times.

For all sizes: continue to work in patt in this way until you have completed row 25 of chart T1. Slip all stitches on to the other needle without knitting them so as to start right side facing, and begin to work in patt from chart T2, beginning at row 1, and repeating the 9 patt stitches across 15(16:17:18) times. Continue until you have completed row 76 of chart T2. (101 rows of Fair Isle pattern now worked altogether.) **Note: from now on, shaping and row counts relate only to pattern rows of chart T2.**

Armhole Shaping
Row 77: (right side facing) cast off 5(8:11:14) sts, patt to end.
Row 78: cast off 5(8:11:14) sts, patt to end.
Rows 79–86: keeping continuity of pattern, cast off 2 sts at beg of next 8 rows: 109(112:115:118) sts.
Now work without shaping until you have completed row 138 of chart T2.

Shoulder Shaping
Rows 139–144: keeping continuity of pattern, cast off 5 sts at beg of next 6 rows: 79(82:85:88) sts.
Row 145: using WR yarn only, K across row (no patterning).
Leave remaining 79(82:85:88) sts on a spare needle or stitch holder.

FRONT
Work exactly as for Back until you have completed row 1 of chart T1. Now change to 3¼ mm needles and work in patt from chart T1 as follows:
Size 1: row 2; repeat sts 18–1 across 7 times, then work sts 18–10 (135 sts).
Row 3: work sts 10–18, then repeat sts 1–18 across 7 times.
Size 2: row 2; repeat sts 18–1 across 8 times (144 sts).
Row 3: repeat sts 1–18 across 8 times.
Size 3: row 2; repeat sts 18–1 across 8 times, then work sts 18–10 (153 sts).
Row 3: work sts 10–18, then repeat sts 1–18 across 8 times.
Size 4: row 2; repeat sts 18–1 across 9 times (162 sts).
Row 3: Repeat sts 1–18 across 9 times.
For all sizes: continue in patt until you have completed row 25 of chart T1. Slip all stitches on to the other needle without knitting them so as to start right side facing and work in patt from chart T2, as for Back, starting at row 1 and continuing until you have completed row 112 of chart T2.

Divide for Neck
Row 113: patt across 47 sts, put next 62(65:68:71) sts on a spare needle or stitch holder.

Left Front
Row 114: (wrong side facing), patt across row.
Row 115: patt across row.
Rows 116–130: keeping armhole edge straight, cast off 3 sts at neck edge on every alternate row 8 times (23 sts on needle).
Row 131: work without shaping.
Rows 132–138: dec 1 st at neck edge on every alternate row 4 times.

Shoulder Shaping
Row 139: cast off 5 sts, patt to end (14 sts).
Row 140: dec 1 st (neck edge), patt to end.

Row 141: cast off 5 sts, patt to end (8 sts).

Row 142: dec 1 st, patt to end.

Row 143: cast off 5 sts, patt to end (2 sts).

Row 144: cast off remaining 2 sts using WR yarn. Slip centre front 15(18:21:24) sts on to a stitch holder, patt across remaining 47 sts.

Right Front

Work to match Left Front, reversing all shapings, casting off last 2 sts on row 145.

SLEEVES

With 2¾ mm needles and HP yarn, cast on 68 sts and work in K1P1 rib in stripes of 2 rows HP, 2 rows WR, until work measures 2 in (5 cm). Change to 3 mm needles. Keeping colour stripe sequence correct, work as follows.

Next row: * K1, inc into next st, rep from * to end (102 sts).

Next row: P across.

Size 1: next row; K6 * K5, inc into next st, rep from * to last 6 sts, K6 (117 sts).

Next row: P across.

Size 2: next row; K5 * K3, inc into next st, rep from * to last st, K1 (126 sts).

Next row: P across.

Size 3: next row; K2 * K2, inc into next st, rep from * to last st, K1 (135 sts).

Next row: P across.

Size 4: next row; K9 * K1, inc into next st, rep from * to last 9 sts, K9 (144 sts).

Next row: P across.

For all sizes: change to 3¼ mm needles and begin to work in pattern from chart T1, starting with row 31 of chart. Work rows 31–36, then begin at row 1 again and work to row 100 (106 rows of pattern worked altogether). **Note: the sleeves are worked using chart T1 only.**

Shape Sleeve Head

Rows 101–102: cast off 6(9:12:15) sts at beg of next 2 rows.

Rows 103–108: cast off 2 sts at beg of every row: 93(96:99:102) sts.

Rows 109–118: cast off 2 sts at beg of every row.

Rows 119–120: cast off 1 st at beg of next 2 rows.

Rows 121–122: cast off 2 sts at beg of next 2 rows.

Rows 123–124: cast off 1 st at beg of next 2 rows.

Rows 125–126: cast off 2 sts at beg of next 2 rows.

Rows 127–128: cast off 1 st at beg of next 2 rows.

Rows 129–130: cast off 2 sts at beg of next 2 rows.

Rows 131–132: cast off 1 st at beg of next 2 rows: 53(56:59:62) sts.

Rows 133–144: cast off 2 sts at beg of every row: 29(32:35:38) sts.

Rows 145–149: cast off 4 sts at beg of next 4 rows.

Cast off remaining 13(16:19:22) sts. Work second sleeve to match.

PICOT NECK EDGE

Join right shoulder seam using back st. With 2¾ mm needles and HP yarn and with right side of work facing, pick up and K 40 sts down left front neck, then work across centre front 15(18:21:24) sts as follows:

Size 1: * K4, K2tog, rep from * once more, K1, K2tog.

Size 2: * K4, K2tog, rep from * twice more.

Size 3: * K4, K2tog, rep from * twice more, K1, K2.

Size 4: * K4, K2tog, rep from * three more times.

For all sizes: pick up and K 40 sts up right side of neck and work across centre back 79(82:85:88) sts as follows:

Size 1: * K4, K2tog 13 times, to end K1. (158 sts on needle).

Size 2: * K4, K2tog 13 times, to last 4 sts, K4. (164 sts on needle).

Size 3: * K4, K2tog 14 times, to end K1. (168 sts on needle).

Size 4: * K4, K2tog 14 times, to end K4. (174 sts on needle).

For all sizes: with HP yarn, continue to work neck edging as follows:

Row 1: P.

Row 2: K.

Row 3: P.

Row 4: K1 * K2tog, rep from * to last st, K1.

Row 5: P1, * YO, P1, rep from * to last st, P1.

Row 6: K.

Row 7: P.

Row 8: K.

Row 9: P.

Row 10: K.

Row 11: cast off knitwise.

TO MAKE UP

Lightly press all pieces with a damp cloth and warm iron. Join left shoulder seam. Sew in sleeves using back stitch. Join side and sleeve seams using back stitch. Fold picot edge inwards and slip stitch neatly into place.

14
Turkish Kelim

As I discovered while I was travelling across Turkey and Syria, the passion for kelims becomes an incurable mania once it takes hold. Turkish kelims or kilims are the flat weave rugs devised by the nomadic Anatolian *Yoruks* of old, which are still woven by their descendants, using traditional patterns and natural dyes brewed from cherry skins, rose roots, poppy petals, lemon skins and pistachio leaves. Kelims have a distinctive style that sets them apart from pile carpets – a simple, almost primitive beauty based on strong geometric forms, bold repeat designs and a superb sense of colour contrast. This style derives from the kelim's origins, for the large fixed looms and non-repeat design cartoons required for elaborate designs were unsuited to the *Yoruk*'s nomadic lifestyle, and curvilinear motifs do not lend themselves well to the flat-weave technique. Relying instead on small portable looms, a repertoire of basic patterns and a repeat technique that made few demands on the memory and was ideal for an interruption-prone life on the move, the *Yoruks* refined the kelim into a textile art form whose bold simplicity many modern collectors prefer to the diffuse complexity of pile carpets.

Happily for the collector, kelims are far less expensive than pile carpets – and happier still for the knitter, kelim patterns translate beautifully into knitting. The only problem is the dizzying one of choice – there are bird pattern kelims from Van, Sumac flower kelims, Thracian kelims covered with diamond medallions and borders, prayer kelims scattered with Tree of Life patterns, and many many more. The kelim from which this design is taken was woven by the Sumacs of northeast Anatolia – the motifs between rows 15–33 and 83–103 are variants of the Ram's Horn pattern, and the horizontal S pattern (rows 6–10) symbolizes eternity or infinity. Even if kelim-collecting is well within your means, there is a very good reason to find something to do with them besides putting them on the floor. Tightly woven in wool without knots or pile to give them substance, kelims do not stand up to heavy wear. This is why many collectors hang their kelims on the wall – but why should your wall be better dressed than you are? Far better, it seems to me, to collect kelim patterns rather than the kelims themselves, knit them up and wear them yourself.

TURKISH KELIM

Chart TK1
Rows 1-172

Colour Key

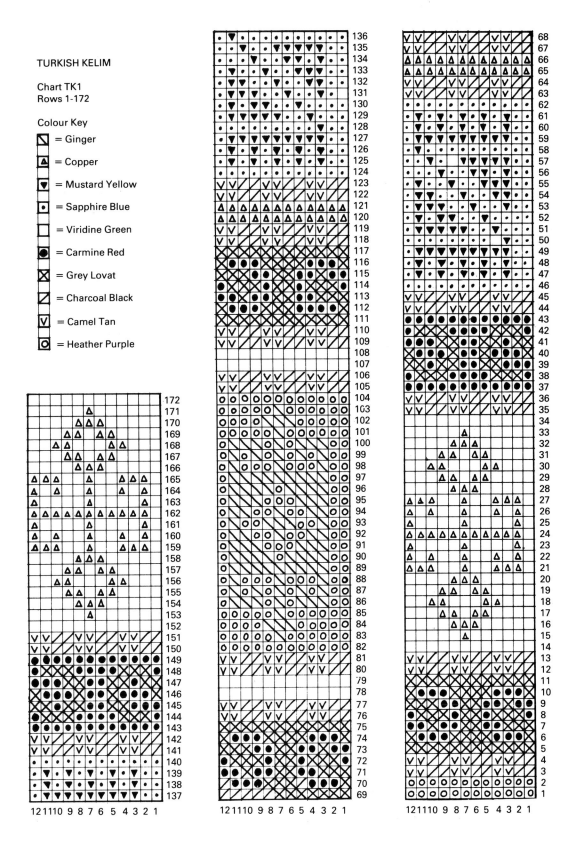

= Ginger

= Copper

= Mustard Yellow

= Sapphire Blue

= Viridine Green

= Carmine Red

= Grey Lovat

= Charcoal Black

= Camel Tan

= Heather Purple

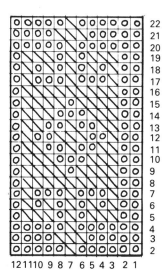

TURKISH KELIM

Chart TK2
Sleeves only
Rows 2-22

TURKISH KELIM SWEATER

YARN COLOURS AND NUMBERS	QUANTITIES REQUIRED IN OUNCES (1 oz = 28.3 g)			
	Size 1	Size 2	Size 3	Size 4
Heather Purple 19	1	2	2	3
Camel Tan FC 45	1	2	2	3
Charcoal Black 81	2	2	3	3
Grey Lovat 30	1	2	2	3
Ginger 32	1	1	2	2
Viridian Green 65	1	2	2	2
Copper 31	1	1	2	2
Carmine Red 72	1	1	2	2
Mustard Yellow 28	1	1	2	2
Sapphire Blue FC 48	1	2	2	2

TENSION 16 sts and 16 rows to 2 in (5 cm) on 3¼ mm needles over Fair Isle pattern. For Vertical Stripe ribbing: 18 sts and 18 rows to 2 in (5 cm) on 2¾ mm needles. Change needle size if necessary to obtain correct tension.

SIZES 4 sizes. Size 1 = 33 in (84 cm), size 2 = 36 in (91.5 cm), size 3 = 39 in (99 cm), size 4 = 42 in (106.5 cm), actual measurements.

ABBREVIATIONS See page 16. *Colours:* CT = Camel Tan, B = Charcoal Black, H = Heather Purple.

NOTES FOR KNITTERS See page 13.

SPECIAL INSTRUCTIONS FOR THIS DESIGN Vertical Stripe ribbing is less stretchy than regular K2P2 ribbing, and cannot be worn turned back at the cuff because of the second colour of yarn which is carried across the back of the ribbing. If you prefer a rib with lots of give and like to wear your cuffs rolled back or pushed up, work regular K2P2 ribbing in horizontal stripes using the colours given for Vertical Stripe ribbing. If you want to knit this design up as a slipover with

Vertical Stripe ribbing, follow the ribbing and increase instructions for the *Whirling Dervish* slipover, but for the remainder of the slipover follow the instructions for *Izmir*.

NEEDLES One pair each size 2¾ mm (No. 12 British, No. 1 American), 3 mm (No. 11 British, No. 2 American) and 3¼ mm (No. 10 British, No. 3 American) needles, and two stitch holders.

BACK

With 2¾ mm needles and CT yarn, cast on 120(132:140:152) sts. Join in B yarn and work in Vertical Stripe ribbing as follows.

Row 1: K2B, P2CT, rep to last 2 sts, P2CT.

Row 2: K2CT, P2B, rep to last 2 sts, P2B.

Repeat rows 1 and 2 until work measures 2½ in (6.5 cm).

Next right side row: (increase row) change to 3 mm needles and H yarn and K across, inc 12(12:16:16) sts evenly over the row: 132(144:156:168) sts.

Next row: P across in H.

Using 3 mm needles on all 1-colour rows and 3¼ mm needles on all 2-colour rows, begin to work in pattern starting with row 2 of chart TK1. On P rows work sts 12–1 across 11(12:13:14) times, on K rows work sts 1–12 across 11(12:13:14) times. Work straight in pattern until you have completed row 98 of chart TK1. *Be sure to maintain continuity of pattern for remainder of work on Back.*

Armhole Shaping

Rows 99–100: cast off 5(7:9:11) sts at beg of each row: 122(130:138:146) sts rem.

Rows 101–114: dec 1 st at beg of each row: 108(116:124:132) sts rem.

Rows 115–118: work in pattern without shaping.

Rows 119–120: dec 1 st at beg of each row: 106(114:122:130) sts rem.

Rows 121–124: work in pattern without shaping.

Rows 125–126: dec 1 st at beg of each row: 104(112:120:128) sts rem.

Rows 127–138: work in pattern without shaping.

Rows 139–140: inc into first st of each row: 106(114:122:130) sts.

Rows 141–148: work in pattern without shaping.

Rows 149–150: inc into first st of each row: 108(116:124:132) sts.

Rows 151–158: work in pattern without shaping.

Rows 159–160: inc into first st of each row: 110(118:126:134) sts.

Rows 161–162: work in pattern without shaping.

Shoulder Shaping

Rows 163–170: cast off 5(6:7:8) sts at beg of each row: 70 sts rem.

Row 171–172: cast off 5 sts at beg of each row: 60 sts rem.

Leave rem 60 sts on spare needle or stitch holder.

FRONT

Work as for Back until you have completed row 142 of chart TK1: 106(114:122:130) sts rem. *Be sure to maintain continuity of pattern throughout.*

Divide for Neck

Row 143: work in pattern across 38(42:46:50) sts, turn, and leave rem 68(72:76:80) sts on spare needle or stitch holder and work on first group of sts as follows.

Left Front

Rows 144–148: dec 1 st at neck edge on every row: 33(37:41:45) sts rem.

Row 149: inc 1 st at beg of row, work across in pattern to last 2 sts, dec 1 st at neck edge: 33(37:41:45) sts.

Rows 150–156: dec 1 st at neck edge on every row: 26(30:34:38) sts rem.

Row 157–158: work in pattern without shaping.

Row 159: inc 1 st at beg of row, work across in pattern to last 2 sts, dec 1 st at neck edge: 26(30:34:38) sts rem.

Row 160: dec 1 st at neck edge, work in pattern across row: 25(29:33:37) sts rem. Now keep neck edge straight for remainder of work.

Rows 161–162: work in pattern without shaping.

Shoulder Shaping

Row 163: cast off 5(6:7:8) sts, work in pattern to end: 20(23:26:29) sts rem.

Row 164: work in pattern without shaping.

Row 165: as row 163: 15(17:19:21) sts rem.

Row 166: work in pattern without shaping.

Row 167: as row 163: 10(11:12:13) sts rem.

Row 168: work in pattern without shaping.

Row 169: as row 163: 5 sts rem.

Row 170: work in pattern without shaping.

Row 171: cast off rem 5 sts.

Right Front

Slip 30 sts for Front Neck on to spare needle or stitch holder, then rejoin yarn to rem 38(42:46:50) sts and work in pattern across row 143. Now work as for Left Front, reversing all shapings and ending by casting off rem 5 sts on row 172.

SLEEVES

With 2¾ mm needles and CT yarn, cast on 52(60:68:72) sts. Join in B yarn and work in Vertical Stripe ribbing as for Front and Back until work measures 2½ in (6.5 cm).

Next right side row: (increase row) change to 3 mm needles and H yarn and K across, inc 8(12:16:24) sts evenly over the row: 60(72:84:96) sts.

Using 3 mm needles on all 1-colour rows and 3¼ mm needles on all 2-colour rows, begin to work in pattern starting with row 2 of chart TK2.

Row 2: work sts 12–1 across 5(6:7:8) times.

Row 3: work sts 1–12 across 5(6:7:8) times.

Rows 4–20: inc 1 st at both ends of row 4 and every following 4th row until you have completed row 20 of chart TK2: 70(82:94:106) sts.

Rows 21–22: work in pattern without shaping.

Now return to row 1 of chart TK1 and continue to work in pattern, inc 1 st at both ends of row 2 and every following 4th row until there are 90(102:114:126) sts on needle. (Row 38 of chart TK1 will now have been worked; from now on all row numbers refer to chart TK1.)

Rows 39–44: work in pattern without shaping.

Rows 45–94: inc 1 st at both ends of row 45 and every following 7th row until there are 106(118:130:142) sts on needle (row 94 of chart TK1).

Rows 95–97: work in pattern without shaping.

Row 98: inc 1 st at both ends of row: 108(120:132:144) sts.

Rows 99–100: work in pattern without shaping.

Shape Sleeve Head

Rows 101–104: cast off 1(3:5:7) sts at beg of each row: 104(108:112:116) sts.

Rows 105–114: cast off 2 sts at beg of each row: 84(88:92:96) sts rem.

Rows 115–116: dec 1 st at beg of each row: 82(86:90:94) sts rem.

Rows 117–118: cast off 2 sts at beg of each row: 78(82:86:90) sts rem.

Rows 119–122: dec 1 st at beg of each row: 74(78:82:86) sts rem.

Rows 123–126: cast off 2 sts at beg of each row: 66(70:74:78) sts rem.

Rows 127–128: dec 1 st at beg of each row: 64(68:72:76) sts rem.

Rows 129–142: cast off 2 sts at beg of each row: 36(40:44:48) sts rem.

Rows 143–144: cast off 5 sts at beg of each row: 26(30:34:38) sts rem.

Rows 145–147: cast off 3(4:5:6) sts at beg of each row: 17(18:19:20) sts rem.

Row 148: cast off rem sts.

Work second sleeve in the same way.

NECKBAND

With 2¾ mm needles and CT yarn and right side of work facing, pick up and K 27 sts down left side of neck, 30 sts from centre front neck and 27 sts up right side of neck: 84 sts. Join in B yarn. Work in Vertical Stripe ribbing as for Front and Back for 10 rows. Cast off neatly in rib.

BACK NECK

With 2¾ mm needles and CT and B yarn, work the 60 sts for Back Neck to match Front Neckband. Cast off neatly in rib.

TO MAKE UP

Gently press all pieces using a warm iron and damp cloth. Join shoulder seams including neck ribbing. Sew sleeves into place along armhole edge then join side and sleeve seams.

15
Flora

THE LOVE of flowers knows no season, and this *Flora* cardigan will give you a garden that will never fade away. Blossoms in any form are a delight to the eye, but if you know the Language of Flowers they can appeal to the heart as well. In Victorian times, every flower was held to have a symbolic meaning – for example, the snowdrop meant Hope and the apple blossom Temptation – and lovers could carry on their courtship and quarrels entirely through the exchange of posies. These floral gifts could convey everything from a single sentiment to a complicated poem, and even the leaves were important. To give a flower with the leaves still on it meant something positive, while to give a flower stripped of its leaves meant something negative. Thus, the present of a pimpernel with leaves meant Assignation; without leaves No Assignation. Today we express our feelings more directly, but I think you will enjoy knowing what *Flora* says in the Language of Flowers. Starting at the bottom, the message reads

Tulip = Beautiful Eyes
German Iris = Flame of Passion
Violets = Constantly In My Mind
Red Rose = Love Triumphant
Pansy = You Occupy All My Thoughts
Carnation = My Heart Is Smitten.

Chart F6

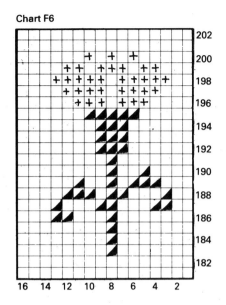

16   14   12   10   8   6   4   2

202 200 198 196 194 192 190 188 186 184 182

Chart F4

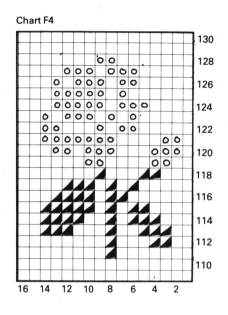

16   14   12   10   8   6   4   2

130 128 126 124 122 120 118 116 114 112 110

Chart F2

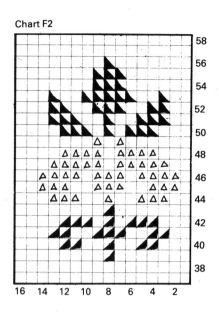

16   14   12   10   8   6   4   2

58 56 54 52 50 48 46 44 42 40 38

Chart F5

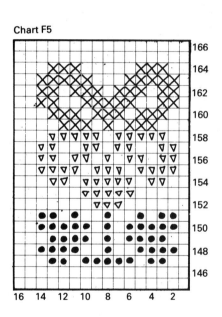

16   14   12   10   8   6   4   2

166 164 162 160 158 156 154 152 150 148 146

Chart F3

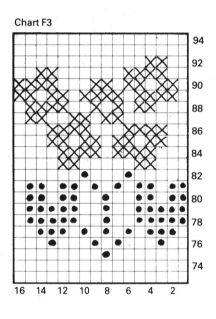

16   14   12   10   8   6   4   2

94 92 90 88 86 84 82 80 78 76 74

Chart F1

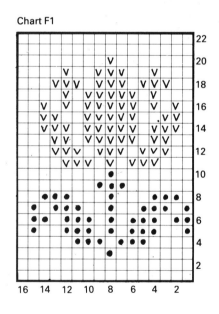

16   14   12   10   8   6   4   2

22 20 18 16 14 12 10 8 6 4 2

FLORA CARDIGAN

Colour Key

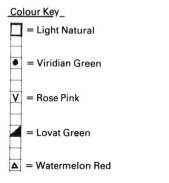

☐ = Light Natural

● = Viridian Green

V = Rose Pink

◤ = Lovat Green

△ = Watermelon Red

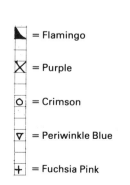

◣ = Flamingo

X = Purple

O = Crimson

▽ = Periwinkle Blue

+ = Fuchsia Pink

FLORA CARDIGAN

YARN COLOURS AND NUMBERS	QUANTITIES REQUIRED IN OUNCES (1 oz = 28.3 g)		
	Size 1	Size 2	Size 3
Light Natural 202	11	12	12
Viridian Green 65	1	1	1
Rose Pink FC 22	1	1	1
Lovat Green 29	1	1	1
Watermelon Red FC 33	1	1	1
Flamingo FC 7	1	1	1
Purple 20	1	1	1
Crimson 55	1	1	2
Periwinkle Blue FC 37	1	1	1
Fuchsia Pink 52	1	1	1

NEEDLES One pair each size 2¼ mm (No. 13 British, No. 0 American), 2¾ mm (No. 12 British, No. 1 American), 3 mm (No. 11 British, No. 2 American), 3¼ mm (No. 10 British, No. 3 American) and 4 mm (No. 8 British, No. 5 American). *Also:* 7 buttons.

TENSION For K1P1 ribbing at welt and cuffs on 2¾ mm needles: 9 sts and 12 rows to 1 in (2.5 cm). For Fair Isle pattern on 3¼ mm needles, 8 sts and 9 rows to 1 in (2.5 cm). For ruching on 4 mm needles, 10 sts and 8 rows to 1 in (2.5 cm). Use larger or smaller needles if necessary to obtain correct tension.

SIZES 3 sizes. Size 1 = 36 in (91.5 cm), size 2 = 40 in (101.5 cm), size 3 = 44 in (111.5 cm), actual measurements. Finished length at centre back, 27 in (68.5 cm).

ABBREVIATIONS See page 16. *Colours:* N = Light Natural, PU = Purple, PB = Periwinkle Blue.

NOTES FOR KNITTERS See page 13.

SPECIAL INSTRUCTIONS FOR THIS DESIGN (1) The fabric of this cardigan consists of 6 bands of 36 rows each. Each band consists of 22 rows of Fair Isle knitting, 4 rows of ribbing, 7 rows of ruching and 3 rows of ribbing. The ruching is worked in Light Natural yarn throughout, but the colour of the K1P1 ribbing above and below the ruching should be worked in the following sequence. First pair of bands in Periwinkle Blue, second pair of bands in Fuchsia Pink, third pair in Rose Pink, fourth pair in Flamingo, fifth pair in Watermelon Red and sixth pair in Periwinkle Blue. (2) The changes in needle size are an important part of the design as they help to keep the fabric regular. Follow the needle change instructions carefully.

BACK

With 2¾ mm needles and N yarn, cast on 118(134:150) sts and work in K1P1 rib for 1 in (2.5 cm). Change to size 3 mm needles and st.st.

Next row (increase row) sizes 1 and 2 only: K2, * inc into next st, K4, rep from * to last 3(2) sts, inc into next st, K2(1): 142(160) sts.

Next row (increase row) size 3 only: K6, * inc into next st, K5, rep from * to end (174) sts.

Next row sizes 1 and 3 only: Inc into first st, P to last st, inc into last st: 144(176) sts.

Next row size 2 only: Purl to end.

Using 3 mm needles for all 1-colour rows and 3¼ mm needles for all 2-colour rows, begin to work in pattern, starting with row 1 of chart F1. On K rows work sts 1–16 across 9(10:11) times. On P rows work sts 16–1 across 9(10:11) times: 144(160:176) sts.

Continue in pattern until row 20 is completed.

Rows 21–22: change to 3 mm needles and N yarn and work in st.st.

Rows 23–26: change to 2¼ mm needles and P B yarn, and work across in K1P1 rib.

Row 27: change to 4 mm needles and N yarn, K2 then knit twice into every st to last 2 sts, K2: 284(316:348) sts.

Rows 28–32: work in st.st and N yarn.

Row 33: change to 2¼ mm needles and P B yarn, K2, then K2tog to last 2 sts, K2: 144(160:176) sts.

Rows 34–36: work across in K1P1 rib.

These 36 rows form the band. Continue until you have worked four complete 36-row bands (144 rows) using charts F2, F3 and F4 and changing the colour of the ribbing as given in Note 1 above.

Armhole Shaping

Rows 145–146: Keeping correct in pattern, cast off 8 sts at beg of each row: 128(144:160) sts.

Rows 147–148: cast off 5 sts at beg of each row: 118(134:150) sts.

Rows 149–158: dec 1 st at beg of each row: 108(124:140) sts.

Continue without further shaping until you have worked 2 more complete bands (charts F5 and F6).

Shoulder Shaping

Change to 3 mm needles and st.st and N yarn.

Rows 217–220: cast off 9(11:13) sts at beg of each row: 72(80:88) sts.

Rows 221–224: cast off 8(10:11) sts at beg of each row.

Row 225: cast off rem 40 sts.

Left Front

With 2¾ mm needles and N yarn, cast on 54(62:70) sts and work in K1P1 rib for 1 in (2.5 cm).

Next row (increase row) sizes 1 and 2 only: K1(5), * inc into next st, K2, rep from * to last 2(6) sts, inc into next st, K1(5): 72(80) sts.

Next row (increase row) size 3 only: K3, * inc into next st, K3, rep from * to last 3 sts, inc into next st, K1, inc into next st. (88 sts).

Next row (all sizes): P.

Using 3 mm needles for all 1-colour rows and 3¼ mm needles for all 2-colour rows, begin to work in pattern, starting with row 1 of chart F1. On K rows work sts 1–16 4(5:5) times, then work sts 1–8 once (nil: once). On P rows work sts 8–1 once (nil: once), then work sts 16–1 4(5:5) times. Work in pattern as for Back until you have worked 4 complete bands (row 144).

Armhole Shaping

Row 145: Keeping correct in pattern, cast off 8 sts at beg of row: 64(72:80) sts.

Row 146: Work in patt without shaping.

Row 147: cast off 5 sts, patt to end row: 59(67:75) sts.

Row 148: as row 146.

Rows 149–158: dec 1 st at beg of next and foll alt rows: 54(62:70) sts.

Continue without further shaping until you have worked row 191.

Neck Shaping

Row 192: Keeping correct in pattern, cast off 8 sts at beg of row: 46(54:62) sts.

Rows 193–196: dec 1 st at neck edge of each row: 42(50:58) sts.

Rows 197–212: dec 1 st at neck edge of next and foll alt rows: 34(42:50) sts.

Continue without shaping until you reach row 216.

Shoulder Shaping

Row 217: change to 3 mm needles and st.st in N yarn. Cast off 9(11:13) sts, patt to end: 25(31:37) sts.

Row 218: Work in st.st.

Row 219: as row 217: 16(20:24) sts.

Row 220: as row 218.

Row 221: cast off 8(10:11) sts, work to end: 8(10:11) sts.

Row 222: as row 218.

Row 223: cast off rem 8(10:11) sts.

RIGHT FRONT

Work as for Left Front reversing all the shapings, and working the Fair Isle pattern by knitting sts 9–16 once (nil: once) and then sts 1–16 4(5:5) times on row 1 and all K rows, and working sts 16–1 4(5:5) times and then sts 16–9 once (nil: once) on all P rows. End by casting off the last sts on row 224.

SLEEVES (All Sizes)

With 2¾ mm needles and N yarn, cast on 64 sts. Work in K1P1 rib for 1 in (2.5 cm). Change to 3 mm needles.

Row 1: K1, * K2, inc into next st, rep from * to last 3 sts, K3 (84 sts).

Row 2: Purl.

Row 3: K1, * inc into next st, K2, rep from * to last 2 sts, inc into next st, K1 (112 sts).

Row 4: change to PU yarn, P across.

Row 5: in PU yarn, K3, * inc into next st, K7, rep from * to last 5 sts, inc into next st, K4 (126 sts).

Row 6: in PU yarn, P1, inc into next st, P to last 2 sts, inc into next st, P1 (128 sts).

Change to 3¼ mm needles and N yarn. Work in pattern, commencing at row 10 of chart F1. Work the 16 patt sts across 8 times. Work in pattern until you have completed the fourth band (row 144).

Shape Sleeve Head

Rows 145–146: Continuing in pattern, cast off 8 sts at beg of next 2 rows (112 sts).

Rows 147–154: Cast off 2 sts at beg of the next 8 rows (96 sts).

Rows 155–178: dec 1 st at beg of each row.

Rows 179–194: dec 1 st at both ends of each row (40 sts).

Row 195: Cast off.

Work second sleeve to match.

NECK RIBBING (All Sizes)

Join shoulder seams. Using 2¾ mm needles and N yarn, with right side of work facing, pick up 48 sts evenly around right front neck edge, 40 sts across back neck, and 48 sts around left front neck edge: 136 sts. Work in K1P1 rib for 1 in (2.5 cm). Cast off neatly in rib.

LEFT FRONT BORDER (All Sizes)

Using 2¾ mm needles and N yarn, cast on 12 sts and work in K1P1 rib until band, when slightly stretched, measures the same as the front edge. Cast off in rib.

RIGHT FRONT BORDER (All Sizes)

Work as for Left Front border, making buttonholes as follows: Rib 4 rows.

Row 5: rib 4, cast off 3, rib 5.

Row 6: rib 5, cast on 3, rib 4.

Continue in rib, working rows 5 and 6 every 4 in (10 cm), the last buttonhole to be ½ in (1.5 cm) below top of band. Cast off in rib.

TO MAKE UP

Carefully press all pieces with a damp cloth and a warm iron, but do not press the ruching and ribbing panels. Sew in sleeves, join underarm and side seams. Sew front borders to front edges, easing to fit. Sew on buttons.

16
Pennsylvania Dutch

AMERICA – a very young country by the standards of Europe and the Orient – is not the first place you would think of looking for traditional folk art designs, but the work of the Pennsylvania Dutch is an exception. 'Pennsylvania Dutch' – a corruption of *Pennsylvania Deutsch* – is the colloquial American term used to describe the German immigrants who settled in what is now the state of Pennsylvania from 1683 onwards, and their descendants. Surrounded by larger communities of settlers from England, the German colonists preferred to keep themselves apart, continuing to speak the German language and to preserve the crafts of their homeland, where a strong tradition of decorative peasant art flourished. Life was hard and at first there was little time for artistic embellishments. But by the American War of Independence in 1776 the Pennsylvania Dutch had developed a distinctive style of folk art that they embroidered on household linens, painted on to pottery, stencilled on furniture and buildings, hammered into ironwork and punched on to tin. Unique in America, Pennsylvania Dutch designs also differed in several respects from the European heritage on which it was based.

The motifs themselves, chief among them the heart and the tulip, did not originate in America, but were traditional patterns in common use throughout Europe. The innovation of the Pennsylvania Dutch was to reduce the motifs to their simplest form, to place them on surfaces with the greatest possible economy, and to carry them out using a very restricted colour palette consisting of red, yellow, blue, black, orange and green. This was in stark contrast to the prevailing style of peasant art in Europe, where the motifs were made as elaborate as possible and splashed over every available surface in a lavish range of shades. Though the Pennsylvania Dutch style had its origins in the impoverished conditions in which the early artisans worked, it soon took root as an art form much preferred by those who appreciated its naivety and freshness, and the style remains very popular in America today. This design was suggested by an old painted dower chest I saw in New York, and includes the most common Pennsylvania Dutch motifs, many of which were deemed by the early German colonists to have a religious significance. The tulip (rows 95–101) was a symbol of bliss in Paradise, the heart (rows 28–36 and 79–86) was emblematic of love and hope of a future life, birds (rows 37–49) symbolized piety and the pomegranate (rows 53–69) was a symbol of fruitfulness and immortality.

PENNSYLVANIA DUTCH WAISTCOAT

Chart PD1
Rows 1-187

Colour Key

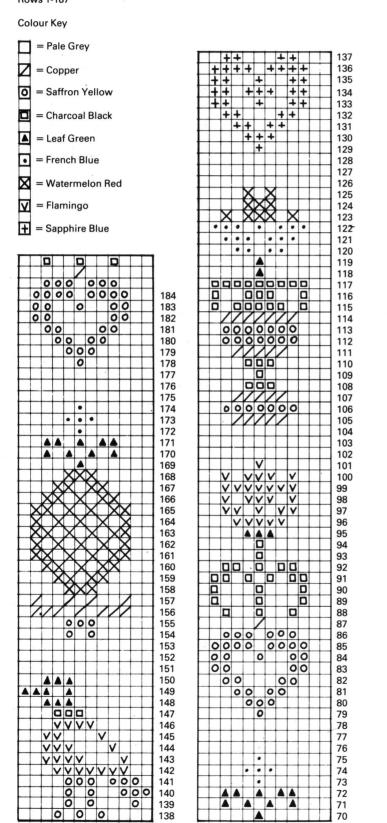
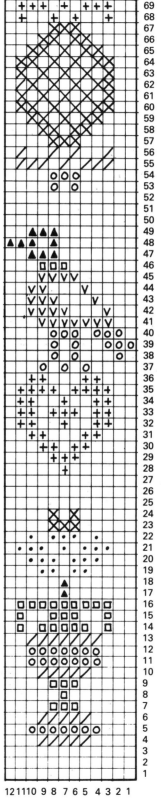

PENNSYLVANIA DUTCH WAISTCOAT

YARN COLOURS AND NUMBERS	QUANTITIES REQUIRED IN OUNCES (1 oz = 28.3 g)			
	Size 1	Size 2	Size 3	Size 4
Pale Grey 203	5	6	7	7
Copper 31	1	1	1	1
Saffron Yellow 90	1	1	1	1
Charcoal Black 81	1	1	1	1
Leaf Green 25	1	1	1	1
French Blue 16	1	1	1	1
Watermelon Red FC 33	1	1	1	1
Flamingo FC 7	1	1	1	1
Sapphire Blue FC 48	1	1	1	1

NEEDLES One pair each size 2¾ mm (No. 12 British, No. 1 American), 3 mm (No. 11 British, No. 2 American) and 3¼ mm (No. 10 British, No. 3 American) needles. *Also:* 5 buttons.

TENSION 16 sts and 16 rows to 2 in (5 cm) on 3¼ mm needles over Fair Isle pattern. For K2P2 ribbing: 9 sts and 9 rows to 1 in (2.5 cm) on 2¾ mm needles. Change needle size if necessary to obtain correct tension.

SIZES 4 sizes. Size 1 = 33 in (84 cm), size 2 = 36 in (91.5 cm), size 3 = 39 in (99 cm), size 4 = 42 in (106.5 cm), actual measurements.

ABBREVIATIONS See page 16. *Colours:* P G = Pale Grey.

NOTES FOR KNITTERS See page 13.

SPECIAL INSTRUCTIONS FOR THIS DESIGN Reverse the direction in which the second bird (rows 130–150) is facing if you want to add more variety to the pattern.

BACK

With 2¾ mm needles and PG yarn, cast on 120(132:140:152) sts and work in K2P2 rib for 2½ in (6.5 cm).

Next row: (increase row) K across, inc 12(12:16:16) sts evenly over the row: 132(144:156:168) sts.

Next row: P across.

Using 3 mm needles on all 1-colour rows and 3¼ mm needles on all 2-colour rows, begin to work in pattern starting with row 1 of chart PD1. On K rows work sts 1–12 across 11(12:13:14) times, on P rows work sts 12–1 across 11(12:13:14) times. Work straight in pattern until you have completed row 104 of chart PD1. *Be sure to maintain continuity of pattern for remainder of work on Back.*

Armhole Shaping

Rows 105–106: cast off 5(7:9:11) sts at beg of each row: 122(130:138:146) sts rem.

Rows 107–110: cast off 4 sts at beg of each row: 106(114:122:130) sts rem.

Rows 111–120: dec 1 st at beg of each row: 96(104:112:120) sts rem.

Rows 121–176: work in pattern without shaping.

Shoulder Shaping

Rows 177–182: cast off 4(5:6:7) sts at beg of each row: 72(74:76:78) sts rem.

Rows 183–184: cast off 3(4:4:5) sts at beg of each row: 66(66:68:68) sts rem.

Rows 185–186: cast off 3(3:4:4) sts at beg of each row, work in pattern to end.

Row 187: cast off rem 60 sts.

LEFT FRONT

With 2¾ mm needles and PG yarn, cast on 60(64:72:76) sts and work in K2P2 rib for 2½ in (6.5 cm).

Next row: (increase row) K across, inc 6(8:6:8) sts evenly over the row: 66(72:78:84) sts.

Next row: P across.

Using 3 mm needles on all 1-colour rows and 3¼ mm needles on all 2-colour rows, begin to work in pattern starting with row 1 of chart PD1, *in the following sequence.*

For sizes 1 and 3 only: on K rows, work sts 1–12 across 5(6) times, then work sts 1–6: 66(78) sts. On P rows work sts 6–1, then work sts 12–1 5(6) times.

For sizes 2 and 4 only: on K rows work sts 1–12 across 6(7) times, on P rows work sts 12–1 across 6(7) times: 72(84) sts.

For all sizes: work straight in pattern until you have completed row 104 of chart PD1. *Be sure to maintain continuity of pattern for remainder of work on Left Front.*

Armhole and Neck Shaping

Row 105: cast off 5(7:9:11) sts at beg of row: 61(65:69:73) sts rem.

Row 106: work in pattern without shaping.

Row 107: cast off 4 sts at beg of row: 57(61:65:69) sts rem.

Row 108: work in pattern without shaping.

Row 109: cast off 4 sts at beg of row: (53:61:65) sts rem.

Row 110: work in pattern without shaping.

Rows 111–119: dec 1 st at beg of each row: 44(48:52:56) sts rem.

Rows 120–170: now keep armhole edge straight for remainder of work and dec 1 st at neck edge on row 120 and every alt row until there are 18(22:26:30) sts on needle. (Row 170 will now have been worked.)

Rows 171–176: work in pattern without shaping.

Shoulder Shaping

Row 177: cast off 4(5:6:7) sts at beg of row: 14(17:20:23) sts rem.

Row 178: work in pattern without shaping.

Row 179: cast off 4(5:6:7) sts at beg of row: 10(12:14:16) sts rem.

Row 180: work in pattern without shaping.

Row 181: cast off 4(5:6:7) sts at beg of row: 6(7:8:9) sts rem.

Row 182: work in pattern without shaping.

Row 183: cast off 3(4:4:5) sts at beg of row: 3(3:4:4) sts rem.

Row 184: work in pattern without shaping.

Row 185: cast off rem 3(3:4:4) sts.

RIGHT FRONT

Work K2P2 ribbing and increase rows as for Left Front, then work in pattern *in the following sequence.*

Sizes 1 and 3 only: on K rows work sts 7–12, then work sts 1–12 5(6) times: 66(78) sts. On P rows work sts 12–1 5(6) times, then work sts 12–7.

Sizes 2 and 4 only: on K rows work sts 1–12 6(7) times, on P rows work sts 12–1 6(7) times: 72(84) sts.

For all sizes: otherwise work as for Left Front, reversing all shapings and ending by casting off rem 3(3:4:4) sts on row 186.

ARMBANDS

Gently press all pieces using a warm iron and damp cloth. Join shoulder seams. With 2¾ mm needles, PG yarn and right side of work facing, pick up and K 148(152:156:160) sts around armhole. Work in K2P2 rib for 9 rows. Cast off loosely in rib. Repeat for other side. Join side seams.

BUTTONHOLE BAND

With 2¾ mm needles and PG yarn, cast on 12 sts and work 4 rows in K2P2 rib.

Row 5: (buttonhole row) rib 4 sts, cast off 3 sts, rib 5 sts.

Row 6: rib 5 sts, cast on 3 sts, rib 4 sts. Make 4 more buttonholes in this way, each 2¾ in or 7 cm from the last. Continue to work in rib until band is of sufficient length when slightly stretched to fit up both fronts and around back neck. Cast off neatly in rib. Attach buttonhole border with a fine slip stitch and press very gently. Sew on buttons opposite buttonholes.

17
Tzigane

SCARLET is a gipsy of a colour, a reckless renegade of a shade that dances circles around the rest of the spectrum, and dares all eyes to look its way. Intoxicating, irrepressible, utterly irresistible – scarlet is more than generous with its favours, for it brings a sparkle to the eye, a lift to the spirits and makes everyone who wears it look marvellous. Yet despite its winning ways, scarlet is often misunderstood in Anglo-Saxon climes, where it is viewed with deep suspicion and treated with icy reserve. In countries where coolness of temperament prevails, scarlet is usually only worn in small touches such as a scarf or a pair of socks, and there are few sadder fashions than that of the plain scarlet dress, left to fend for itself, as though no other colour would wish to be seen with it.

They know far better in Hungary and Romania, where the fondness for scarlet amounts to a national passion that they indulge with complete abandon by lavishing it all over everything they wear and use. They particularly love to use scarlet as a background for shades of pink, blue, yellow and green – volatile mixtures that clash with panache and glow with vibrant gaiety. Floral motifs are the favourite form for these exhilarating colour combinations, and the effect is so bewitching that many designers, Kenzo and Yves Saint Laurent prime among them, frequently include variations of the Hungarian gipsy look in their collections.

This design was inspired by a Romanian kelim woven in Oltenia, a region whose carpets are prized above all others for their bright colours and distinctive floral patterns. The six-petalled flowers bracketed top and bottom by broad double leaves and the diamond flowers on curious spiky stems are among the most popular Oltenian motifs. Like nature, these designs abhor a vacuum, either of colour or of pattern. In its native setting, a kelim like this would be surrounded by painted furniture, embroidered textiles and patterned pottery, while a skirt in a fabric bearing this design would be worn with a large flower-pattern shawl, a blouse embroidered with scarlet and a flower print scarf. *Tzigane* looks very chic worn with black and scarlet, but it looks most dramatic worn with as many patterns and colours as possible, in the gipsy fashion.

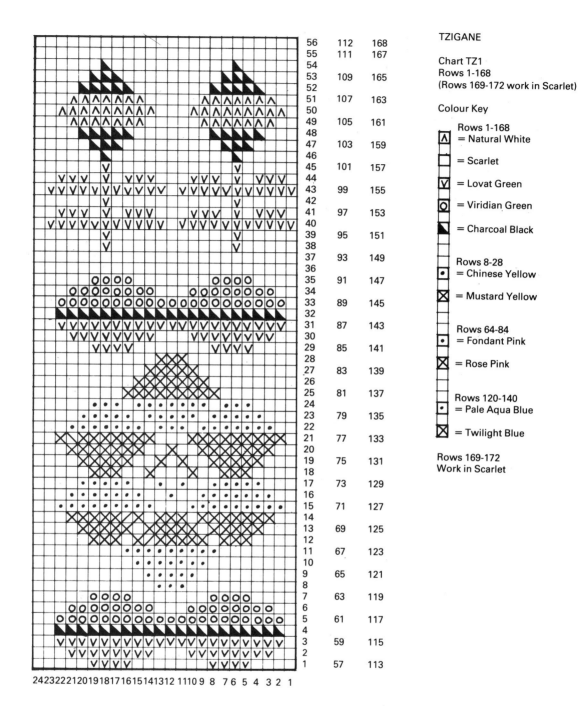

56	112	168
55	111	167
54		
53	109	165
52		
51	107	163
50		
49	105	161
48		
47	103	159
46		
45	101	157
44		
43	99	155
42		
41	97	153
40		
39	95	151
38		
37	93	149
36		
35	91	147
34		
33	89	145
32		
31	87	143
30		
29	85	141
28		
27	83	139
26		
25	81	137
24		
23	79	135
22		
21	77	133
20		
19	75	131
18		
17	73	129
16		
15	71	127
14		
13	69	125
12		
11	67	123
10		
9	65	121
8		
7	63	119
6		
5	61	117
4		
3	59	115
2		
1	57	113

24 23 22 21 20 19 18 17 16 15 14 13 12 11 10 9 8 7 6 5 4 3 2 1

TZIGANE

Chart TZ1
Rows 1-168
(Rows 169-172 work in Scarlet)

Colour Key

Rows 1-168
Λ = Natural White

☐ = Scarlet

V = Lovat Green

Ⓞ = Viridian Green

◨ = Charcoal Black

Rows 8-28
• = Chinese Yellow

⊠ = Mustard Yellow

Rows 64-84
• = Fondant Pink

⊠ = Rose Pink

Rows 120-140
• = Pale Aqua Blue

⊠ = Twilight Blue

Rows 169-172
Work in Scarlet

110

TZIGANE SLIPOVER

YARN COLOURS AND NUMBERS	QUANTITIES REQUIRED IN OUNCES (1 oz = 28.3 g)			
	Size 1	Size 2	Size 3	Size 4
Scarlet 93	3	4	4	5
Charcoal Black 81	1	1	2	2
Viridian Green 65	1	1	2	2
Lovat Green 29	1	1	2	2
Twilight Blue 33	1	1	1	1
Pale Aqua Blue 75	1	1	1	1
Mustard Yellow 28	1	1	1	1
Chinese Yellow 23	1	1	1	1
Natural White 1a	1	1	1	1
Rose Pink FC 22	1	1	1	1
Fondant Pink 70	1	1	1	1

NEEDLES One pair each size 2¾ mm (No. 12 British, No. 1 American), 3 mm (No. 11 British, No. 2 American) and 3¼ mm (No. 10 British, No. 3 American) needles, and a stitch holder.

TENSION 16 sts and 16 rows to 2 in (5 cm) on 3¼ mm needles over Fair Isle pattern. For K2P2 ribbing: 9 sts and 9 rows to 1 in (2.5 cm) on 2¾ mm needles. Change needle size if necessary to obtain correct tension.

SIZES 4 sizes. Size 1 = 33 in (84 cm), size 2 = 36 in (91.5 cm), size 3 = 39 in (99 cm), size 4 = 42 in (106.5 cm), actual measurements.

ABBREVIATIONS See page 16. *Colours:* CB = Charcoal Black, VG = Viridian Green, SC = Scarlet.

NOTES FOR KNITTERS See page 13.

BACK

With 2¾ mm needles and CB yarn, cast on 120(132:140:152) sts and work in K2P2 rib as follows.

Rows 1–2: rib in CB.
Rows 3–4: rib in VG.
Rows 5–6: rib in SC.
Rows 7–8: rib in CB.
Rows 9–10: rib in VG.
Rows 11–12: rib in SC.
Rows 13–14: rib in CB.
Rows 15–16: rib in VG.
Rows 17–18: rib in SC.
Next row: (increase row) in CB, K across, inc 12(12:16:16) sts evenly over the row: 132(144:156:168) sts.
Next row: P across in CB.

Using 3 mm needles on all 1-colour rows and 3¼ mm needles on all 2-colour rows, begin to work in pattern starting with row 1 of chart TZ1 *in the following sequence.*

For sizes 1 and 3 only: on K rows work sts 1–24 across 5(6) times, then work sts 1–12. On P rows work sts 12–1, then work sts 24–1 across 5(6) times: 132(156) sts.

For sizes 2 and 4 only: on K rows work sts 1–24 across 6(7) times, on P rows work sts 24–1 across 6(7) times: 144(168) sts. Work straight in pattern until you have completed row 90 of chart TZ1. *Be sure to maintain continuity of pattern for remainder of work on Back.*

Armhole Shaping

Rows 91–92: cast off 5(7:9:11) sts at beg of each row: 122(130:138:146) sts rem.
Rows 93–96: cast off 4 sts at beg of each row: 106(114:122:130) sts rem.
Rows 97–106: dec 1 st at beg of each row: 96(104:112:120) sts rem.
Rows 107–162: work in pattern without shaping.

Shoulder Shaping

Rows 163–168: cast off 4(5:6:7) sts at beg of each row: 72(74:76:78) sts rem.
Rows 169–170: cast off 3(4:4:5) sts at beg of each row: 66(66:68:68) sts rem.
Rows 171–172: cast off 3(3:4:4) sts at beg of each row, work in pattern to end: 60 sts rem.

Back Neck

Change to 2¾ mm needles and CB yarn and work the 60 sts for back neck in K2P2 rib as follows.

Rows 1–2: rib in CB.
Rows 3–4: rib in VG.
Rows 5–6: rib in SC.
Rows 7–8: rib in CB.
Rows 9–10: rib in VG.
Row 11: cast off in rib in CI

FRONT

Work ribbing and increase rows as for Back, then begin to work in pattern starting with row 1 of chart TZ1 *in the following sequence.*

For sizes 1 and 3 only: on K rows work sts 13–24, then work sts 1–24 across 5(6) times. On P rows work sts 24–1 across 5(6) times, then work sts 24–13: 132(156) sts.

For sizes 2 and 4 only: on K rows work sts 1–24 across 6(7) times, on P rows work sts 24–1 across 6(7) times; 144(168) sts. Otherwise work as for Back until you have completed row 142 of chart TZ1: 96(104:112:120) sts rem. *Be sure to maintain continuity of pattern throughout.*

Divide for Neck

Row 143: work in pattern across 33(37:41:45) sts, turn, leave rem 63(67:71:75) sts on a spare needle or stitch holder and work on first group of sts as follows.

Left Front

Rows 144–158: dec 1 st at neck edge on every row: 18(22:26:30) sts rem.
Rows 159–162: work in pattern without shaping.

Shoulder Shaping

Row 163: cast off 4(5:6:7) sts at beg of row: 14(17:20:23) sts rem.
Row 164: work in pattern without shaping.
Row 165: as row 163: 10(12:14:16) sts rem.
Row 166: as row 164.
Row 167: as row 163: 6(7:8:9) sts rem.
Row 168: as row 164.
Row 169: cast off 3(4:4:5) sts at beg of row: 3(3:4:4) sts rem.
Row 170: as row 164.
Row 171: cast off rem sts.

Right Front

Slip 30 sts for Front Neck on to a stitch holder. Rejoin yarn to second group of 33(37:41:45) sts and work in pattern across row 143. Now work as for Left Front, reversing all shapings and ending by casting off rem sts on row 172.

FRONT NECKBAND

With 2¾ mm needles, CB yarn and right side of work facing, pick up and K27 sts down left side of neck, 30 sts from centre front neck and 27 sts up right side of neck: 84 sts. Work in K2P2 rib as for Back Neck. Cast off in rib in CB on the 11th row.

ARMBANDS

Gently press all pieces with a warm iron and damp cloth. Join shoulder seams including neck ribbing. With 2¾ mm needles, CB yarn and right side of work facing, pick up and K148(152:156:160) sts around armhole. Work in K2P2 rib as for Back Neck. Cast off loosely in rib in CB on the 11th row. Repeat for other side.

TO MAKE UP

Join side seams.

18
Persian Garden

FAR FROM being a stay-at-home art, knitting is very much bound up with the romance of travel, as the story behind this design shows. Artistic designs and techniques are extremely good travellers, and from earliest times they have been passed on from hand to hand along the trade routes that link East and West. The intricate oriental type of colour knitting that reproduces the patterns found on Eastern carpets can still be found along the old routes between the Black Sea and the high mountains of the Northwest Frontier, and of all the designs that have travelled these byways the best known is the curved teardrop shape called the *boteh*. The *boteh* motif originated in Persia, where it was used on carpets and on woven, knitted and embroidered textiles, often in combination with flower patterns and striped borders. From Persia the *boteh* pattern was taken to India, where in time it became the prime design motif in the finely woven floral shawls of Kashmir. By 1760 Kashmiri *boteh* shawls were finding their way to Europe in ships of the British East India Company, and by 1800 the shawls had become the indispensable Western fashion accessory that they were to remain for over a hundred years. The weavers of Paisley in Scotland were quick to seize on the commercial possibilities of the new vogue, and by 1808 they had begun to produce woven *boteh* shawls copied from Kashmiri patterns. The Scottish shawls were so successful that the *boteh* pattern became known in Europe and America as the 'paisley' pattern, and European paisley shawls were ultimately so sought-after that they were exported to Persia – where the story began! Few motifs have been so well-loved, for so long, as the *boteh* – an enjoyment tht can only be enhanced by following the oriental practice of using *boteh* patterns in knitting. This design is based on antique Persian tribal rugs and I think you will find that, like a magic carpet, it will take you anywhere in the world with style.

PERSIAN GARDEN

Chart P1, 18 sts and 29 rows.

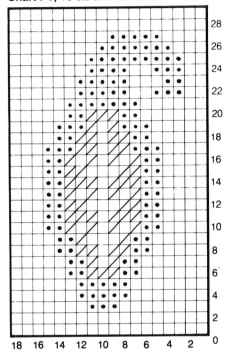

Chart P2, 18 sts and 32 rows.

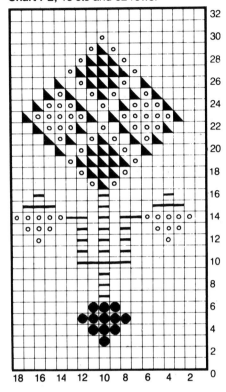

**Persian Garden Sweater
Colour Key**

☐ = Navy **or** Pale Grey

▣ = Carmine Red

◪ = Viridian Green

◣ = Watermelon Red

◙ = Rose Pink

▤ = Lovat Green

● = Mustard on Navy colourway, **or**
Navy on Pale Grey colourway

◖ = Flamingo

◫ = Turquoise Blue

⊞ = Heather Purple

115

Chart P3, 18 sts and 29 rows.

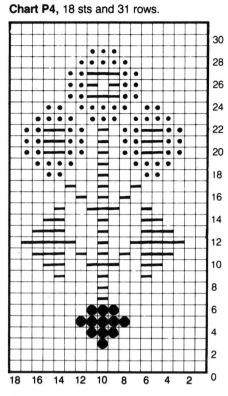

Chart P4, 18 sts and 31 rows.

Chart P5, 18 sts and 29 rows.

Chart P6, 18 sts and 32 rows.

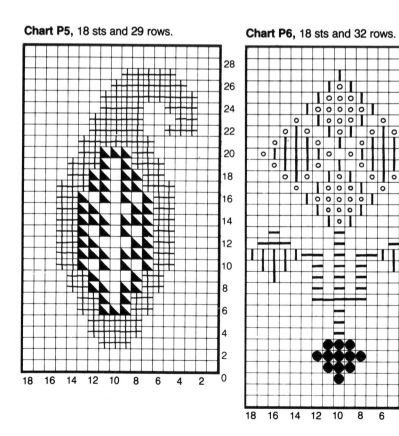

PERSIAN GARDEN SWEATER

YARN COLOURS AND NUMBERS	QUANTITIES REQUIRED IN OUNCES (1 oz = 28.3 g)		
	Size 1	Size 2	Size 3
Navy Blue 21			
or			
Pale Grey 203	8	9	10
Mustard Yellow 28			
or			
Navy Blue 21	1	1	1
Viridian Green 65	1	1	1
Carmine Red 72	2	2	2
Lovat Green 29	2	2	2
Rose Pink F C 22	1	1	1
Watermelon Red F C 33	1	1	1
Flamingo F C 7	1	1	1
Turquoise Blue 48	1	1	1
Heather Purple 19	1	1	1

NEEDLES One pair each size 2¾ mm (No. 12 British, No. 1 American), 3 mm (No. 11 British, No. 2 American) and 3¼ mm (No. 10 British, No. 3 American) needles.

TENSION 18 sts and 16 rows to 2 in (5 cm) on 3¼ mm needles over Fair Isle pattern. For Vertical Stripe ribbing: 18 sts and 18 rows to 2 in (5 cm) on 2¾ mm needles. Change needle size if necessary to obtain correct tension.

Sizes 3 sizes. Size 1 = 32 in (81.5 cm), size 2 = 36 in (91.5 cm), size 3 = 40 in (101.5 cm) actual measurements.

ABBREVIATIONS See page 16. *Colours:* G = Pale Grey, N = Navy, C = Carmine Red.

NOTES FOR KNITTERS See page 13.

SPECIAL INSTRUCTIONS FOR THIS DESIGN After working chart P1, row numbers (odd or even) do not always correspond with K and P rows.

BACK

With 2¾ mm needles and G or N yarn, cast on 114(124:134) sts and work in Vertical Stripe ribbing as follows:
Row 1: * K2 in C, P2 in G or N, rep from * to end.
Row 2: * K2 in G or N, P2 in C, rep from * to end.
Rep rows 1 and 2 until work measures 2½ in (6.5 cm) ending with a row 2. Change to 3 mm needles and work as follows, using G or N yarn.
Size 1: K12 * K2, inc into next st, rep from * to last 12 sts, K12 (144 sts).
Size 2: K5 * K2, inc into next st, rep from * to last 5 sts, K5 (162 sts).
Size 3: inc in first st, * K2, inc into next st, rep from * to last st, inc in last st (180 sts).
For all sizes: next row; P across. Using 3 mm needles for all 1-colour rows and 3¼ mm needles for all 2-colour rows, begin to work in pattern from chart P2, starting with row 1 and repeating sts 1–18 8(9:10) times across the row. Work in patt until you have completed chart P2, then work charts P3 and P4 and rows 1–6 of chart P5. (98 rows of pattern have now been worked in all).

Armhole Shaping

Rows 99–100: keeping continuity of pattern, cast off 7(9:11) sts at beg of each row: 130(144:158) sts.
Rows 101–114: dec 1 st at beg of every row: 116(130:144) sts.
Rows 115–118: work without shaping.
Rows 119–120: dec 1 st at beg of each row: 114(128:142) sts.
Rows 121–124: work without shaping. (Start to work from chart P6 on row 122.)
Rows 125–126: dec 1 st at beg of each row: 112(126:140) sts.
Rows 127–138: work without shaping.
Rows 139–140: inc into first st of each row: 114(128:142) sts.
Rows 141–148: work without shaping.
Rows 149–150: inc into first st of each row: 116(130:144) sts.
Rows 151–156: work without shaping. (Change to chart P1 on row 154.)

Neck Shaping

Row 157: patt across 47(51:55) sts, cast off the next 22(28:34) sts and leave remaining 47(51:55) sts on a stitch holder. Working on first group of sts only, proceed as follows (right shoulder).
Row 158: cast off 4 sts (neck edge), patt to end.
Row 159: inc into first st, patt to end: 44(48:52) sts.
Row 160: cast off 4 sts, patt to end: 40(44:48) sts.
Row 161: patt across row.
Row 162: cast off 4 sts, patt to end: 36(40:44) sts.

Shoulder Shaping

Row 163: cast off 5(6:7) sts (shoulder edge), patt to end: 31(34:37) sts.
Row 164: cast off 4 sts (neck edge), patt to end: 27(30:33) sts.
Row 165: as row 163: 22(24:26) sts.
Row 166: as row 164: 18(20:22) sts.
Row 167: as row 163: 13(14:15) sts.
Row 168: as row 164: 9(10:11) sts.
Row 169: as row 163: 4 sts rem.
Row 170: cast off.
Rejoin yarn to neck edge of 47(51:55) sts on spare needle (right side facing) and work to correspond, from row 157, reversing all shapings.

FRONT

Work exactly as for Back as far as row 136: 112(126:140) sts.

Divide for Neck

Row 137: work across 45(49:53) sts, cast off the next 22(28:34) sts, leave the remaining sts on a stitch holder.

Left Front

Row 138: cast off 4 sts (neck edge), patt to end: 41(45:49) sts.

Row 139: inc into first st, patt to end: 42(46:50) sts.

Row 140: cast off 4 sts, patt to end: 38(42:46) sts.

Row 141: patt across row.

Row 142: cast off 2 sts, patt to end: 36(40:44) sts.

Rows 143–148: keeping continuity of patt, rep shaping for rows 141 and 142 3 more times: 30(34:38) sts.

Row 149: inc into first st, patt to end: 31(35:39) sts.

Row 150: cast off 2 sts, patt to end: 29(33:37) sts.

Row 151: patt across row.

Row 152: cast off 2 sts, patt to end: 27(31:35) sts.

Row 153: patt across row.

Row 154: cast off 2 sts, patt to end. (Change to chart P1 on row 154.) 25(29:33) sts.

Rows 155–157: work without shaping.

Row 158: dec 1 st, patt to end: 24(28:32) sts.

Row 159: inc into first st, patt to end: 25(29:33) sts.

Rows 160–161: work without shaping.

Row 162: dec 1 st (neck edge), patt to end: 24(28:32) sts.

Shoulder Shaping

Row 163: cast off 5(6:7) sts, patt to end.

Row 164: patt across row.

Rows 165–170: keeping continuity of patt, rep shaping for rows 163 and 164 3 more times, casting off last 4 sts on row 170.

Right Front

Rejoin yarn to neck edge of remaining 45(49:53) sts and patt to correspond with left shoulder, reversing all shapings.

SLEEVES

With 2¾ mm needles and G or N yarn, cast on 54(60:66) sts and work in 2-colour Vertical Stripe rib as for the Back, until work measures 1½ in (4 cm). Change to 3 mm needles and work in G or N yarn as follows:

Size 1: * K2, inc into next st, rep from * to end (72 sts).

Size 2: * K1, inc into next st, rep from * to end (90 sts).

Size 3: * K1, inc into next st, rep from * to end (99 sts).

Size 3 only:

next row: P across.

Size 3 only: next row; * K10, inc into next st, rep from * to end (108 sts).

For all sizes: next row; P across.

Using 3 mm needles for all 1-colour rows, and 3¼ mm needles for all 2-colour rows, proceed to work in pattern from chart P1, starting with row 1. Repeat sts 1–18 4(5:6) times across the row. Inc 1 st at both ends of row 4, and every following 4th row until there are 90(108:126) sts on needle (row 36), *incorporating the extra stitches into the pattern.*

Rows 37–41: work 5 rows without shaping.

Row 42: inc 1 st at both ends of row. Continue in patt, inc 1 st at both ends of every 7th row until there are 116(134:152) sts on needle (row 126).

Shape Sleeve Head

Rows 127–130: work in patt without shaping.

Rows 132–134: cast off 5(8:10) sts at beg of next 4 rows: 96(102:112) sts.

Rows 135–144: cast off 2 sts at beg of next 10 rows: 76(82:92) sts.

Rows 145–146: cast off 1 st at beg of next 2 rows: 74(80:90) sts.

Rows 147–148: cast off 2 sts at beg of next 2 rows: 70(76:86) sts.

Rows 149–152: cast off 1 st at beg of next 4 rows: 66(72:82) sts.

Rows 153–156: cast off 2 sts at beg of next 4 rows: 58(64:74) sts.

Rows 157–158: cast off 1 st at beg of next 2 rows: 56(62:72) sts.

Rows 159–170: cast off 2 sts at beg of next 12 rows: 32(38:48) sts.

Rows 171–172: cast off 3 sts at beg of next 2 rows: 26(32:42) sts.

Rows 173–175: cast off 4 sts at beg of next 3 rows.

Cast off remaining 14(20:30) sts.

Work second sleeve to match.

NECKBAND

Sew up right shoulder using back stitch. With 2¾ mm needles and G or N yarn and with right side of work facing, pick up and K40 sts down left side of front neck, pick up and K22 (28:34) sts across centre front neck, and 40 sts up right side of front neck, then 28 sts down right side of back neck, 22(28:34) sts across centre back neck and 28 sts up left side of neck: 180(192:204) sts on needle.

Next row: P, using G or N yarn. Now proceed to work in Vertical Stripe rib pattern as for Back for 8 rows.

Next row: K, using G or N yarn. Cast off knitways in G or N yarn, using a 3 mm needle.

TO MAKE UP

Lightly press all pieces using a warm iron and damp cloth. Join neck edging and left shoulder seam using back stitch. Sew sleeves into place, then join side and sleeve seams using back stitch throughout.

19
Christmas Cracker

Is it wickedly impractical and extravagant to have a sweater you wear only a few days a year? I don't think so – particularly when those days come at Christmas time. I *adore* Christmas, and from December 1 to Twelfth Night in January, no Scrooge is safe from the scourge of my seasonal high spirits. I can't wait to leaf through my Christmas cookbook, put a holly wreath on the door and open the first window on my Advent calendar. Out comes the battered suitcase full of treasured Christmas tree ornaments, boxes of bright ribbons and rolls of pretty paper. And into the house comes a procession of interesting shopping bags, mysterious parcels, letters and cards by the score. There are parties to give and to go to, friends to see, stockings to fill, pantomimes to rehearse and carols to sing. I love it all – except the brittle white icing on Christmas cakes, people who hand out lists of what they want to be given, and people who sneak a look at their presents before Christmas morning.

However, high days and holidays make special demands on your appearance, and from this point of view Christmas can be less than a pure pleasure. You want to look festive – but long dresses are hopeless for climbing up a ladder to trim the tree or hang mistletoe in the hall, party frocks are quite unsuitable for dashing in and out of the kitchen, and even the most elegant dressing gown doesn't strike quite the right note over Christmas brunch. Worst of all, with the inevitable arrival of unexpected callers, you have to be prepared to look festive at a moment's notice. My solution is this Christmas waistcoat. I decided on a button-front so it wouldn't have to be pulled over the head, spoiling a special hairdo or makeup, but as the pattern is a 12-stitch repeat you can easily turn it into a sweater or slipover if you prefer. You can slip out of *Christmas Cracker* if you find yourself getting overheated, pop it back on when you hear the doorbell go, and it's absolutely certain to make you look the very picture of seasonal good cheer. Happy Christmas!

CHRISTMAS CRACKER

Chart CCR1
Rows 1-187

Colour Key

◪ = Moorit Brown

⊞ = French Blue

◩ = Bright Mauve

· = Navy Blue

▲ = Saffron Yellow

∨ = Scarlet

⊠ = Viridian Green

□ = Sand Beige

⊙ = Lovat Green

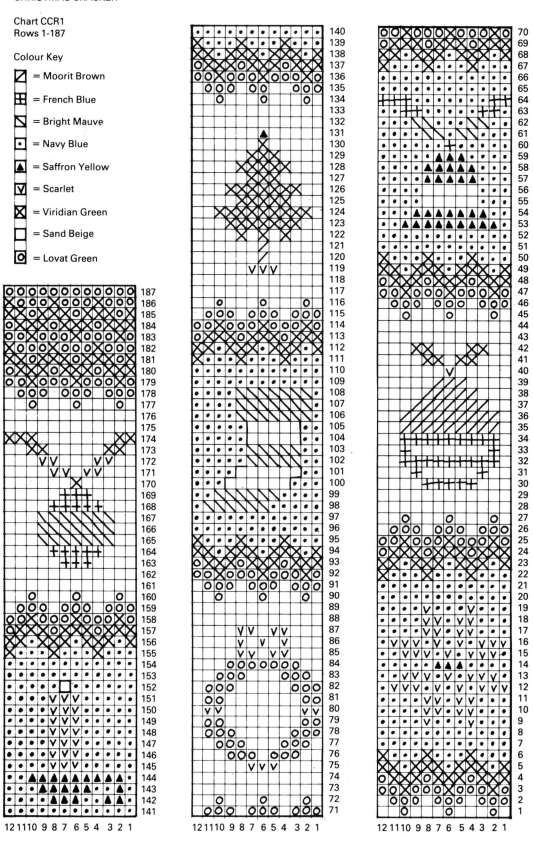

CHRISTMAS CRACKER WAISTCOAT

YARN COLOURS AND NUMBERS	QUANTITIES REQUIRED IN OUNCES (1 oz = 28.3 g)			
	Size 1	Size 2	Size 3	Size 4
Sand Beige F C 43	3	4	4	5
Navy Blue 21	1	2	2	2
Viridian Green 65	1	1	1	2
Lovat Green 29	1	1	1	2
Scarlet 93	1	1	1	1
Saffron Yellow 90	1	1	1	1
French Blue 16	1	1	1	1
Moorit Brown 4	1	1	1	1
Bright Mauve 44	1	1	1	1

NEEDLES One pair each size 2¾ mm (No. 12 British, No. 1 American), 3 mm (No. 11 British, No. 2 American) and 3¼ mm (No. 10 British, No. 3 American) needles. *Also:* 5 buttons.

TENSION 16 sts and 16 rows to 2 in (5 cm) on 3¼ mm needles over Fair Isle pattern. For K2P2 ribbing: 9 sts and 9 rows to 1 in (2.5 cm) on 2¾ mm needles. Change needle size if necessary to obtain correct tension.

SIZES 4 sizes. Size 1 = 33 in (84 cm), size 2 = 36 in (91.5 cm), size 3 = 39 in (99 cm), size 4 = 42 in (106.5 cm), actual measurements.

ABBREVIATIONS See page 16. *Colours:* S B = Sand Beige.

NOTES FOR KNITTERS See page 13.

BACK

With 2¾ mm needles and S B yarn, cast on 120(132:140:152) sts and work in K2P2 rib for 2½ in (6.5 cm).

Next row: (increase row) K across, inc 12(2:16:16) sts evenly over the row: 132(144:156:168) sts.

Next row: P across.

Using 3 mm needles on all 1-colour rows and 3¼ mm needles on all 2-colour rows, begin to work in pattern starting with row 1 of chart CCR1. On K rows work sts 1–12 across 11(12:13:14) times, on P rows work sts 12–1 across 11(12:13:14) times. Work straight in pattern until you have completed row 104 of chart CCR1. *Be sure to maintain continuity of pattern for remainder of work on Back.*

Armhole Shaping

Rows 105–106: cast off 5(7:9:11) sts at beg of each row: 122(130:138:146) sts rem.

Rows 107–110: cast off 4 sts at beg of each row: 106(114:122:130) sts rem.

Rows 111–120: dec 1 st at beg of each row: 96(104:112:120) sts rem.

Rows 121–176: work in pattern without shaping.

Shoulder Shaping

Rows 177–182: cast off 4(5:6:7) sts at beg of each row: 72(74:76:78) sts rem.

Rows 183–184: cast off 3(4:4:5) sts at beg of each row: 66(66:48:68) sts rem.

Rows 185–186: cast off 3(3:4:4) sts at beg of each row, work in pattern to end.

Row 187: cast off rem 60 sts.

LEFT FRONT

With 2¾ mm needles and S B yarn, cast on 60(64:72:76) sts and work in K2P2 rib for 2½ in (6.5 cm).

Next row: (increase row) K across, inc 6(8:6:8) sts evenly over the row: 66(72:78:84) sts.

Next row: P across.

Using 3 mm needles on all 1-colour rows and 3¼ mm needles on all 2-colour rows, begin to work in pattern starting with row 1 of chart CCR1, *in the following sequence.*

For sizes 1 and 3 only: on K rows, work sts 1–12 across 5(6) times, then work sts 1–6: 66(78) sts. On P rows work sts 6–1, then work sts 12–1 5(6) times.

For sizes 2 and 4 only: on K rows work sts 1–12 across 6(7) times, on P rows work sts 12–1 across 6(7) times: 72(84) sts.

For all sizes: work straight in pattern until you have completed row 104 of chart CCR1. *Be sure to maintain continuity of pattern for remainder of work on Left Front.*

Armhole and Neck Shaping

Row 105: cast off 5(7:9:11) sts at beg of row: 61(65:69:73) sts rem.

Row 106: work in pattern without shaping.

Row 107: cast off 4 sts at beg of row: 57(61:65:69) sts.

Row 108: work in pattern without shaping.

Row 109: cast off 4 sts at beg of row: 53(57:61:65) sts.

Row 110: work in pattern without shaping.

Rows 111–119: dec 1 st at beg of each row: 44(48:52:56) sts rem.

Rows 120–170: now keep armhole edge straight for remainder of work and dec 1 st at neck edge on row 120 and every alt row until there are 18(22:26:30) sts on needle. (Row 170 will now have been worked.)

Rows 171–176: work in pattern without shaping.

Shoulder Shaping

Row 177: cast off 4(5:6:7) sts at beg of row: 14(17:20:23) sts rem.

Row 178: work in pattern without shaping.

Row 179: cast off 4(5:6:7) sts at beg of row: 10(12:14:16) sts rem.

Row 180: work in pattern without shaping.

Rows 181: cast off 4(5:6:7) sts at beg of row: 6(7:8:9) sts rem.

Row 182: work in pattern without shaping.

Row 183: cast off 3(4:4:5) sts at beg of row: 3(3:4:4) sts rem.

Row 184: work in pattern without shaping.

Row 185: cast off rem 3(3:4:4) sts.

RIGHT FRONT

Work K2P2 ribbing and increase rows as for Left Front, then begin to work in pattern *in the following sequence.*

Sizes 1 and 3 only: on K rows, work sts 7–12, then work sts 1–12 5(6) times: 66(78) sts. On P rows work sts 12–1 5(6) times, then work sts 12–7.

Sizes 2 and 4 only: on K rows work sts 1–12 6(7) times, on P rows work sts 12–1 6(7) times: 72(84) sts.

For all sizes: otherwise work as for Left Front, reversing all shapings and ending by casting off rem 3(3:4:4) sts on row 186.

ARMBANDS

Gently press all pieces using a warm iron and damp cloth. Join shoulder seams. With 2¾ mm needles, SB yarn and right side of work facing, pick up 148(152:156:160) sts around armhole. Work in K2P2 rib for 9 rows. Cast off loosely in rib. Repeat for other side. Join side seams.

BUTTONHOLE BAND

With 2¾ mm needles and SB yarn cast on 12 sts and work 4 rows in K2P2 rib.

Row 5: (buttonhole row) rib 4 sts, cast off 3 sts, rib 5 sts.

Row 6: rib 5 sts, cast on 3 sts, rib 4 sts. Make 4 more buttonholes in this way, each 2¾ in or 7 cm from the last. Continue to work in rib until band is of sufficient length when slightly stretched to fit up both fronts and around back neck. Cast off neatly in rib. Attach buttonhole border with a fine slip stitch and press very gently. Sew on buttons opposite buttonholes.

20
Gingham

GINGHAM is one of the world's great classic fabrics and, like many seemingly familiar things, turns out to have rather exotic roots. Gingham comes from the Malay word *gingan*, and even today throughout Indonesia and Malaya a gingham fabric in black, white and grey plays an important part in religious ceremonies and ritual dances, where it is said to symbolize the perfect balance of light and dark, male and female and good and evil. Certainly gingham looks quite magical in the *kechak* or monkey dance of Bali, where I watched spellbound as a group of boys and young men dressed in sarongs of black check gingham leapt gracefully about the moonlit temple courtyard chanting *ke-chak-chak-chak* in strange but lovely harmonies.

Transplanted to Britain and woven in the great centres of Glasgow and Lancashire, gingham threw off its sombre colourings and emerged in the pretty shades that look so well when made up into frocks, shirts, tablecloths, curtains, cushions, quilts and children's soft toys. Gingham always seems crisp, fresh, bright, and buoyant, and since it translates beautifully into knitting there is no reason at all why cotton should be allowed a monopoly on the pattern. Gingham enjoyed a tremendous vogue during the late 1930s when it was much in demand for *appliqué* needlework, either as a background for plain cut-outs or as the fabric for cut-outs that were sewn to a plain background with fancy stitches. A 1930s *appliqué* tablecloth was the inspiration for this design – a merry A-B-C theme with small-check apples, butterflies, brollies, boats and cats bordered with wide gingham stripes in four colours and trimmed with a knitted-in blanket stitch.

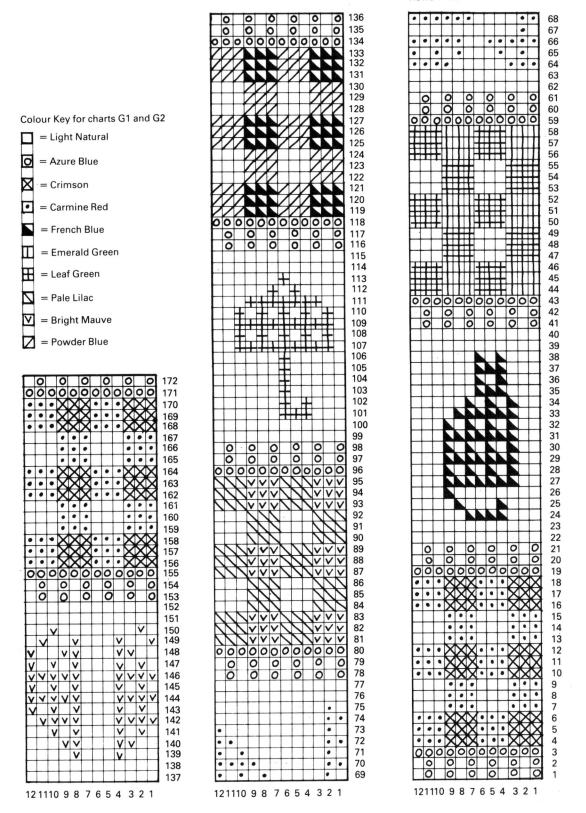

Colour Key for charts G1 and G2

☐ = Light Natural

◰ = Azure Blue

⊠ = Crimson

▣ = Carmine Red

◣ = French Blue

Ⅲ = Emerald Green

⊞ = Leaf Green

◺ = Pale Lilac

Ⅴ = Bright Mauve

◿ = Powder Blue

Chart G1
Rows 1-172

GINGHAM SWEATER

YARN COLOURS AND NUMBERS	QUANTITIES REQUIRED IN OUNCES (1 oz = 28.3 g)			
	Size 1	Size 2	Size 3	Size 4
Light Natural 202	5	6	6	7
Azure Blue 17	1	1	2	2
Crimson 55	1	1	1	1
Carmine Red 72	1	1	2	2
French Blue 16	1	1	1	1
Emerald Green 79	1	1	1	1
Leaf Green 25	1	1	2	2
Pale Lilac 49	1	1	1	1
Bright Mauve 44	1	1	1	1
Powder Blue F C 49	1	1	1	1

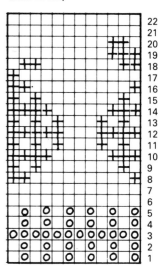

NEEDLES One pair each size 2¾ mm (No. 12 British, No. 1 American), 3 mm (No. 11 British, No. 2 American) and 3¼ mm (No. 10 British, No. 3 American) needles, and a stitch holder.

TENSION 16 sts and 16 rows to 2 in (5 cm) on 3¼ mm needles over Fair Isle pattern. For K1P1 ribbing: 10 sts and 11 rows to 1 in (2.5 cm) on 2¾ mm needles. Change needle size if necessary to obtain correct tension.

SIZES 4 sizes. Size 1 = 33 in (84 cm), size 2 = 36 in (91.5 cm), size 3 = 39 in (99 cm), size 4 = 42 in (106.5 cm), actual measurements.

ABBREVIATIONS See page 16. *Colours:* L N = Light Natural.

NOTES FOR KNITTERS See page 13.

SPECIAL INSTRUCTIONS FOR THIS DESIGN If you want to use a K2P2 rib instead of a K1P1 rib, work as follows. **BACK and FRONT:** cast on 120(132:140:152) sts. **Increase row:** inc 12(12:16:16) sts evenly over the row. **SLEEVES:** cast on 52(60:68:72) sts. **Increase row:** inc 8(12:16:24) sts evenly over the row. **NECK RIBBING:** pick up 84 sts around front neck.

BACK

With 2¾ mm nedles and LN yarn, cast on 118(130:140:152) sts and work in K1P1 rib for 2½ in (6.5 cm).

Next row: (increase row) K across, inc 14(14:16:16) sts evenly over the row: 132(144:156:168) sts.

Next row: P across.

Using 3 mm needles on all 1-colour rows and 3¼ mm needles on all 2-colour rows begin to work in pattern starting with row 1 of chart G1. On K rows work sts 1–12 cross 11(12:13:14) times, on P rows work sts 12–1 across 11(12:13:14) times. Work straight in pattern until you have completed row 98 of chart G1. *Be sure to maintain continuity of pattern for remainder of work on Back.*

Armhole Shaping

Rows 99–100: cast off 5(7:9:11) sts at beg of each row: 122(130:138:146) sts rem.

Rows 101–114: dec 1 st at beg of each row: 108(116:124:132) sts rem.

Rows 115–118: work in pattern without shaping.

Rows 119–120: dec 1 st at beg of each row: 106(114:122:130) sts rem.

Rows 121–124: work in pattern without shaping.

Rows 125–126: dec 1 st at beg of each row: 104(112:120:128) sts rem.

Rows 127–138: work in pattern without shaping.

Rows 139–140: inc into first st of each row: 106(114:122:130) sts.

Rows 141–148: work in pattern without shaping.

Rows 149–150: inc into first st of each row: 108(116:124:132) sts.

Rows 151–158: work in pattern without shaping.

Rows 159–160: inc into first st of each row: 110(118:126:134) sts.

Rows 161–162: work in pattern without shaping.

Shoulder Shaping

Rows 163–170: cast off 5(6:7:8) sts at beg of each row: 70 sts rem.

Rows 171–172: cast off 5 sts at beg of each row: 60 sts rem.

Back Neck

With 2¾ mm needles and LN yarn, work the 60 sts for back neck in K1P1 rib for 9 rows. Cast off neatly in rib on the 10th row.

FRONT

Work as for Back until you have completed row 142 of chart G1: 106(114:122:130) sts rem. *Be sure to maintain continuity of pattern throughout.*

Divide for Neck

Row 143: work in pattern across 38(42:46:50) sts, turn, and leave rem 68(72:76:80) sts on spare needle or stitch holder and work on first group of sts as follows.

Left Front

Rows 144–148: dec 1 st at neck edge on every row: 33(37:41:45) sts rem.

Row 149: inc 1 st at beg of row, work across in pattern to last 2 sts, dec 1 st at neck edge: 33(37:41:45) sts.

Rows 150–156: dec 1 st at neck edge on every row: 26(30:34:38) sts rem.

Rows 157–158: work in pattern without shaping.

Row 159: inc 1 st at beg of row, work across in pattern to last 2 sts, dec 1 st at neck edge: 26(30:34:38) sts.

Row 160: dec 1 st at neck edge, work in pattern across row: 25(29:33:37) sts rem. Now keep neck edge straight for remainder of work.

Rows 161–162: work in pattern without shaping.

Shoulder Shaping

Row 163: cast off 5(6:7:8) sts, work in pattern to end: 20(23:26:29) sts rem.

Row 164: work in pattern without shaping.

Row 165: as row 163: 15(17:19:21) sts rem.

Row 166: work in pattern without shaping.

Row 167: as row 163: 10(11:12:13) sts rem.

Row 168: work in pattern without shaping.

Row 169: as row 163: 5 sts rem.

Row 170: work in pattern without shaping.

Row 171: cast off rem 5 sts.

Right Front

Slip 30 sts for Front Neck on to spare needle or stitch holder, then rejoin yarn to rem 38(42:46:50) sts and work in pattern across row 143. Now work as for Left Front, reversing all shapings and ending by casting off rem 5 sts on row 172.

SLEEVES

With 2¾ mm needles and LN yarn, cast on 54(60:66:72) sts and work in K1P1 rib for 2½ in (6.5 cm).

Next row: (increase row) K across, inc 6(12:18:24) sts evenly over the row: 60(72:84:96) sts.

Next row: P across.

Using 3 mm needles on all 1-colour rows and 3¼ mm needles on all 2-colour rows, begin to work in pattern starting with row 1 of chart G2.

Row 1: work sts 1–12 across 5(6:7:8) times.

Row 2: work sts 12–1 across 5(6:7:8) times.

Row 3: as row 1.

Rows 4–20: inc 1 st at both ends of row 4 and every following 4th row until you have completed row 20 of chart G2: 70(82:94:106) sts.

Rows 21–22: work in pattern without shaping.

Now return to row 1 of chart G1 and continue to work in pattern, inc 1 st at both ends of row 2 and every following 4th row until there are 90(102:114:126) sts on needle. (Row 38 of chart G1 will now have been worked.)

Rows 39–44: work in pattern without shaping.

Rows 45–94: inc 1 st at both ends of row 45 and every following 7th row until there are 106(118:130:142) sts on needle. (Row 94 of chart G1.)

Rows 95–97: work in pattern without shaping.

Row 98: inc 1 st at both ends of row: 108(120:132:144) sts.

Rows 99–100: work in pattern without shaping.

Shape Sleeve Head

Rows 101–104: cast off 1(3:5:7) sts at beg of each row: 104(108:112:116) sts.

Rows 105–114: cast off 2 sts at beg of each row: 84(88:92:96) sts rem.

Rows 115–116: dec 1 st at beg of each row: 82(86:90:94) sts rem.

Rows 117–118: cast off 2 sts at beg of each row: 78(82:86:90) sts rem.

Rows 119–122: dec 1 st at beg of each row: 74(78:82:86) sts rem.

Rows 123–126: cast off 2 sts at beg of each row: 66(70:74:78) sts rem.

Rows 127–128: dec 1 st at beg of each row: 64(68:72:76) sts rem.

Rows 129–142: cast off 2 sts at beg of each row: 36(40:44:48) sts rem.

Rows 143–144: cast off 5 sts at beg of each row: 26(30:34:38) sts rem.

Rows 145–147: cast off 3(4:5:6) sts at beg of each row: 17(18:19:20) sts rem.

Row 148: cast off rem sts.

Work second sleeve in the same way.

NECKBAND

With 2¾ mm needles, LN yarn and right side of work facing, pick up and K 28 sts down left side of neck, 30 sts from centre front neck and 28 sts up right side of neck: 86 sts. Work in K1P1 rib for 9 rows. Cast off neatly in rib on the 10th row.

TO MAKE UP

Gently press all pieces using a warm iron and damp cloth. Join shoulder seams including neck ribbing. Sew sleeves into place along armhole edge then join side and sleeve seams.

21
Blue Willow

THE BLUE WILLOW pattern is one of the best-loved designs in the world, and it looks just as charming in knitting as it does on china ware. The china pattern was first devised in England in the early nineteenth century, and time has not diminished the appeal of its happy combination of Chinese motifs and Victorian prettiness. But Blue Willow is more than a pretty pattern. The willow tree, pagoda and other figures on a piece of Willow ware all tell a story – the legend of the Blue Willow.

Long ago, in the land of China, there lived a wicked Mandarin and his beautiful daughter, Li-Chi. High walls enclosed the Mandarin's estate, and inside could be found all the delights that riches could buy. There were sumptuous silks and sparkling jewels, groves of trees where birds sang sweetly from dawn to dusk, perfumed gardens and a limpid lake spanned by a graceful bridge. There was everything but happiness. For although Li-Chi had been promised to an old and ugly suitor, she had fallen in love with her father's handsome secretary, Chang. When the Mandarin discovered their feelings for each other, he sent Chang away and locked Li-Chi in a tiny chamber at the top of a tall pagoda, vowing to keep her there until she agreed to marry the man he had chosen for her. A friendly gardener was hiding behind an orange tree that stood near the pagoda. As soon as it was dark, he called up to Li-Chi and offered his help. 'Go and find Chang', cried Li-Chi through her tears, 'and ask him to come to me when the willow leaves begin to fall.' Chang came at the appointed time and released Li-Chi from her prison. They paused for a single kiss, then fled towards the bridge and freedom. But the Mandarin happened upon them, and a chase ensued. By the time they reached the bridge he had almost overtaken them, and all would have been lost if the Gods had not taken pity on the young lovers and turned them into a pair of birds who soared up into the sky, free to love each other forever.

Chart BW1
192 Rows

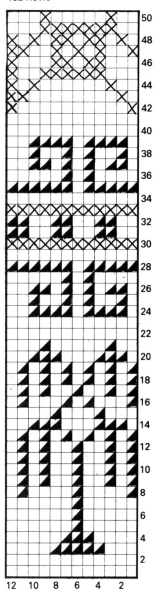

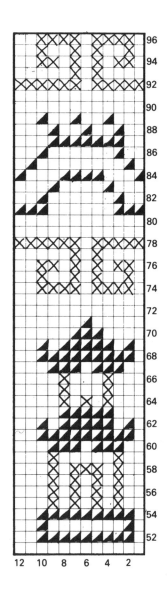

<u>Colour Key</u>

◨ = Azure Blue

☒ = French Blue

☐ = Light Natural

Chart BW2
9 Rows

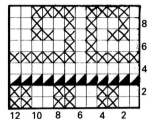

End Chart B1

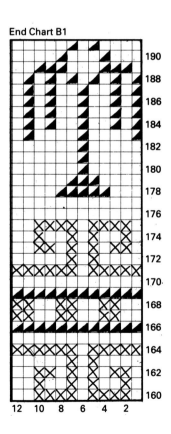

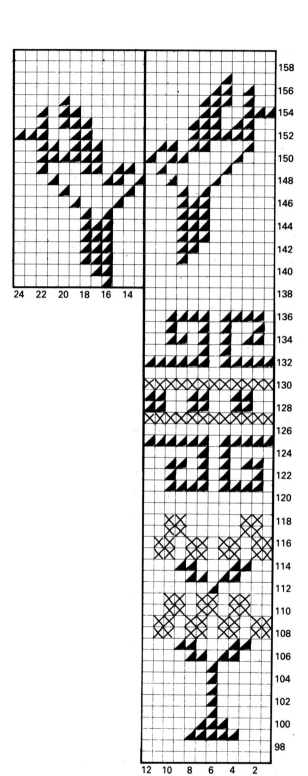

BLUE WILLOW CARDIGAN

YARN COLOURS AND NUMBERS

YARN COLOURS AND NUMBERS	QUANTITIES REQUIRED IN OUNCES (1 oz = 28.3 g)		
	Size 1	Size 2	Size 3
Light Natural 202	8	8	9
Azure Blue 17	4	4	5
French Blue 16	2	2	3

NEEDLES One pair each size 2¾ mm (No. 12 British, No. 1 American), 3 mm (No. 11 British, No. 2 American) and 3¼ mm (No. 10 British, No. 3 American) needles. *Also:* 5 buttons.

TENSION 16 sts and 18 rows to 2 in (5 cm) on 3¼ mm needles over Fair Isle pattern. For K1P1 ribbing: 10 sts and 11 rows to 1 in (2.5 cm) on 2¾ mm needles. Change needle size if necessary to obtain correct tension.

SIZES 3 sizes. Size 1 = 33 in (84 cm), size 2 = 36 in (91.5 cm), size 3 = 39 in (99 cm), actual measurements.

ABBREVIATIONS See page 16. *Colours:* N = Light Natural, AB = Azure Blue.

NOTES FOR KNITTERS See page 13.

SPECIAL INSTRUCTIONS FOR THIS DESIGN Odd-numbered rows are K rows and even-numbered rows are P rows except for when working the sleeves after completing chart B2. Use 3 mm needles on all 1-colour rows. Because of rows 139–159, this design should be treated as a 24-stitch repeat.

BACK

With 2¾ mm needles and N yarn, cast on 132(144:156) sts and work in K1P1 rib for 2¾ in (7 cm). Change to 3¼ mm needles and proceed to work in st.st and pattern beginning at row 1 of chart BW1. Work sts 1–12 of row 1 across 11(12:13) repeats in all. Work sts 12–1 of row 2 across 11(12:13) repeats in all. Continue in pattern until you have completed 106(110:114) pattern rows.

Armhole Shaping

Keeping correct in pattern, cast off 5(8:11) sts at beg of the next 2 rows. Now dec 1 st at beg of the next 14 rows: 108 (114:120) sts. Continue straight in pattern for 56 rows.

Shoulder Shaping

Keeping correct in pattern, cast off 10 sts at beg of next 6 rows. Cast off remaining 48(54:60) sts.

LEFT FRONT

With 2¾ mm needles and N yarn, cast on 66(72:78) sts and work in K1P1 rib for 2¾ in (7 cm). Change to 3¼ mm needles and st.st and proceed to work in pattern from chart BW1, starting at row 1, as follows:

Size 1: Row 1: work sts 1–12 (5 times), then work sts 1–6 (66 sts).

Row 2: work sts 6–1, then work sts 12–1 (5 times).

Size 2: Row 1: work sts 1–12 (6 times) (72 sts).

Row 2: work sts 12–1 (6 times).

Size 3: Row 1: work sts 1–12 (6 times), then work sts 1–6 (78 sts).

Row 2: work sts 6–1, then work sts 12–1 (6 times).

For all sizes: continue in this way until you have completed 96(98:98) pattern rows and begin neck shaping.

Neck and Armhole Shaping

Keeping correct in pattern, dec 1 st at neck edge on next and every following 3rd row until 30 sts remain. At the same time, when 106(110:114) pattern rows have been worked, shape armhole as follows. Keeping correct in pattern, cast off 5(8:11) sts at beg of next right side row. Now dec 1 st at armhole edge on next right side row 7 times (14 rows). Keep armhole edge straight and work as for Back to shoulder shaping.

Shoulder Shaping

Keeping correct in pattern, cast off 10 sts at beg of next 3 right side rows (all sts will now be cast off).

RIGHT FRONT

With 2¾ mm needles and N yarn, cast on 66(72:78) sts and work in K1P1 rib for 2¾ in (7 cm). Change to 3¼ mm needles and st.st and proceed to work in pattern from chart BW1, starting at row 1, as follows:

Size 1: Row 1: work sts 7–12, then work sts 1–12 (5 times) (66 sts).

Row 2: work sts 12–1 (5 times), then work sts 12–7.

Size 2: Row 1: work sts 1–12 (6 times) (72 sts).

Row 2: work sts 12–1 (6 times).

Size 3: Row 1: work sts 7–12, then work sts 1–12 (6 times) (78 sts).

Row 2: work sts 12–1 (6 times), then work sts 12–7.

For all sizes: following this stitch sequence, work Right Front to match the Left Front, reversing all shapings.

SLEEVES

Pattern sequence for sleeves: work rows 1–9 of chart BW2, then return to row 1 of chart BW1. With 2¾ mm needles and N yarn, cast on 68(72:74) sts and work in K1P1 rib for 2¾ in (7 cm). Change to size 3¼ mm needles and P 1 row in AB. Now work in pattern and st.st, using the sequence as above.

Size 1: Row 1: work sts 9–12, then sts 1–12 (5 times) then sts 1–4 (68 sts).

Row 2: (inc into first and last st of row) work pattern sts 5–1, then sts 12–1 (5 times), then sts 12–8 (70 sts).

Size 2: Row 1: work sts 1–12 (6 times) (72 sts).

Row 2: (inc into first and last st of row) work st 1, then sts 12–1 (6 times), then st 12 (74 sts).

Size 3: Row 1: work st 12, then sts 1–12 (6 times) then st 1 (74 sts).

Row 2: (inc into first and last st of row) work sts 2–1, then sts 12–1 (6 times), then sts 12–11 (76 sts).

For all sizes: keeping correct in pattern, inc 1 st at both ends of every 6th row until there are 110 sts. Now work straight until 114(118:122) rows of pattern have been completed.

Shape Sleeve Head

Keeping correct in pattern, cast off 7 sts at beg of next 2 rows.

Now dec 1 st at beg of every row until 48 sts remain.

Cast off 3 sts at beg of next 6 rows.

Cast off remaining 30 sts.

Work second sleeve to match.

Now carefully press pieces with a warm iron and damp cloth, omitting the ribbing. Join shoulder seams, sew sleeves into position along armhole edge, then join side and sleeve seams.

BUTTONHOLE BORDER

With 2¾ mm needles and N yarn, cast on 12 sts and work 4 rows in K1P1 rib.

Row 5: (buttonhole row) rib 4 sts, cast off 3 sts, rib 5 sts.

Row 6: rib 5 sts, cast on 3 sts, rib 4 sts.

Make 4 more buttonholes in this way, each 2¾ in or 7 cm from the last. Continue to work in rib until neckband is of sufficient length, when slightly stretched, to fit up both fronts and around back neck. Cast off neatly in rib.

TO FINISH

Attach the buttonhole border with a fine slip stitch and press gently. Sew on buttons opposite buttonholes.

22
Harvest Home

B Y RIGHTS, autumn ought to be a dismal time of year – the rich flower colours of summer drain into the earth, and daylight steals ever earlier away, pursued by the first winter frosts. Yet just when nature seems at its bleakest the landscape takes on a quiet beauty, the bare woodland glade with its carpet of brown leaves reveals an unexpected richness of tone and shade, and bright red berries cluster in the hedgerows as squirrels scamper after late fallen nuts. Lights seen through the mist look warm and welcoming, the chill gives early evenings an air of anticipation and a splendid new season is upon us, with its own colours, customs, pleasures and pastimes, all to be enjoyed to the full. It is a time of gentle pursuits and cosy conviviality – of bonfires and thanksgiving suppers, of filling the larder with the fruits of summer and of decorating rooms with arrangements of dried flowers and grasses – the time of Harvest Home.

The season of plenty was the inspiration for this sweater, which carries a design of autumn berries, cornucopias or horns of plenty, squirrels and nuts, sheaves of grain, evergreen trees and my particular favourite among the everlasting flowers – the bright orange Chinese Lantern, or *Physalis franchetii*. I adore dried floral decorations, particularly as the French do them – truly heroic arrangements that boast ears of dried maize and branches of fluffy white cotton bolls as well as the more usual dried flowers, pods, ferns and grasses. In Paris at autumn, florists offer delightful bouquets of maize, cotton bolls and grasses to take to friends or hostesses. Such a present might not be to everyone's liking, but it is a custom I find tremendously appealing for it pays tribute, as does this design, to the special charms of this golden season.

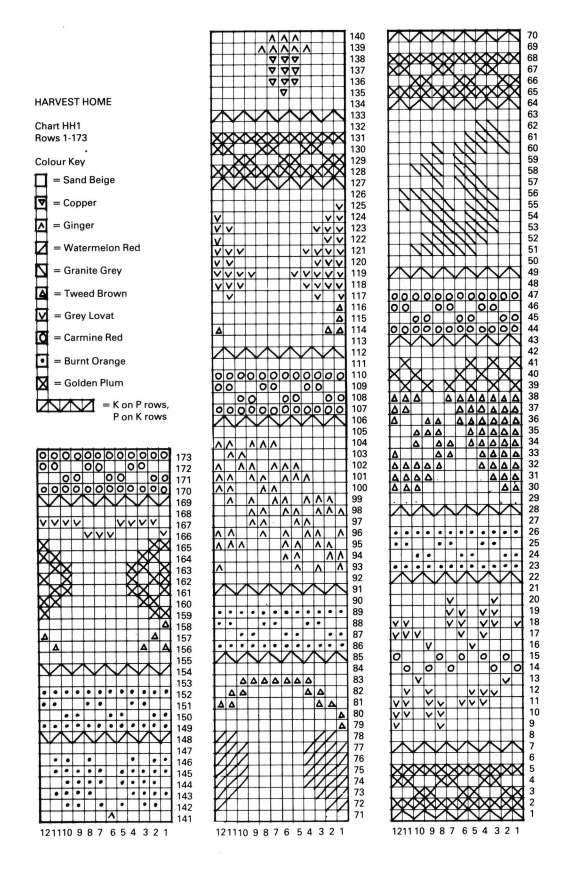

HARVEST HOME

Chart HH1
Rows 1-173

Colour Key

☐ = Sand Beige

▽ = Copper

◮ = Ginger

◿ = Watermelon Red

◺ = Granite Grey

◮ = Tweed Brown

∨ = Grey Lovat

◖ = Carmine Red

▣ = Burnt Orange

☒ = Golden Plum

◸◹◺◿ = K on P rows,
P on K rows

HARVEST HOME SWEATER

YARN COLOURS AND NUMBERS	QUANTITIES REQUIRED IN OUNCES (1 oz = 28.3 g)		
	Size 1	Size 2	Size 3
Sand Beige FC43	7	8	9
Golden Plum FC10	1	1	1
Grey Lovat 30	1	1	1
Carmine Red 72	1	1	1
Burnt Orange FC38	1	1	1
Tweed Brown FC46	1	1	2
Granite Grey 27	1	1	1
Watermelon Red FC33	1	1	1
Ginger 32	1	1	1
Copper 31	1	1	1

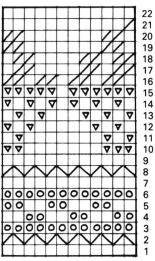

NEEDLES One pair each size 2¾ mm (No. 12 British, No. 1 American), 3 mm (No. 11 British, No. 2 American) and 3¼ mm (No. 10 British, No. 3 American) plus set of 4 doublepointed 2¾ mm needles and 1 extra doublepointed 2¾ mm needle and a stitch holder. *Also:* length of ribbon for threading through collar.

TENSION 16 sts and 16 rows to 2 in (5 cm) on 3¼ mm needles over Fair Isle pattern. For K1P1 ribbing: 10 sts and 11 rows to 1 in (2.5 cm) on 2¾ mm needles. Change needle size if necessary to obtain correct tension.

SIZES 3 sizes. Size 1 = 36 in (91.5 cm), size 2 = 39 in (99 cm), size 3 = 42 in (106.5 cm), actual measurements.

ABBREVIATIONS See page 16. *Colours:* SB = Sand Beige.

NOTES FOR KNITTERS See page 13.

SPECIAL INSTRUCTIONS FOR THIS DESIGN (1) If you prefer red squirrels to grey ones, work the squirrels (rows 51–62) in Copper yarn. If you do, you will not need the Granite Grey yarn. (2) The rows marked with a zigzag on the charts are to be worked in reverse st.st in SB yarn, to give a ridged effect.

BACK

With 2¾ mm needles and S B yarn, cast on 130(140:152) sts and work in K1P1 rib for 2½ in (6.5 cm).

Next row (increase row) K across, inc 14(16:16) sts evenly across the row: 144(156:168) sts.
Next row: P across.
Using 3 mm needles on all 1-colour rows and 3¼ mm needles on all 2-colour rows, begin to work in pattern starting with row 1 of chart HH1. On K rows work sts 1–12 across 12(13:14) times, on P rows work sts 12–1 across 12(13:14) times. Work straight in pattern until you have completed row 98 of chart HH1. *Be sure to maintain continuity of pattern for remainder of work on Back.*

Armhole Shaping

Rows 99–100: cast off 7(9:11) sts at beg of each row: 130(138:146) sts rem.
Rows 101–114: dec 1 st at beg of each row: 116(124:132) sts rem.
Rows 115–118: work in pattern without shaping.
Rows 119–120: dec 1 st at beg of each row: 114(122:130) sts rem.
Rows 121–124: work in pattern without shaping.
Rows 125–126: dec 1 st at beg of each row: 112(120:128) sts rem.
Rows 127–138: work in pattern without shaping.
Rows 139–140: inc into first st of each row: 114(122:130) sts.
Rows 141–148: work in pattern without shaping.
Rows 149–150: inc into first st of each row: 116(124:132) sts.
Rows 151–158: work in pattern without shaping.
Rows 159–160: inc into first st of each row: 118(126:134) sts.
Rows 161–162: work in pattern without shaping.

Shoulder Shaping

Rows 163–170: cast off 5(6:7) sts at beg of each row: 78 sts rem.
Row 171: cast off 6 sts at beg of row: 72 sts rem.
Row 172: cast off 9 sts at beg of row: 63 sts rem.
Row 173: cast off 3 sts at beg of row, work in pattern to end: 60 sts rem.
Leave rem 60 sts on a stitch holder.

FRONT

Work as for Back until you have completed row 144 of chart HH1; 114(122:130) sts. *Be sure to maintain continuity of pattern throughout.*

Divide for Neck

Row 145: work in pattern across 47(51:55) sts. Cast off the next 20 sts, leave rem 47(51:55) sts on a stitch holder and work on first group of sts as follows.

Left Front

Row 146: cast off 5 sts (neck edge), work in pattern to end: 42(46:50) sts rem.
Row 147: work in pattern without shaping.
Row 148: cast off 4 sts, work in pattern to end: 38(42:46) sts.
Row 149: inc into first st (armhole edge), work in pattern to end: 39(43:47) sts.
Rows 150–156: keeping armhole edge straight, dec 2 sts at neck edge on row 150 and every alt row 3 more times: 31(35:39) sts.
Rows 157–158: work in pattern without shaping.
Row 159: inc into first st, work in pattern to end: 32(36:40) sts.
Row 160: dec 2 sts at neck edge, work in pattern to end: 30(34:38) sts.
Rows 161–162: work in pattern without shaping.

Shoulder Shaping

Row 163: cast off 5(6:7) sts, work in pattern to end: 25(28:31) sts.
Row 164: dec 1 st, work in pattern to end: 24(27:30) sts.
Row 165: as row 163: 19(21:23) sts rem.
Row 166: work in pattern without shaping.
Row 167: as row 163: 14(15:16) sts rem.
Row 168: as row 166.
Row 169: as row 163: 9 sts rem.
Row 170: as row 166.
Row 171: cast off 6 sts, work in pattern to end: 3 sts rem.
Row 172: as row 166.
Row 173: cast off rem 3 sts.

Right Front

Rejoin yarn to second group of 47(51:55) sts and work in pattern across row 145. Now work as for Left Front, reversing all shapings and ending by casting off rem 9 sts on row 172.

SLEEVES

With 2¾ mm needles and S B yarn, cast on 60(66:72) sts and work in K1P1 rib for 2½ in (6.5 cm).
Next row: (increase row) K across, inc 12(18:24) sts evenly over the row: 72(84:96) sts.
Next row: P across.
Using 3 mm needles on all 1-colour rows and 3¼ mm needles on all 2-colour rows, begin to work in pattern starting with row 1 of chart HH2.
Row 1: work sts 1–12 across 6(7:8) times.
Row 2: work sts 12–1 across 6(7:8) times.
Row 3: as row 1.
Rows 4–20: inc 1 st at both ends of row 4 and every following 4th row until you have completed row 20 of chart HH2: 82(94:106) sts.
Rows 21–22: work in pattern without shaping.
Now return to row 1 of chart HH1 and continue to work in pattern, inc 1 st at both ends of row 2 and every following 4th row until there are 102(114:126) sts on needle. (Row 38 of chart HH1 will now have been worked.)
Rows 39–44: work in pattern without shaping.
Rows 45–94: inc 1 st at both ends of row 45 and every following 7th row until there are 118(130:142) sts on needle. (Row 94 of chart HH1 will now have been worked.)
Rows 95–97: work in pattern without shaping.
Row 98: inc 1 st at both ends of row: 120(132:144) sts.
Rows 99–100: work in pattern without shaping.

Shape Sleeve Head

Rows 101–104: cast off 3(5:7) sts at beg of each row: 108(112:116) sts.

Rows 105–114: cast off 2 sts at beg of each row: 88(92:96) sts rem.

Rows 115–116: dec 1 st at beg of each row: 86(90:94) sts rem.

Rows 117–118: cast off 2 sts at beg of each row: 82(86:90) sts rem.

Rows 119–122: dec 1 st at beg of each row: 78(82:86) sts.

Rows 123–126: cast off 2 sts at beg of each row: 70(74:78) sts rem.

Rows 127–128: dec 1 st at beg of each row: 68(72:76) sts rem.

Rows 129–142: cast off 2 sts at beg of each row: 40(44:48) sts rem.

Rows 143–144: cast off 5 sts at beg of each row: 30(34:38) sts rem.

Rows 145–147: cast off 4(5:6) sts at beg of each row: 18(19:20) sts rem.

Row 148: cast off rem sts.

Work second sleeve in the same way.

NECKBAND

Sew up the shoulder seams using back stitch. With S B yarn and set of 4 plus 1 doublepointed 2¾ mm needles, pick up and K 20 sts across centre front neck on to first needle. Using S B yarn and with right side of work facing, pick up and K 33 sts up right side of front neck on to 2nd needle, 60 sts across back neck on to 3rd needle and 33 sts down left side of front neck on to 4th needle. Turn work and proceed as follows.

Row 1: working in K1P1 rib, rib 33 sts from 4th needle, 60 sts from 3rd needle, 33 sts from 2nd needle. Then rib 2 sts from centre front 20 sts (leaving 18 sts on doublepointed needle at centre front).

Row 2: (right side) rib sts from 2nd, 3rd and 4th needles, then rib 2 sts from centre front 18 sts (leaving 16 sts on doublepointed needle at centre front).

Continue to rib neck band in this way, taking 2 sts from centre front sts on doublepointed needle at the end of every row until you have worked 10 rows in all, when every stitch will have been taken up from the centre front. Cast off neatly in rib.

COLLAR

With 3 mm needles and S B yarn, cast on 16 sts and P 1 row. Proceed to work in pattern as follows:

Row 1: (wrong side) K1 SL.1 K1 psso, Y O twice, K2tog P8, inc into next st, K2.

Row 2: K14 P1 K2.

Row 3: K1 SL.1 K1 psso, Y O twice, K2tog P9, inc into next st, K2.

Row 4: K12, turn, P9, inc into next st, K2.

Row 5: K16 P1 K2.

Row 6: K1 SL.1 K1 psso, Y O twice, K2tog P12 K2.

Row 7: K13, turn, P9 P2tog K2.

Row 8: K15 P1 K2.

Row 9: K1 SL.1 K1 psso, Y O twice, K2tog P9, P2tog K2.

Row 10: K14 P1 K2.

Row 11: K1 SL.1 K1 psso, Y O twice, K2tog P8, P2tog K2.

Row 12: K13 P1 K2.

Row 13: K1 SL.1 K1 psso, Y O twice, K2tog K11.

Row 14: K2 P8, turn, K10.

Row 15: K2 P8, turn, K10.

Row 16: K2 P9 K2 P1 K2.

These 16 rows form the collar pattern. Repeat them 10 times, then work rows 1–13. Cast off knitwise.

TO MAKE UP

Lightly press all pieces using a warm iron and damp cloth. Sew in sleeves using back stitch. Sew up sleeve seams and side seams using back stitch. Oversew collar to neckband, placing collar just inside the top of the rib neckband, beginning and ending at the centre front of neck. Thread ribbon through holes, leaving ends long enough to tie in a bow at centre front.

23
Paisley Stripe

THERE ARE some motifs that present a perpetual challenge at which designers hurl themselves over and over again, rather like Don Quixote and the windmill. One is the rose, and another is the paisley. Apart from its exotic origins and history, the paisley as a pattern has much to recommend it – elegance of form, vitality of movement and infinite adaptability. It is also maddeningly elusive and wickedly persistent, for there is no such thing as the definitive paisley – just variations on an endless theme. Once you have done one, the others rise up to haunt you. After I completed *Persian Garden*, the paisley continued to lurk at the back of my mind, bedevilling my dreams and demanding another outing in a different form – simpler, bolder and this time in only two colours of yarn per row.

Inspiration came at the hands of Isabella Beeton who, when she was not in the kitchen writing her famous cookery book, was one of England's first fashion editors. Isabella's husband Samuel was a publishing entrepreneur who founded a stable of successful magazines in the 1850s and 1860s including *Boys Own*, *The Queen* and the *Englishwomen's Domestic Magazine*, which was the first popular magazine for women. Edited by Isabella after her marriage, its regular features on fiction, fashion, food, society, topics of general interest and even an agony column established the prototype for all women's magazines of today, and was a good deal more interesting than many. Paris fashions were reported monthly in minute detail, the magazine carried pictures of current styles backed up by paper patterns available by mail order, and each issue included handcoloured needlework patterns from France and Germany. It was among these that I found the basis for this design – a paisley stripe slipper for a man, worked in single wool on canvas – which I adapted and put on to a waistcoat shape, as the waistcoat's points reminded me of the elegant cut of the slipper's instep. Thanks to Isabella, I no longer see paisleys in my sleep – at least, not for the moment. Since one good turn deserves another, I pass on an excellent piece of advice from the *Englishwoman's Domestic Magazine* which works a treat when choosing yarns:

> *One hint, in conclusion, may be useful to ladies when they go shopping. After they have been looking at silks or other fabrics which run upon one colour, the eye gets fatigued and cannot appreciate the various shades set before it. The best way to restore the 'tone' of the eye is to allow it to rest for some time on green or grey, when it will be so much refreshed that the colours, which a few minutes before appeared dull, now brighten up and are seen in their proper tint.*

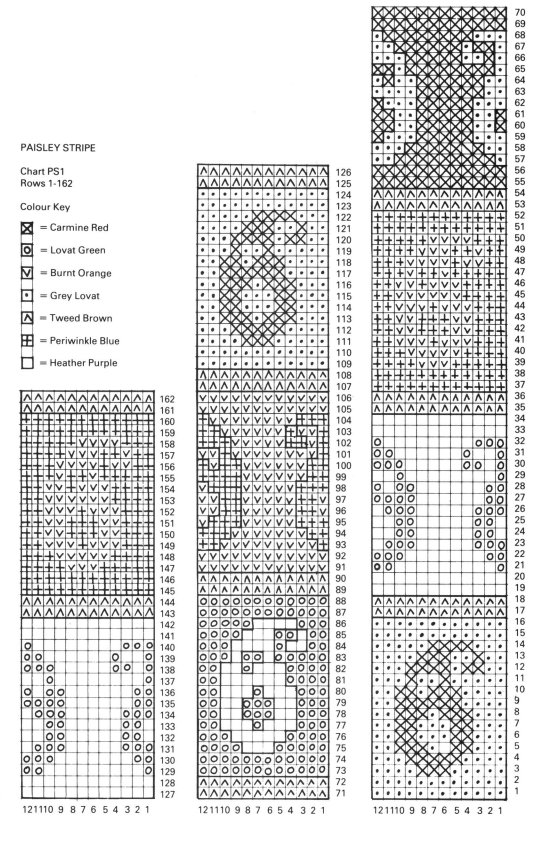

PAISLEY STRIPE

Chart PS1
Rows 1-162

Colour Key

⊠ = Carmine Red

O = Lovat Green

∨ = Burnt Orange

⋅ = Grey Lovat

∧ = Tweed Brown

⊞ = Periwinkle Blue

☐ = Heather Purple

PAISLEY STRIPE
Chart PS2
Right Front
Rows 1-31
Sizes 1 and 3 only

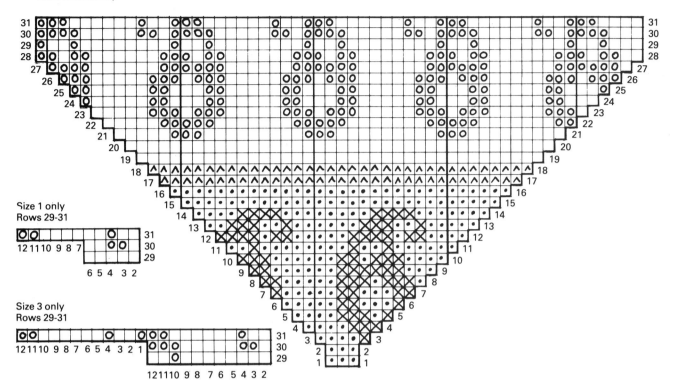

Size 1 only
Rows 29-31

Size 3 only
Rows 29-31

PAISLEY STRIPE
Chart PS3
Right Front
Rows 1-31
Sizes 1 and 3 only

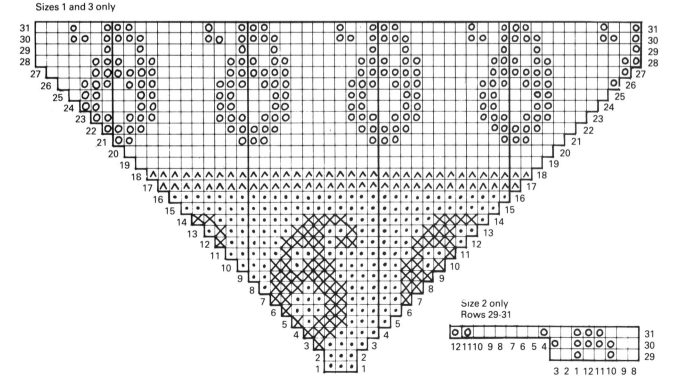

Size 2 only
Rows 29-31

PAISLEY STRIPE
Chart PS4
Left Front
Rows 1-32
Sizes 1 and 3 only

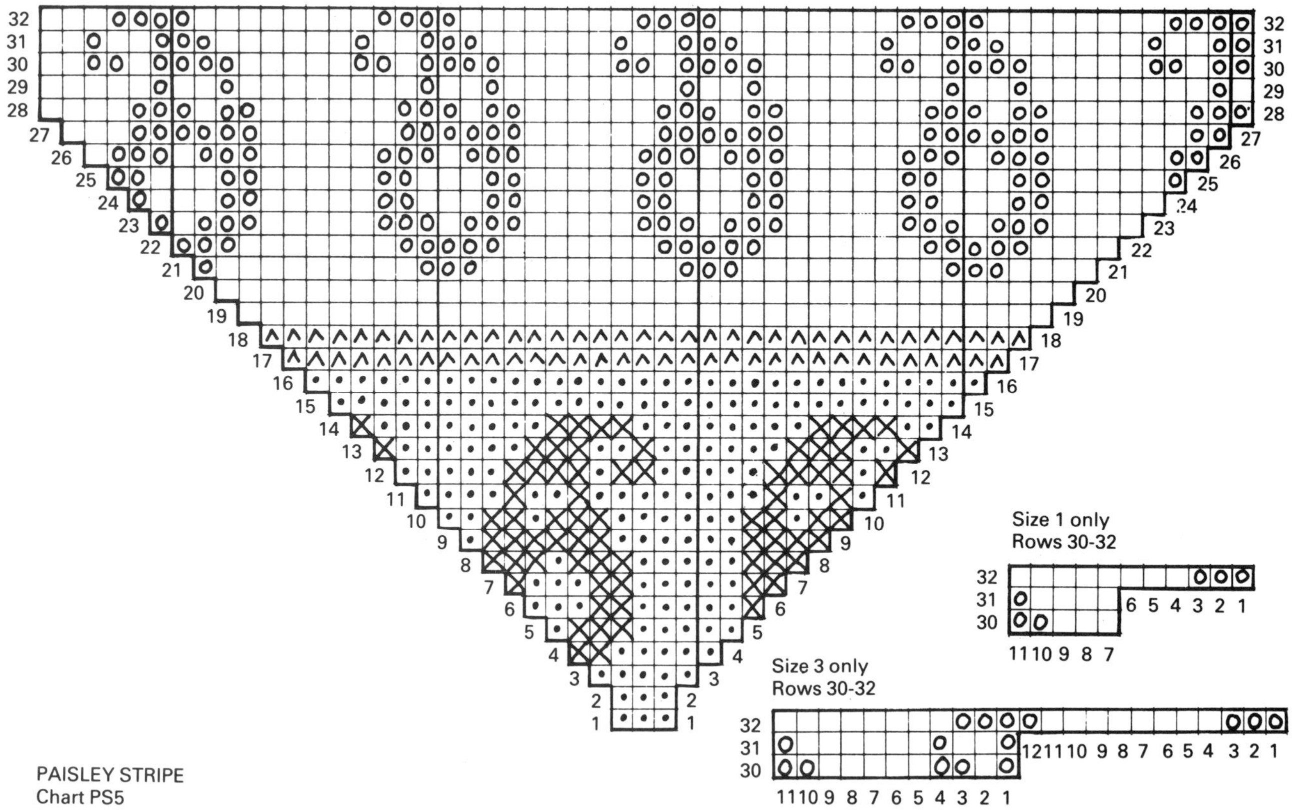

Size 1 only
Rows 30-32

Size 3 only
Rows 30-32

PAISLEY STRIPE
Chart PS5
Left Front
Rows 1-32
Size 2 only

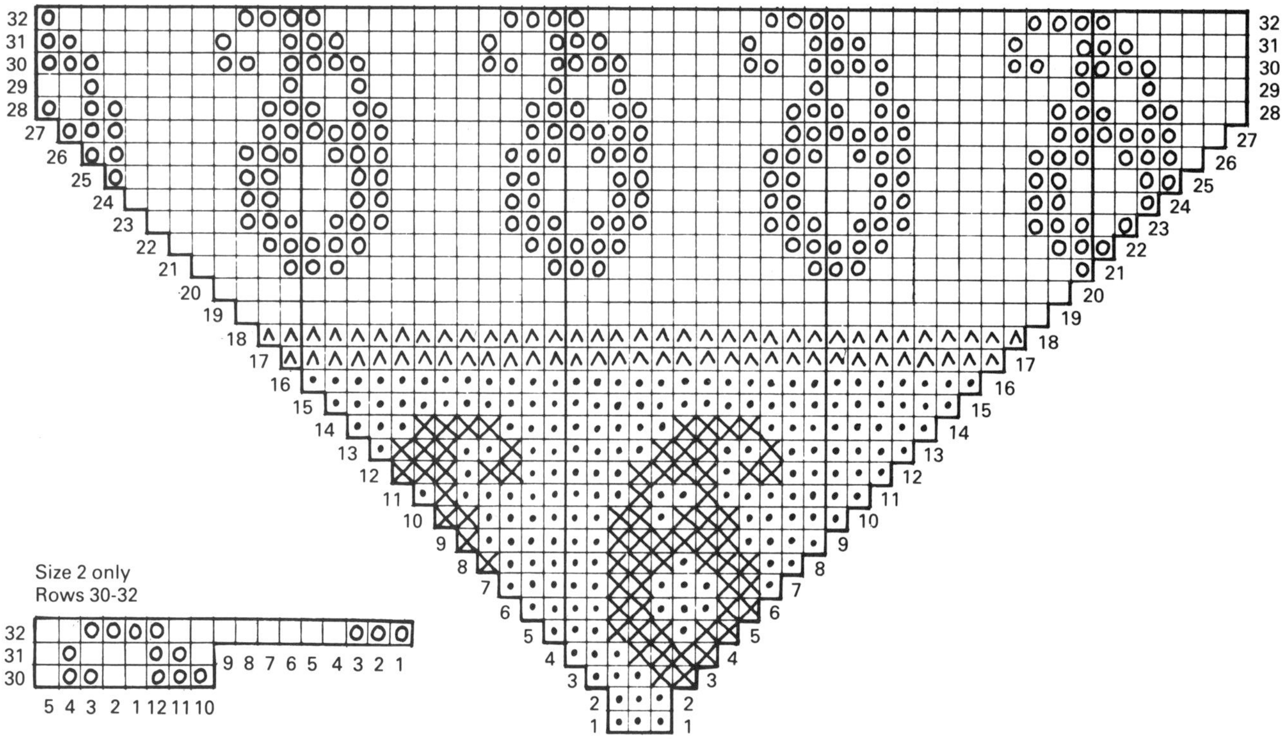

Size 2 only
Rows 30-32

148

PAISLEY STRIPE POINTED WAISTCOAT

YARN COLOURS AND NUMBERS	QUANTITIES REQUIRED IN OUNCES (1 oz = 28 g)		
	Size 1	Size 2	Size 3
Carmine Red 72	1	1	1
Lovat Green 29	1	1	1
Burnt Orange F C 38	1	1	1
Grey Lovat 30	1	1	1
Tweed Brown F C 46	2	2	2
Periwinkle Blue F C 37	1	1	2
Heather Purple 19	1	1	1

NEEDLES One pair each size 2¾ mm (No. 12 British, No. 1 American), 3 mm (No. 11 British, No. 2 American) and 3¼ mm (No. 10 British, No. 3 American) needles. *Also:* 5 buttons.

TENSION 16 sts and 16 rows to 2 in (5 cm) on 3¼ mm needles over Fair Isle pattern. Change needle size if necessary to obtain correct tension.

SIZES 3 sizes. Size 1 = 33 in (84 cm), size 2 = 36 in (91.5 cm), size 3 = 39 in (99 cm), actual measurements.

ABBREVIATIONS See page 16. *Colours:* HP = Heather Purple, GL = Grey Lovat, TB = Tweed Brown.

NOTES FOR KNITTERS See page 13.

SPECIAL INSTRUCTIONS FOR THIS DESIGN This waistcoat has been designed to be very short at the back, and is meant to sit above the back waist like a bolero. Knitted to correct tension, the back length from the centre back neck to the first row of pattern (not including neckband and bottom border) should measure approximately 16¼ in (41 cm). If you would like to increase the length, add 16 rows in the following way. Work as given for Back and Fronts, but do not begin armhole shaping until rows 109–110. Adjust all other shapings accordingly. Work to the end of chart PS1, then finish by repeating rows 55–70 of chart PS1. I do not recommend that you increase the length any further, as the waistcoast points will then sit much too low at the front. A lengthened waistcoat will require six buttons.

BACK

With 2¾ mm needles and HP yarn cast on 132(144:156) sts. Using 3 mm needles on all 1-colour rows and 3¼ mm needles on all 2-colour rows begin to work in pattern starting with **row 32** of chart PS1. Work sts 12–1 across 11(12:13) times.

Next row: work sts 1–12 across 11(12:13) times: 132(144:156) sts. Work straight in pattern until you have completed row 92 of chart PS1. *Be sure to maintain continuity of pattern for remainder of work on Back.*

Armhole Shaping

Rows 93–94: cast off 5(7:9) sts at beg of each row: 122(130:138) sts rem.

Rows 95–98: cast off 4 sts at beg of each row: 106(114:122) sts rem.

Rows 99–102: dec 1 st at both ends of each row: 98(106:114) sts rem.

Rows 103–158: work straight in pattern.

Shoulder Shaping

Rows 159–162: cast off 13(15:17) sts at beg of each row: 46 sts rem.

Row 163: cast off rem 46 sts.

RIGHT FRONT

With 2¾ mm needles and GL yarn, cast on 3 sts.

Next row: K 3 sts.

Next row: P 3 sts. Using 3 mm needles on all 1-colour rows and 3¼ mm needles on all 2-colour rows, work waistcoat point using chart PS2 for sizes 1 and 3 and chart PS3 for size 2. Begin on row 3 of chart for your size and inc 1 st at both ends of every row as shown. Work as shown until you have completed row 28 of chart for your size.

Row 29: work across 55 sts in pattern, then cast on 5(8:11) sts as shown.

Row 30: work across 60(63:66) sts in pattern.

Row 31: work across 60(63:66) sts in pattern, then cast on 6(9:12) sts as shown. There should now be 66(72:78) sts on needle.

Row 32: now change to chart PS1 and continue to work in pattern starting with row 32 of chart PS1, *in the following sequence.*

Sizes 1 and 3 only: work sts 12–1 5(6) times, then work sts 12–7: 66(78) sts.

Size 2 only: work sts 12–1 across 6 times (72 sts).

Row 33: Sizes 1 and 3 only: work sts 7–12, then work sts 1–12 5(6) times.

Size 2 only: work sts 1–12 across 6 times.

Rows 34–93: work straight in pattern. *Be sure to maintain continuity of pattern for remainder of work on Right Front.*

Armhole and Neck Shaping

Row 94: cast off 5(7:9) sts at beg of row: 61(65:69) sts rem.

Row 95: dec 1 st at beg of row (neck edge), work across in pattern: 60(64:68) sts rem.

Row 96: cast off 4 sts at beg of row, work across in pattern: 56(60:64) sts rem.

Row 97: dec 1 st at beg of row (neck edge), work across in pattern: 55(59:63) sts rem.

Row 98: cast off 4 sts at beg of row, work across in pattern: 51(55:59) sts rem.

Row 99: dec 1 st at *both* ends of row: 49(53:57) sts rem.

Row 100: dec 1 st at beg of row: 48(52:56) sts rem.

Row 101: dec 1 st at *both* ends of row: 46(50:54) sts rem.

Row 102: dec 1 st at beg of row: 45(49:53) sts rem.

Rows 103–139: keep armhole edge straight for remainder of work and dec 1 st at neck edge on row 103 and every alt row until there are 26(30:34) sts on needle. (Row 139 of chart PS1 will now have been worked.)

Rows 140–159: work straight in pattern.

Shoulder Shaping

Row 160: cast off 13(15:17) sts at beg of row, work across in pattern.

Row 161: work across in pattern.

Row 162: cast off rem 13(15:17) sts.

LEFT FRONT

Rows 1–28: work waistcoat point using chart PS4 for sizes 1 and 3 and chart PS5 for size 2.

Row 29: work in pattern without shaping.

Row 30: work across 55 sts in pattern, then cast on 5(8:11) sts as shown.

Row 31: work across 60(63:66) sts in pattern.

Row 32: work across 60(63:66) sts in pattern, then cast on 6(9:12) sts as shown. There should now be 66(72:78) sts on needle.

Row 33: now change to chart PS1 and continue to work in pattern starting with row 33 of chart PS1, *in the following sequence.*

Sizes 1 and 3 only: work sts 1–12 5(6) times, then work sts 1–6: 66(78) sts.

Size 2 only: work sts 1–12 6 times (72 sts).

Row 34: Sizes 1 and 3 only: work sts 6–1, then work sts 12–1 5(6) times.

Size 2 only: work sts 12–1 6 times.

Be sure to maintain continuity of pattern for remainder of work on Left Front. Now work as for Right Front, reversing all shapings and ending by casting off rem 13(15:17) sts on row 161.

ARMBANDS

Gently press all pieces with a warm iron and damp cloth. Join shoulder seams. With 2¾ mm needles, TB yarn and right side of work facing, pick up and K 138(142:146) sts around armhole edge.

Row 1: P all sts.
Rows 2–4: K all sts.
Row 5: P all sts.
Row 6: K all sts.
Row 7: P all sts.
Row 8: K across, inc 20 sts evenly over the row.
Row 9: P all sts.
Cast off neatly. Repeat for other side.

LEFT BORDER AND NECKBAND

Join side seams. With 2¾ mm needles and TB yarn, cast on 11 sts.

Row 1: sl.1 K1 * P1 K1, rep from * to last st, K1.

Row 2: sl.1 * P1 K1, rep from * to end.

Repeat rows 1 and 2 until border when slightly stretched fits along lower edge from left side seam to base of point, ending with a row 1. *Shape point as follows:*

1st row: rib 2, turn.
2nd row: sl.1 K1.
3rd row: rib 4, turn.
4th row: sl.1, rib to end.
5th row: rib 6, turn.
6th row: sl.1, rib to end.
7th row: rib 8, turn.
8th row: sl.1, rib to end.
9th row: rib 10, turn.
10th row: sl.1, rib to end.

Now continue in rib on all sts until border when slightly stretched fits from left side seam, along front lower point, up front edge and round to centre back of neck. Cast off in rib. Sew border into place. Mark position for 5 buttons; bottom button just above pattern row 28, top button just below pattern row 95, remaining buttons spaced evenly between.

RIGHT BORDER AND NECKBAND

Work as for Left Border, repeating rows 1 and 2 until border when slightly stretched fits from left side seam along lower back edge to base of point ending with a row 2. Shape point as given for Left Border. Continue in rib, working buttonholes opposite button markers as follows.

1st row: rib 4, cast off 3 sts, rib to end.
2nd row: rib across, casting on 3 sts above those cast off on 1st row. Complete as for Left Border.

TO MAKE UP

Sew Right Border into place, joining borders at back of neck and at left side seam. Sew on buttons opposite buttonholes. Finish by turning armbands through and sewing them down along inside edges of Back and Fronts.

24
Lucrezia

THE COURTLY CLOTHES of Baroque Europe were among the most splendid the world has ever seen – glorious creations in richly-coloured silks, satins and brocades shot through with threads of silver and gold. Meticulous attention was paid to every aspect of the toilette, and as fine hands were considered a mark of distinction, magnificent gloves were indispensable accessories for courtiers of both sexes. Some of the loveliest gloves were knitted in intricate patterns with fine coloured silks, and the motifs used in *Lucrezia* are from a rare and priceless example in the Robert Spence Collection of gloves, the property of the Worshipful Company of Glovers of London, held in the reserve collection of the Museum of London. Dating from the early eighteenth century and probably of Italian origin, this man's glove is worked in fine silk on the tiny scale of 32 stitches and 36 rows to the inch. Beautifully shaped with a flaring gauntlet cuff and lined throughout in cream silk, the glove bears a design of stylized flowers, leaves, tiny birds and animals in colours on a cream ground, using two and sometimes three colours of yarn on every row. The flowers have an almost tropical opulence, and each of the fingers carries a different bloom on a long blue or green stem, bounded above and below by a band of geometric pattern. Four of these bands have been incorporated into this design, along with three of the finger flowers, the shorter flower that decorates the thumb and the vertical lines of rosettes that were used for shaping the fingers. Worked here in pure Shetland wool, *Lucrezia* preserves the colouring of the original as far as possible, and conveys something of the style of those sumptuous times when the art of Western colour knitting reached its height.

Chart L-1, rows 9-76.

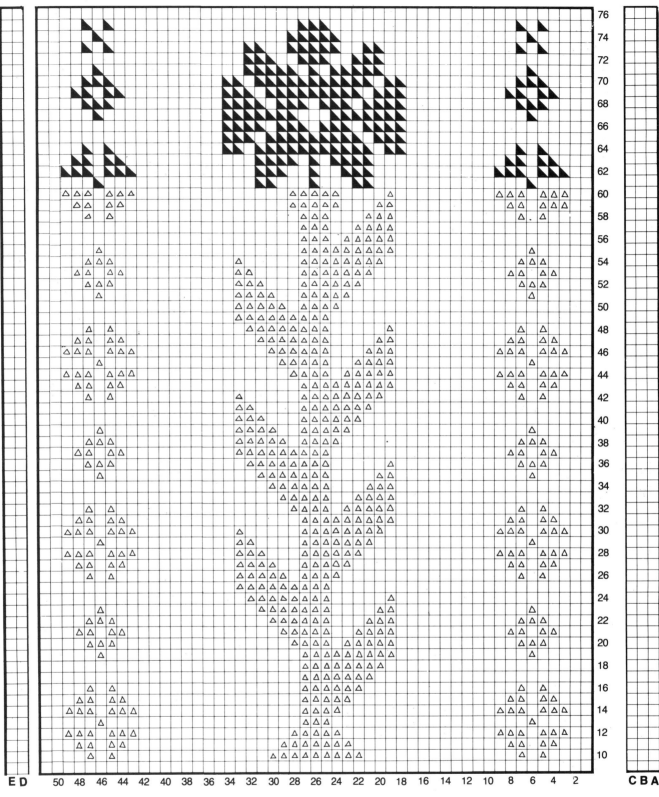

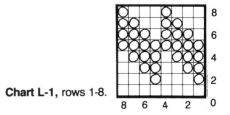

Chart L-1, rows 1-8.

Chart L-1, rows 150-159.

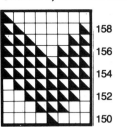

Chart L-1, rows 77-87.

Chart L-1, rows 88-149.

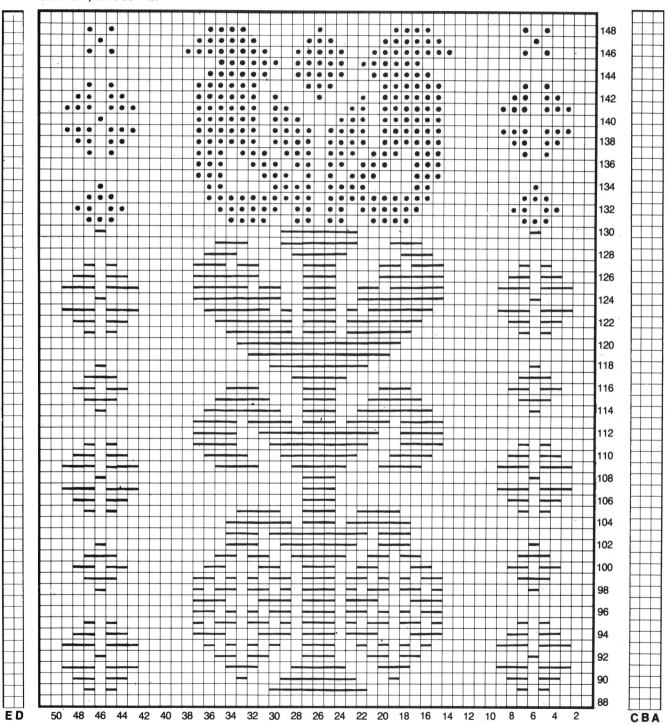

**Lucrezia Coat
Colour Key**

☐ = Light Natural

△ = Sapphire Blue

◯ = Flamingo.

⊙ = Carmine Red

▭ = Lovat Green

◉ = Rose Pink

◣ = Watermelon Red

Note: sts A-C and D-E are **only** worked on the Back, and only between rows 9-76, 88-149, 160-222 and 236-284.

Chart L-1, rows 223-235.

Chart L-1, rows 160-222.

ED   50 48 46 44 42 40 38 36 34 32 30 28 26 24 22 20 18 16 14 12 10 8   6   4   2   CBA

156

Chart L-2 (Back only), rows 236-284, sts E-92.

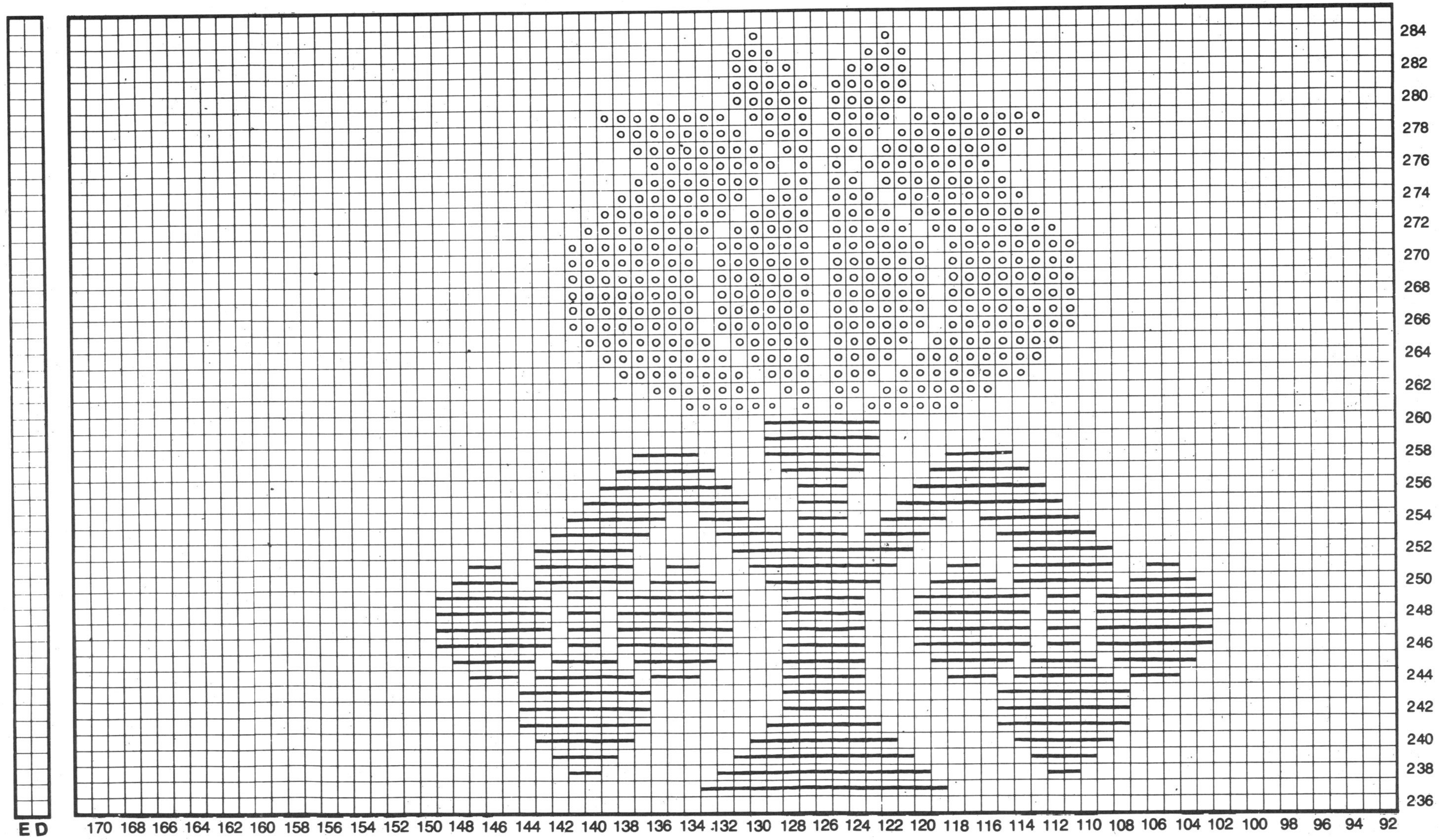

Chart L-2 (Back only) rows 236-284, sts 91-A.

Work sts 4-20 as for sts 1-3

158

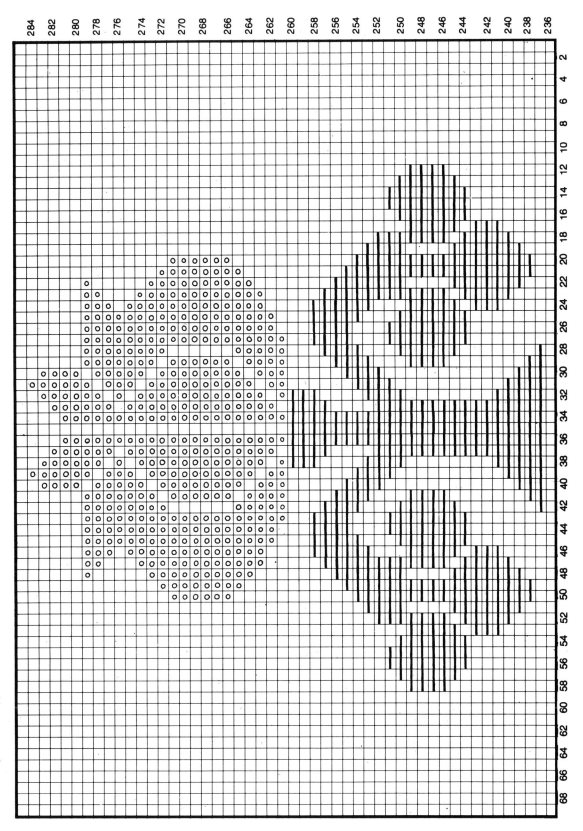

Chart L-3 (Fronts only), rows 236-284.

159

LUCREZIA COAT

YARN COLOURS AND NUMBERS	QUANTITIES REQUIRED IN OUNCES (1 oz = 28.3 g)
Light Natural 202	14
Sapphire Blue F C 48	7
Flamingo F C 7	2
Carmine Red 72	5
Lovat Green 29	2
Rose Pink F C 22	1
Watermelon Red F C 33	2

NEEDLES One pair each size 2¾ mm (No. 12 British, No. 1 American), 3 mm (No. 11 British, No. 2 American) and 3¼ mm (No. 10 British, No. 3 American) needles.

TENSION 15 sts and 15.3 rows to 2 in (5 cm) on 3¼ mm needles over Fair Isle pattern. 8 sts and 11 rows to 1 in (2.5 cm) on 2¾ mm needles for front edgings. Change needle size if necessary to obtain correct tension.

SIZE 1 size. To fit bust sizes 34–42 in (86.5–106.5 cm). Back length: 39 in (99 cm) measured laid flat. Width all round 47 in (119 cm).

ABBREVIATIONS See page 16. *Colours:* N = Light Natural, C = Carmine Red, B = Sapphire Blue.

NOTES FOR KNITTERS See page 13.

BACK

With 2¾ mm needles and N yarn, cast on 176 sts. K1 row, working into the backs of the sts to give a neat edge. Continue in st.st for 2 in (5 cm), ending with a K row.

Next row: K1 row (this forms the division for the hem). Now change to 3¼ mm needles and proceed to work in st.st and pattern from chart L1, starting with row 1 as follows.

Row 1: K sts 1–8 across, 22 repeats in all (176 sts).

Row 2: P sts 8–1 across, 22 repeats in all. Continue in this way until you have completed row 8.

Row 9: work sts A–C. Then work sts 1–11 once. Now work sts 12–51 across, 4 repeats in all. Complete row by working sts D–E (176 sts).

Row 10: work sts E–D, then work sts 51–12 across 4 repeats in all, then work sts 11–1 once, then complete row by working sts C–A.

Work until you have completed row 76. Continue to work in pattern in this way: work **rows 77–87, 150–159** and **223–235** as for rows 1–8, and **rows 88–149** and **160–222** as for rows 9–76. Proceed in pattern until you have completed row 235 of chart L1, then work rows **236–284** from chart L2.

Row 285: change to 3 mm needles and N yarn and plain st.st for remainder of work, starting with this K row.

Row 286: P across.

Neck shaping

Row 287: work 75 sts, cast off next 26 sts, work remaining 75 sts. Leaving first group of sts on a stitch holder, work on last group of sts as follows: work in st.st for another 12 rows, dec 1 st at neck edge on next and every other row.

Row 299: cast off remaining 69 sts. Work other side to match.

FRONTS

Left Front

With 2¾ mm needles and N Yarn, cast on 69 sts and work hem as for Back. Change to size 3¼ mm needles and begin to work in pattern from chart L-1 starting with row 1 as follows.

Rows 1–8: work all K rows as follows. K sts 4–8, then repeat sts 1–8 across 8 times in all. Work all P rows as follows: P sts 8–1 across 8 repeats in all, complete row by working sts 8–4 (69 sts).

Row 9: work sts 12–40, then work sts 1–11, complete row by working sts 12 –40 again (69 sts).

Row 10: work sts 40–12, then sts 11–1, complete row by working sts 40–12 again. Continue in this way until you have worked row 76.

Then continue to work in pattern as follows: work **rows 77–87, 150–159** and **223–235** as for rows 1–8. Work **rows 88–149** and **160–222** as for rows 9–76. Proceed in pattern until you have completed row 235 of chart L1.

Work **rows 236–284** from chart L3.

Row 285: change to 3 mm needles and N yarn and plain st.st for remainder of work, starting with this K row.

Rows 286–303: work in plain st.st in N.

Row 304: cast off.

Right Front

Work hem as for Left Front.

Rows 1–8, 77–87, 150–159 and **223–235:** work all K rows as follows: K sts 1–8 across 8 times, complete row by working sts 1–5. Work all P rows as follows: P sts 5–1, then repeat sts 8–1 across 8 times (69 sts).

Rows 9–76, 88–149 and **160–222** are worked as for Left Front. Work **rows 236–284** from chart L3.

Row 285: change to 3 mm needles and N yarn and plain st.st and complete as for Left Front.

SLEEVES

With 2¾ mm needles and C yarn, cast on 64 sts and work in K1P1 rib as follows: 12 rows in C, 12 rows in B. Change to 3 mm needles and plain st.st and in B yarn work as follows:

Row 1: * K twice into next st, K3, rep from * to end of row (80 sts).

Row 2: P across.

Repeat rows 1 and 2 twice more (125 sts).

Row 7: * K twice into next st, K4, rep from * to end of row (150 sts).

Row 8: P across.

Row 9: * K twice into next st, K2, rep from * to end of row (200 sts).

Change to 3¼ mm needles and N and C yarn, and begin to work in pattern from chart L1, starting with row 131 as follows:

Row 131: work sts 1–40 across, 5 repeats in all (200 sts).

Row 132: work sts 40–1 across, 5 repeats in all. Continue in this way until you have completed row 149 of chart L1.

Row 150: work sts 8–1 across 25 repeats in all (200 sts).

Row 151: work sts 1–8 across, 25 repeats in all. Continue in this way until you have worked **row 159.**

Work **rows 160–222** as for rows 141–149. Work **rows 223–235** as for rows 150–159.

Row 236: work in N.

Row 237: cast off in N.

Work second sleeve to match.

FRONT EDGINGS

With 2¾ mm needles and B yarn, cast on 43 sts and work as follows:

Row 1: K21 P1 K21 (the odd st in the middle marks the fold).

Row 2: P21 K1 P21.

Repeat rows 1–2, working 16 rows in B, then 16 rows in C, until the band, when slightly stretched, measures the same as the front edge. Work another 2½ in (6.5 cm) in colour sequence, then cast off. Work another band to match. Take 18 strands of yarn, each 16 in (41 cm) long, either using C or B or a mixture of colours. Divide into sections of 6 strands and plait to within 2 in (5 cm) of the end. Make a knot and trim the end to neaten. Make a second plait to match.

TO MAKE UP

Lightly press all pieces with a damp cloth and a warm iron. Join shoulder seams. Sew in sleeves. Join underarm and side seams. Press hems in half and slip stitch up. Press edgings in half, join the two pieces together, place this seam level with centre back, pin long edges down fronts, easing to fit, then slip stitch into place. Attach ties 20 in (51 cm) from hem, at the inside of the front bands where the edging seam is. This coat should be stored flat, and should not be kept on a clothes hanger.

25
Chivalry

THE COMBINATION of flowers and geometric bands was what I liked most about *Lucrezia*, and when I finished the coat I decided to do another design along the same lines, but on a smaller scale. Zigzags are the nicest geometric patterns to work with because they have two very useful properties – the natural undulation of the bands balances the lines of straight-across patterns and, when zigzag bands are staggered as they are here, they make a natural frame for the motifs placed between the zigzag rows. After the lush foliage of *Lucrezia*, I used very simple stylized leaves to throw attention on to the flowers themselves, which are taken from Italian brocades. Since most of the colours in *Lucrezia* are light ones, I decided to go towards the other end of the spectrum and, using the Sapphire Blue as a starting point, chose the rich, deep colours you see in bunches of anemones. Despite the pale background, the result is what I would call a dark sweater, one that seems to me ideally suited to brunettes.

Note that this design increases to the widest point of the sleeves before the working in pattern begins, so all you have to do is work straight until you begin to decrease for the sleeve head. If you are one of the many knitters who find increasing in pattern at the beginning of sleeves tedious and loathsome, you might like to adapt this method for other sweaters in the collection.

CHIVALRY

Chart CV1
Rows 1–172

Colour Key

☐ = Light Natural

◩ = Fuchsia Pink

▲ = Crimson

⊡ = Viridian Green

⊙ = Purple

V = Bright Mauve

△ = Lovat Green

⊠ = Sapphire Blue

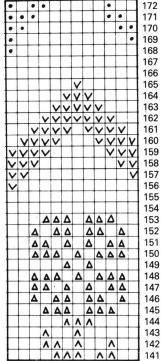

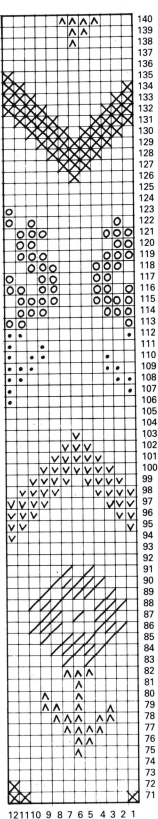

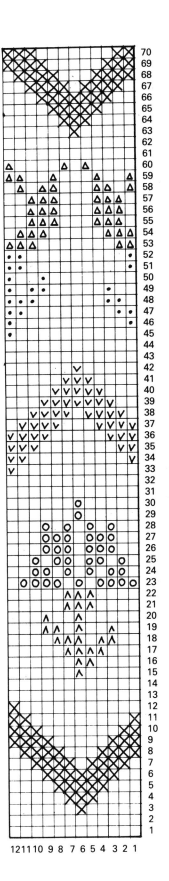

CHIVALRY SWEATER

YARN COLOURS AND NUMBERS	QUANTITIES REQUIRED IN OUNCES (1 oz = 28.3 g)			
	Size 1	Size 2	Size 3	Size 4
Fuchsia Pink 52	1	1	1	1
Purple 20	1	1	2	2
Crimson 55	1	1	1	1
Lovat Green 29	1	1	1	2
Viridian Green 65	1	1	1	2
Sapphire Blue FC 48	1	1	1	1
Bright Mauve 44	1	1	1	1
Light Natural 202	6	7	8	8

NEEDLES One pair each size 2¾ mm (No. 12 British, No. 1 American), 3 mm (No. 11 British, No. 2 American) and 3¼ mm (No. 10 British, No. 3 American) needles, and two stitch holders.

TENSION 16 sts and 16 rows to 2 in (5 cm) on 3¼ mm needles over Fair Isle pattern. For K2P2 ribbing: 9 sts and 9 rows to 1 in (2.5 cm) on 2¾ mm needles. Change needle size if necessary to obtain correct tension.

SIZES 4 sizes. Size 1 = 33 in (84 cm), size 2 = 36 in (91.5 cm), size 3 = 39 in (99 cm), size 4 = 42 in (106.5 cm), actual measurements.

ABBREVIATIONS See page 16. *Colours:* SB = Sapphire Blue, PU = Purple, LN = Light Natural, BM = Bright Mauve.

NOTES FOR KNITTERS See page 13.

CHIVALRY

Chart CV2
Sleeves Only

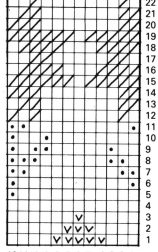

BACK

With 2¾ mm needles and SB yarn, cast on 120(132:140:152) sts and work 2 rows in K2P2 rib.

Rows 3–4: rib in PU.
Rows 5–6: rib in BM.
Rows 7–8: rib in SB.
Rows 9–10: rib in PU.
Rows 11–12: rib in BM.
Rows 13–14: rib in SB.
Rows 15–16: rib in PU.
Next row: (increase row) change to LN yarn and K across, inc 12(12:16:16) sts evenly over the row: 132(144:156:168) sts.
Next row: P across in LN.

Using 3 mm needles on all 1-colour rows and 3¼ mm needles on all 2-colour rows, begin to work in pattern starting with **row 3** of chart CV1. On K rows work sts 1–12 across 11(12:13:14) times, on P rows work sts 12–1 across 11(12:13:14) times. Work straight in pattern until you have completed row 98 of chart CV1. *Be sure to maintain continuity of pattern for remainder of work on Back.*

Armhole Shaping

Rows 99–100: cast off 5(7:9:11) sts at beg of each row: 122(130:138:146) sts rem.
Rows 101–114: dec 1 st at beg of each row: 108(116:124:132) sts rem.
Rows 115–118: work in pattern without shaping.
Rows 119–120: dec 1 st at beg of each row: 106(114:122:130) sts rem.
Rows 121–124: work in pattern without shaping.
Rows 125–126: dec 1 st at beg of each row: 104(112:120:128) sts rem.
Rows 127–138: work in pattern without shaping.
Rows 139–140: inc into first st of each row: 106(114:122:130) sts.
Rows 141–148: work in pattern without shaping.
Rows 149–150: inc into first st of each row: 108(116:124:132) sts.
Rows 151–158: work in pattern without shaping.
Rows 159–160: inc into first st of each row: 110(118:126:134) sts.
Rows 161–162: work in pattern without shaping.

Shoulder Shaping

Rows 163–170: cast off 5(6:7:8) sts at beg of each row: 70 sts rem.
Rows 171–172: cast off 5 sts at beg of each row: 60 sts rem.

Back Neck

Change to 2¾ mm needles and SB yarn and work in K2P2 rib for 2 rows.
Rows 3–4: rib in PU.
Rows 5–6: rib in BM.
Rows 7–8: rib in SB.
Rows 9–10: rib in PU. Cast off neatly in rib.

FRONT

Work as for Back until you have completed row 142 of chart CV1: 106(114:122:130) sts rem. *Be sure to maintain continuity of pattern throughout.*

Divide for Neck

Row 143: work in pattern across 38(42:46:50) sts, turn, and leave rem 68(72:76:80) sts on spare needle or stitch holder and work on first group of sts as follows.

Left Front

Rows 144–148: dec 1 st at neck edge on every row: 33(37:41:45) sts rem.
Row 149: inc 1 st at beg of row, work across in pattern to last 2 sts, dec 1 st at neck edge: 33(37:41:45) sts.
Rows 150–156: dec 1 st at neck edge on every row: 26(30:34:38) sts rem.
Rows 157–158: work in pattern without shaping.
Row 159: inc 1 st at beg of row, work across in pattern to last 2 sts, dec 1 st at neck edge: 26(30:34:38) sts rem.
Row 160: dec 1 st at neck edge, work in pattern across row: 25(29:33:37) sts rem. Now keep neck edge straight for remainder of work.
Rows 161–162: work in pattern without shaping.

Shoulder Shaping

Row 163: cast off 5(6:7:8) sts, work in pattern to end: 20(23:26:29) sts rem.
Row 164: work in pattern without shaping.
Row 165: as row 163: 15(17:19:21) sts rem.
Row 166: work in pattern without shaping.
Row 167: as row 163: 10(11:12:13) sts rem.
Row 168: work in pattern without shaping.
Row 169: as row 163: 5 sts rem.
Row 170: work in pattern without shaping.
Row 171: cat off rem 5 sts.

Right Front

Slip 30 sts for Front Neck on to spare needle or stitch holder, then rejoin yarn to rem 38(42:46:50) sts and work in pattern across row 143. Now work as for Left Front, reversing all shapings and ending by casting off rem 5 sts on row 172.

SLEEVES

With 2¾ mm needles and SB yarn cast on 52(60:68:72) sts and work 2 rows in K2P2 rib.
Rows 3–4: rib in PU.
Rows 5–6: rib in BM.
Rows 7–8: rib in SB.
Rows 9–10: rib in PU.
Rows 11–12: rib in BM.
Row 13: (increase row) change to SB yarn and 3 mm needles and K across, inc 28(30:32:36) sts evenly over the row: 80(90:100:108) sts.
Row 14: P across in SB.
Row 15: (increase row) change to PU yarn and K across, inc 28(30:32:36) sts evenly over the row: 108(120:132:144) sts.
Row 16: P across in PU.
Using 3 mm needles on all 1-colour rows and 3¼ mm needles on all 2-colour rows begin to work in pattern starting with row 1 of chart CV2. On K rows work sts 1–12 across 9(10:11:12) times, on P rows work sts 12–1 across 9(10:11:12) times. Work straight in pattern until you have completed row 22 of chart CV2, then return to chart CV1 and continue to work straight in pattern until you have completed row 100 of chart CV1.

Shape Sleeve Head

Rows 101–104: cast off 1(3:5:7) sts at beg of each row: 104(108:112:116) sts.
Rows 105–114: cast off 2 sts at beg of each row: 84(88:92:96) sts rem.
Rows 115–116: dec 1 st at beg of each row: 82(86:90:94) sts rem.
Rows 117–118: cast off 2 sts at beg of each row: 78(82:86:90) sts rem.
Rows 119–122: dec 1 st at beg of each row: 74(78:82:86) sts rem.
Rows 123–126: cast off 2 sts at beg of each row: 66(70:74:78) sts rem.
Rows 127–128: dec 1 st at beg of each row: 64(68:72:76) sts rem.
Rows 129–142: cast off 2 sts at beg of each row: 36(40:44:48) sts rem.
Rows 143–144: cast off 5 sts at beg of each row: 26(30:34:38) sts rem.
Rows 145–147: cast off 3(4:5:6) sts at beg of each row: 17(18:19:20) sts rem.
Row 148: cast off rem sts.
Work second sleeve in the same way.

FRONT NECKBAND

With 2¾ mm needles, SB yarn and right side of work facing, pick up and K 27 sts down left side of neck, 30 sts from centre front neck and 27 sts up right side of neck (84 sts). Work 2 rows in K2P2 rib.
Rows 3–4: rib in PU.
Rows 5–6: rib in BM.
Rows 7–8: rib in SB.
Rows 9–10: rib in PU. Cast off neatly in rib.

TO MAKE UP

Gently press all pieces using a warm iron and damp cloth. Join shoulder seams including neck ribbing. Sew sleeves into place along armhole edge, then join side and sleeve seams.

26
Lantern Festival

Not all colour schemes from the orient are as subtle as that of *Chow Chow* or as elegantly simple as that of *Blue Willow*. Closely allied to the bright colours favoured in Eastern Europe and Central Asia is what might be called the festive palette of the Far East, in which intense pinks, reds and yellows – thought to be auspicious or lucky colours – predominate. The colour scheme for *Lantern Festival* was suggested by a traditional woven fabric from Korea comprised of blue, fuchsia, yellow, crimson, green, scarlet and white stripes, that looks like a silken rainbow. The fabric is used for the wide sleeves of the national dress, or *hanbo*, worn by girls and young women, the brilliance of the sleeves being heightened by long skirts in a toning colour – usually scarlet or fuchsia – the costume being completed by a luxurious silk tassel, elegantly knotted using the *maedup* technique, which is worn just below the fastening of the neck.

The pattern of straight and broken lines that come between the lanterns are figures of great antiquity and many meanings. Devised in China over three thousand years ago, they originated as simple signs used in oracular consultations and gradually evolved into a complex system in which eight sets of three broken or straight lines in different combinations – called trigrams – came to symbolize all things in heaven and earth. The trigrams appear on this design in ascending order: *Ch'ien* (the Creative), *K'un* (the Receptive), *Chên* (the Arousing), *K'an* (the Abysmal), *Kên* (Keeping Still), *Sun* (the Gentle), *Li* (the Clinging) and *Tui* (the Joyous). Each trigram is associated with particular attributes, cardinal directions, natural elements and many other things. In fortune telling, the trigrams are combined into 6-line pairs – called hexagrams – of which there are 64 different combinations. The hexagrams represent the set of all possible situations in which a person might find themselves, and over the centuries many volumes of commentaries have been written on the courses of action appropriate to each situation and its corresponding hexagram. In ascending order, the hexagrams on this design are Peace, Difficulty at the Beginning, Gradual Progress and Revolution. The hexagrams are much consulted in oriental fortune telling today, in the East through soothsayers and in the west through the use of the *I Ching* or *Book of Changes*. Whether or not you are interested in fortune telling, it is fascinating to reflect that the two simplest elements in design – straight and broken lines – could have given rise to such an intricate system of belief.

LANTERN FESTIVAL

Chart LF1
Rows 1-172

Colour Key

Ʌ = Flamingo

◣ = Fondant Pink

△ = Scarlet

V = Emerald Green

• = Bright Mauve

⊠ = Azure Blue

⧄ = Turquoise Green

◉ = Fuchsia Pink

☐ = Chinese Yellow

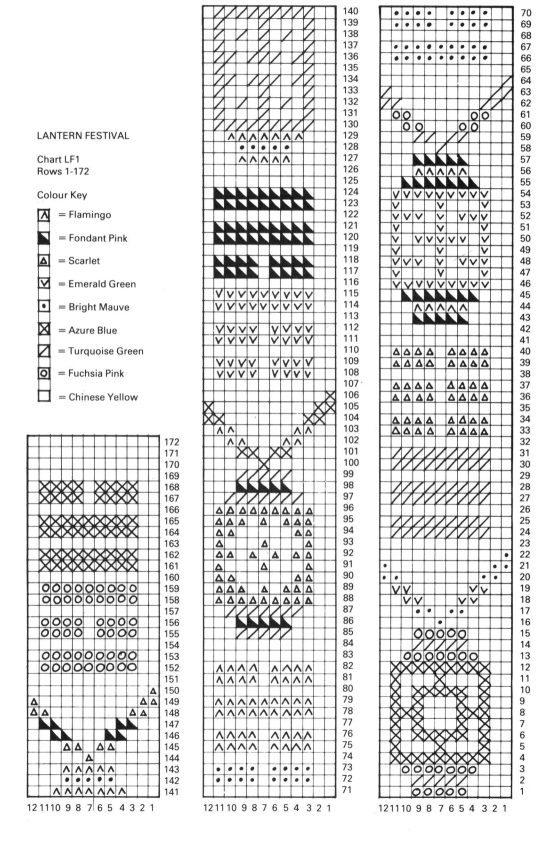

LANTERN FESTIVAL SLIPOVER

YARN COLOURS AND NUMBERS	QUANTITIES REQUIRED IN OUNCES (1 oz = 28.3 g)			
	Size 1	Size 2	Size 3	Size 4
Chinese Yellow 23	3	4	4	5
Fuchsia Pink 52	1	1	1	1
Emerald Green 79	1	1	1	2
Bright Mauve 44	1	1	1	1
Flamingo FC7	1	1	1	1
Fondant Pink 70	1	1	1	1
Azure Blue 17	1	1	1	2
Scarlet 93	1	1	1	2
Turquoise Green 71	1	1	1	1

NEEDLES One pair each size 2¾ mm (No. 12 British, No. 1 American), 3 mm (No. 11 British, No. 2 American) and 3¼ mm (No. 10 British, No. 3 American) needles, and a stitch holder.

TENSION 16 sts and 16 rows to 2 in (5 cm) on 3¼ mm needles over Fair Isle pattern. For K2P2 ribbing: 9 sts and 9 rows to 1 in (2.5 cm) on 2¾ mm needles. Change needle size if necessary to obtain correct tension.

SIZES 4 sizes. Size 1 = 33 in (84 cm), size 2 = 36 in (91.5 cm), size 3 = 39 in (99 cm), size 4 = 42 in (106.5 cm), actual measurements.

ABBREVIATIONS See page 16. *Colours:* EG = Emerald Green, SC = Scarlet, ab = Azure Blue, FP = Fuchsia Pink, CY = Chinese Yellow.

NOTES FOR KNITTERS See page 13.

BACK

With 2¾ mm needles and EG yarn, cast on 120(132:140:152) sts and work in K2P2 rib as follows.

Rows 1–2: rib in EG.

Rows 3–4: rib in SC.

Rows 5–6: rib in AB.

Rows 7–8: rib in FP.

Rows 9–10: rib in CY.

Rows 11–12: rib in EG.

Rows 13–14: rib in SC.

Rows 15–16: rib in AB.

Rows 17–18: rib in FP.

Next row: (increase row) in CY, K across, inc 12(12:16:16) sts evenly over the row: 132(144:156:168) sts.

Next row: P across in CY.

Using 3 mm needles on all 1-colour rows and 3¼ mm needles on all 2-colour rows, begin to work in pattern starting with row 1 of chart LF1. On K rows work sts 1–12 across 11(12:13:14) times, on P rows work sts 12–1 across 11(12:13:14) times. Work straight in pattern until you have completed row 90 of chart LF1. *Be sure to maintain continuity of pattern for remainder of work on Back.*

Armhole Shaping

Rows 91–92: cast off 5(7:9:11) sts at beg of each row: 122(130:138:146) sts rem.

Rows 93–96: cast off 4 sts at beg of each row: 106(114:122:130) sts rem.

Rows 97–106: dec 1 st at beg of each row for 10 rows: 96(104:112:120) sts rem.

Rows 107–162: work in pattern without shaping.

Shoulder Shaping

Rows 163–168: cast off 4(5:6:7) sts at beg of each row: 72(74:76:78) sts rem.

Rows 169–170: cast off 3(4:4:5) sts at beg of each row: 66(66:68:68) sts rem.

Rows 171–172: cast off 3(3:4:4) sts at beg of each row, work in pattern to end: 60 sts rem.

Back Neck

Change to 2¾ mm needles and work the 60 sts for Back Neck in K2P2 rib as follows.

Rows 1–2: rib in SC.

Rows 3–4: rib in AB.

Rows 5–6: rib in FP.

Rows 7–8: rib in CY. Cast off in rib in CY on the 9th row.

FRONT

Work as for Back until you have completed row 142 of chart LF1: 96(104:112:120) sts rem. *Be sure to maintain continuity of pattern throughout.*

Divide for Neck

Row 143: work in pattern across 33(37:41:45) sts, turn, leave rem 63(67:71:75) sts on a spare needle or stitch holder and work on first group of sts as follows.

Left Front

Rows 144–158: dec 1 st at neck edge on every row: 18(22:26:39) sts rem.
Rows 159–162: work in pattern without shaping.

Shoulder Shaping

Row 163: cast off 4(5:6:7) sts at beg of row: 14(17:20:23) sts rem.
Row 164: work in pattern without shaping.
Row 165: as row 163: 10(12:14:16) sts rem.
Row 166: as row 164.
Row 167: as row 163: 6(7:8:9) sts rem.
Row 168: as row 164.
Row 169: cast off 3(4:4:5) sts at beg of row: 3(3:4:4) sts rem.
Row 170: as row 164.
Row 171: cast off rem sts.

Right Front

Slip 30 sts for Front Neck on to a stitch holder. Rejoin yarn to second group of 33(37:41:45) sts and work in pattern across row 143. Now work as for Left Front, reversing all shapings and ending by casting off rem sts on row 172.

FRONT NECKBAND

With 2¾ mm needles, SC yarn and right side of work facing, pick up and K 27 sts down left side of neck, 30 sts from centre front neck and 27 sts up right side of neck: 84 sts. Work in K2P2 rib as follows.
Rows 1–2: rib in SC.
Rows 3–4: rib in AB.
Rows 5–6: rib in FP.
Rows 7–8: rib in EG.
Cast off in rib in EG on the 9th row.

ARMBANDS

Gently press all pieces with a warm iron and damp cloth. Join shoulder seams, including neck ribbing. With 2¾ mm needles, SC yarn and right side of work facing, pick up and K148(152:156:160) sts around armhole. Work 8 rows of K2P2 ribbing as given for Front Neckband. Cast off loosely in rib in EG on the 9th row. Repeat for other side.

TO MAKE UP

Join side seams.

27
Transylvania

THIS DESIGN is based on the traditional Hungarian *cifraszür* – to my mind the most flamboyantly romantic man's coat in all the world. These long, straight-cut woollen coats had been worn by Hungarian horsemen and herdsmen since medieval times, always in a distinctive fahion – draped across the shoulders, with arms *not* in the sleeves, the coat being held in place by ties across the front. Originally plain and made in grey, black or white fabric, *szür* coats were gradually embellished with decoration until, by the end of the eighteenth century, they had evolved into the magnificent mantles that were the pride of Hungarian manhood. In some parts of Hungary, embroidery was the preferred method of decoration, and coats were worked with bright roses, rosemary leaves, tulips, carnations, swirling foliage and often the Hungarian coat of arms. In other regions *appliqué* work took precedence, and the coats would be enriched with intricate panels cut from broadcloth or felt which were sewn on to the hem, the edge of the sleeves, up the fronts and on to the rectangular panel at the top of the back. Young peasant men could not marry until they possessed a *cifraszür*, noblemen wore them as a matter of national honour, many famous Hungarian highwaymen first took to the road in an effort to obtain the money to purchase these costly but most covetable of coats and *cifraszürs* even accompanied their owners to the grave, placed upon the coffin like a shield or a flag.

This coat is modelled on *cifraszürs* from Transylvania, where the finest *szür* fabric was woven and where *appliqué* work in just one colour was the favoured style, the Transylvanian *szür* being further distinguished by long triangular panels up the fronts and long edgings that curve up around the sides and back of the neck. Transylvania, you may recall, was the fifteenth-century home of the wicked Prince Vlad Dracul – the original Dracula – who inflicted terrible tortures on all those who displeased him. When I was first drawing up the chart for this design, it acquired the nickname of 'Vlad the Impaler' for reasons that should be obvious. However, with that behind me, I can assure you that working out the chart was the most difficult part, and although the pattern is intricate, this is compensated for by the fact that no shaping is required.

TRANSYLVANIA
Chart TY2

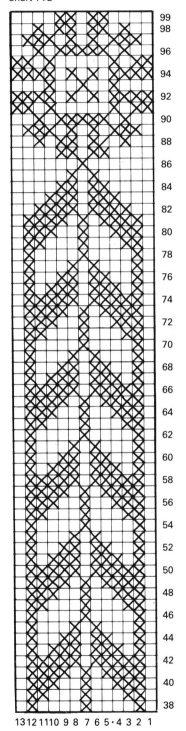

99
98
96
94
92
90
88
86
84
82
80
78
76
74
72
70
68
66
64
62
60
58
56
54
52
50
48
46
44
42
40
38

13 12 11 10 9 8 7 6 5 · 4 3 2 1

TRANSYLVANIA

Chart TY1

Colour Key

  = Black

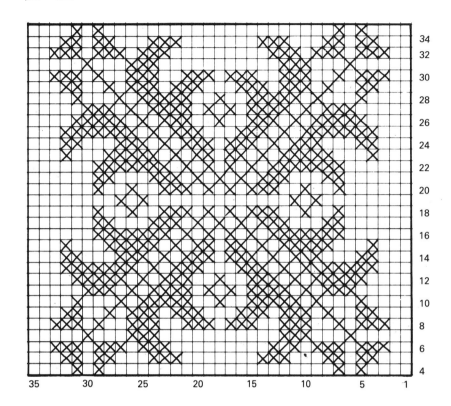 = Scarlet

34
32
30
28
26
24
22
20
18
16
14
12
10
8
6
4

35   30   25   20   15   10   5   1

175

TRANSYLVANIA
Chart TY3

TRANSYLVANIA

Chart TY4

| 50 | 45 | 40 | 35 | 30 | 25 | 20 | 15 | 10 | 5 | 1 |

197 250
195 248
193 246
191 244
189 242
187 240
185 238
183 236
181 234
179 232
177 230
175 228
173 226
171 224
169 222
167 220
165 218
163 216
161 214
159 212
157 210
155 208
153 206
151 204
149 202
147 200
145 198

| 50 | 45 | 40 | 35 | 30 | 25 | 20 | 15 | 10 | 5 | 1 |

TRANSYLVANIA

Chart TY4A

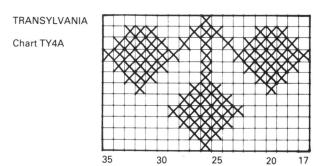

| 35 | 30 | 25 | 20 | 17 |

Chart TY4B

35   30   25   20   17

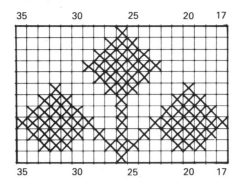

35   30   25   20   17

Chart TY5

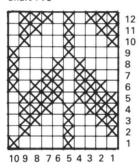

12
11
10
9
8
7
6
5
4
3
2
1

10 9 8 7 6 5 4 3 2 1

Chart TY6

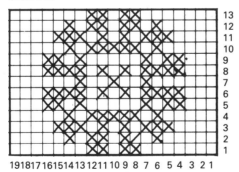

13
12
11
10
9
8
7
6
5
4
3
2
1

19 18 17 16 15 14 13 12 11 10 9 8 7 6 5 4 3 2 1

TRANSYLVANIA
Chart TY7
Right Front
Rows 1-135

135
130
125
120
115
110
105
101
95
90
85
80
75
70
65
60
55
50
45
40
35
30
25
20
15
10
5
1

TRANSYLVANIA
Chart TY8
Left Front
Rows 136-270

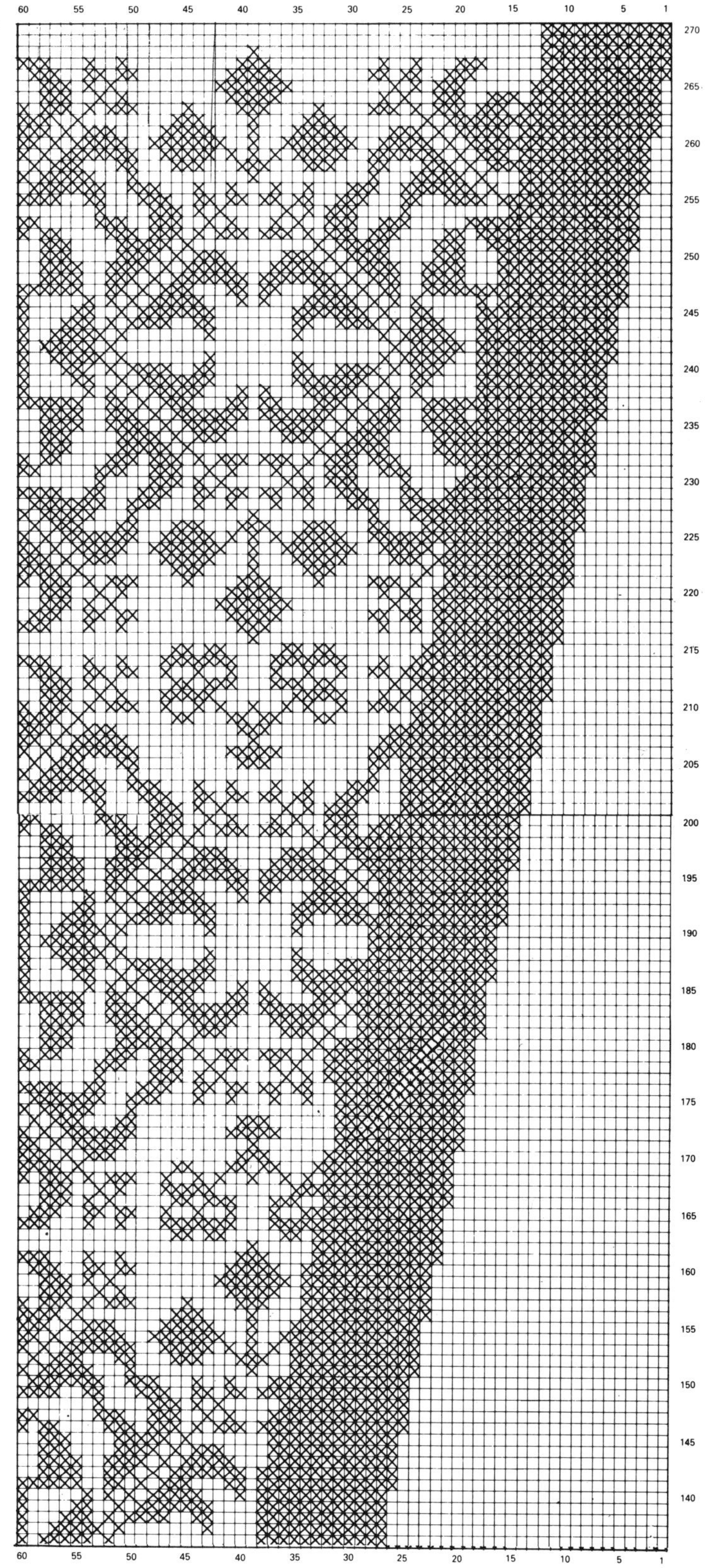

TRANSYLVANIA COAT

YARN COLOURS AND NUMBERS	QUANTITIES REQUIRED IN OUNCES (1 oz = 28 g)
Scarlet 93	10
Charcoal Black 81	12

NEEDLES One pair each size 2¾ mm (No. 12 British, No. 1 American), 3 mm (No. 11 British, No. 2 American) and 3¼ mm (No. 10 British, No. 3 American) needles and a stitch holder.

TENSION 16 sts and 18 rows to 2 in (5 cm) on 3¼ mm needles over Fair Isle pattern. 8 sts and 11 rows to 1 in (2.5 cm) on 2¾ mm needles for front edgings. Change needle size if necessary to obtain correct tension.

SIZES one size, to fit bust measurement 34–42 in (86.5–106.5 cm). Back length: 28 in (71 cm). Width all round 44 in (112 cm).

ABBREVIATIONS See page 16. *Colours:* SC = Scarlet, CB = Charcoal Black.

NOTES FOR KNITTERS See page 13.

SPECIAL INSTRUCTIONS FOR THIS DESIGN When working the triangular panels on the Fronts, carry the scarlet yarn to the end of each row; do not carry it up the back of the work. On the Back, carry the CB yarn to the end of the row between rows 145–250.

BACK

With 2¾ mm needles and CB yarn, cast on 176 sts and K1 row, working into the backs of the sts to give a neat edge. Continue in stocking stitch for 2 in (5 cm), ending with a P row.

Next row: P1 row (this forms the division for hem). Change to 3 mm needles and SC yarn and work as follows.

Rows 1–2: work in SC.

Row 3: work in CB.

Row 4: change to 3¼ mm needles and begin to work in pattern from chart TY1, starting with row 4 of chart. Work sts 35–1 across 5 times, then P 1 st in CB (176 sts).

Row 5: K1 st in CB, then work sts 1–35 of chart TY1 across 5 times. Work in pattern until you have completed row 34 of chart TY1.

Row 35: change to 3 mm needles and K 1 row in CB.

Rows 36–37: work in SC.

Row 38: change to 3¼ mm needles, join in CB yarn, and begin to work in pattern as follows. Work 11 sts in CB. Work sts 13–1 of chart TY2. Work 39 sts in CB. Work sts 49–1 of chart TY3. Work 39 sts in CB. Work sts 13–1 of chart TY2 again. Work 12 sts in CB (176 sts).

Row 39: work 12 sts in CB. Work sts 1–13 of chart TY2. Work 39 sts in CB. Work sts 1–49 of chart TY3. Work 39 sts in CB. Work sts 1–13 of chart TY2 again. Work 11 sts in CB.

Work in pattern until you have completed row 99 of charts TY2 and TY3.

Row 100: work 63 sts in CB. Work sts 49–1 of chart TY3. Work 64 sts in CB (176 sts).

Row 101: work 64 sts in CB. Work sts 1–49 of chart TY3. Work 64 sts in CB. Work in pattern until you have completed row 116 of chart TY3.

Rows 117–129: change to 3 mm needles and work 13 rows in CB.

Rows 130–143: work 14 rows in SC.

Row 144: work in CB.

Row 145: change to 3¼ mm needles, join in SC yarn, and work in pattern as follows. Work 13 sts in SC. Work sts 1–50 of chart TY4 as shown on main part of chart. Work sts 1–50 again, but for sts 17–35 of rows 145–156, substitute the pattern shown on chart TY4A. Now work sts 1–50 a third time as shown on main part of chart. Complete row by working 13 sts in SC.

Row 146: work 13 sts in SC. Work sts 50–1 of chart TY4 as shown on main part of chart. Work sts 50–1 again, but for sts 35–17 of rows 146–156 substitute the pattern shown on chart TY4A. Work sts 50–1 a third time as shown on main part of chart. Complete row by working 13 sts in SC.

Continue to work in pattern in this way, starting and ending each row with 13 sts in SC. Between rows 186–197, substitute chart TY4B for sts 35–17 on P rows and sts 17–35 on K rows in the second repeat, as given for rows 145–156 and chart TY4A.

Row 198: work 13 sts in SC. Work sts 50–36 as shown on main chart. Work sts 35–17 from chart TY4A, then work sts 16–1 from main chart. Work sts 50–1 as shown on main chart. Work sts 50–36, then sts 35–17 from chart TY4A, then sts 16–1 from main chart. Complete row by working 13 sts in SC.

Row 199: work 13 sts in SC. Work sts 1–16 as shown on main chart, work sts 17–35 from chart TY4A, then work sts 36–50 from main chart. Work sts 1–50 as shown on main chart. Work sts 1–16, work sts 17–35 from chart TY4A, then work sts 36–50 from main chart. Work 13 sts in SC.

Continue to work in pattern, beginning and ending each row with 13 sts in SC. Between rows 239–250, substitute chart TY4B for sts 17–35 on K rows and 35–17 on P rows in the first and third repeat as given for rows 198–209 and chart TY4A.

Row 251: change to 3 mm needles and work in CB.

Row 252: work in SC.

Divide for Neck

Row 253: in SC K 66 sts, cast off 44 sts, K 66 sts (176 sts). Place first group of 66 sts on a stitch holder and work on second group of 66 sts as follows.

Row 254: work sts 10–1 of chart TY5 across 6 times, then work sts 10–5 (66 sts).

Rows 255–265: maintaining continuity of pattern, dec 1 st at neck edge on row 255 and every alt row until you have completed row 265 (60 sts rem). Cast off rem 60 sts, rejoin yarn to second group of 66 sts and work to match.

FRONTS

Right Front

With 2¾ mm needles and CB yarn, cast on 60 sts and K 1 row, working into the backs of the sts to give a neat edge. Continue in stocking stitch for 2 in (5 cm), ending with a P row.

Next row: P 1 row (this forms the division for hem). Change to 3 mm needles and SC yarn and begin to work from chart TY7, starting with row 1 of chart. Work in pattern until you have completed row 270 of chart, then cast off. Work *Left Front* in the same way, using chart TY8.

SLEEVES

With 2¾ mm needles and CB yarn cast on 192 sts and K 1 row, working into the back of the sts to give a neat edge. Continue in stocking stitch for 1½ in (3.75 cm) ending with a P row.

Next row: P 1 row (this forms the division of hem). Change to 3 mm needles and SC yarn.

Rows 1–2: work in SC.

Rows 3–6: work in CB.

Rows 7–19: change to 3¼ mm needles, join in SC yarn and work in pattern as follows. On K rows work 1 st in CB, then work sts 1–19 of chart TY6 across 10 times, then work 1 st in CB (192 sts). On P rows work 1 st in CB, then work sts 19–1 of chart TY6 across 10 times, then work 1 st in CB.

Rows 20–43: change to 3 mm needles and work 24 rows in CB.

Row 44: change to 3¼ mm needles, join in SC yarn and work in pattern as follows. Work 8 sts in CB, then work sts 49–1 of row 68 of chart TY3 *but using CB for those sts marked O on the chart on all repeats.* Work 15 sts in CB. Work sts 49–1 of row 68 again. Work 15 sts in CB. Work sts 49–1 of row 68 a third time, end row by working 7 sts in CB (192 sts).

Row 45: work 7 sts in CB. Work sts 1–49 of row 69 of chart TY3, *but using CB for those sts marked O on the chart on all repeats.* Work 15 sts in CB. Work sts 1–49 of row 69 again. Work 15 sts in CB. Work sts 1–49 of row 69 a third time, end by working 8 sts in CB.

Continue to work in pattern in this way (using black for all sts marked O on row 70 of chart TY3 on all repeats) until you have completed row 116 of chart TY3 (row 92 of sleeves).

Rows 93–117: change to 3 mm needles, work 25 rows in CB.

Row 118: cast off all sts.

Work second sleeve to match.

FRONT EDGINGS

With 2¾ mm needles and SC yarn, cast on 43 sts and work as follows.

Row 1: K21, P1, K21 (the odd stitch in the middle marks the fold line).

Row 2: P21, K1, P21.

Repeat rows 1 and 2 until the band, when slightly stretched, measures the same as the front edge. Work another 2½ in (6.5 cm), then cast off. Work another band to match.

TIES

Take 12 strands of yarn, each 8 in (20.5 cm) long, in a mixture of CB and SC. Divide strands into 3 sections of 4 strands each, and plait to within 2 in (5 cm) of the end. Make a knot and trim the ends to neaten. Make a second tie in the same way.

TO MAKE UP

Gently press all pieces with a warm iron and damp cloth. Join shoulder seams. Sew in sleeves. Join underarm and side seams. Press up hems and slip stitch into place. Press edgings in half, join the two edging pieces together, place this seam level with centre back, pin long edges down fronts, easing to fit, and slip stitch into place. Attach ties to front edges 20 in (51 cm) from hem.

Shetland yarn and where to get it

All the designs in this collection are knitted in Shetland 2-ply jumper weight wool. It is recommended, but not essential, that you use the same yarn when knitting up the designs – see (13) in *Notes For Knitters* (p. 13). Several spinners do Shetland yarn, but if you want to use exactly the same yarn as I have, you can obtain it mail order. For details, 2-ply jumper weight yarn shade cards and list of current prices, write to:

Department CK
T. M. Hunter Ltd.
Sutherland Wool Mills
Brora, Scotland KW9 6NA

Caring for Shetland knitwear

Shetland knitwear should be washed by hand. Use soap flakes or a washing agent recommended for hand-washing woollies. Dissolve the soap flakes or washing agent thoroughly in hot water, then add cold water to reduce the temperature to 40°C (104° C) – just hot enough for your hands. There must be sufficient water to cover the sweater completely. *Never* use a bleaching agent. Allow the washing agent to remove the dirt – *do not rub* the sweater as this will damage the fibres. Gently ease the sweater in the washing liquid – do not lift it in and out or pull it about roughly as this may cause stretching. Lift the sweater from the washing water carefully, and squeeze it *gently* to remove as much moisture as possible. Rinse in at least three different lots of clean warm water until the rinsing water is clear. On removing the sweater from the final rise, squeeze it gently – *never* wring it – and roll in a clean dry white towel. This should remove most of the moisture. Do *not* spin dry. Lay the sweater out flat on a clean towel and carefully ease it into the correct shape. In this flat position, the final drying must be carried out slowly in an airing cupboard or warm room, or outside in the shade. Do not dry in direct sunlight, or in front of a fire of any type. Do not hang knitwear on a line to dry. Press under a damp cloth with a medium iron (180°C). Frequent washing is recommended; never allow your sweater to become too soiled.

On going into business

I often receive letters from people wanting to know how to start out in the handknitting business, and when I do I always think of Noel Coward's song *Don't Put Your Daughter On the Stage Mrs Worthington*, particularly the refrain:

Don't put your daughter on the stage, Mrs Worthington
Don't put your daughter on the stage,
The profession is overcrowded
And the struggle's pretty tough
And admitting the fact
She's burning to act,
That isn't quite enough

© 1935 Chappell & Co. Ltd.

However, the Master's sage advice never stopped a born actor or actress from flinging themselves at the footlights, nor is mine going to dissuade anyone who really wants to from having a crack at fashion. Just consider these points before you take the plunge.

(1) Remember, fashion is a *business*. Do not even *think* of venturing into commerce without arming yourself in advance with every piece of business advice and aid you can possibly acquire.

(2) Do not underprice yourself. When selling your first designs, the temptation is to make them as inexpensive – and therefore as attractive – as possible. Unfortunately, this usually results in your selling your work at cost-price or less – meaning that the more you sell, the less you earn. When costing a design, add up the cost of all materials, your design and administration time (*don't* throw these in for free), telephone and postage, the cost of having the designs knitted up, cost if any for advertising or publicity – then double it at a minimum, and triple it if you can.

(3) Learn to pace yourself. Lots of fledgling designers begin with heaps of good ideas, launch them – then find their inspiration drying up as commercial pressures take their toll. Every designer has a duff season occasionally, but if you are just starting out, your first bad season can all too easily be your last. Try to work up a few fall-back designs to hold in reserve should you need them; if you have eight good designs, float four for the first collection, four for the second. Even if you don't dry up, remember that the fashion press and buyers have an insatiable appetite for *new* things. However good it is, if they've seen a design before, they won't be too keen to take it up after it's been out awhile.

(4) Publicity matters. The fact that your designs might be the best in the world is no good to you unless the world knows about them. Don't wait for publicity to come to you – go out and seek it. You can't afford to be shy.

(5) Choose your suppliers and outlets carefully. Only work with reliable suppliers and shops who have a proven track record.

(6) When ordering supplies, buy less rather than more. Do not be tempted to overbuy yarn just because the bulk rate is cheaper per ounce than the smaller quantities. In the beginning, it is always safer to go for smaller amounts at the higher price – it works out much cheaper in the end than buying vast amounts that you don't use, and then can't return. The designer equivalent of an albatross around the neck is 100 pounds of unwanted Mouse Brown yarn languishing in the living room.

(7) Don't give up – success is 1% inspiration and 99% tenacity.

Acknowledgments

Many people have been helpful and inspirational to me in my work as a designer. However, I would like to single out the following for an especial mention. They are my chief and best knitter, Eileen Sturgess, and Anne Frost – without whom this book would never have knitted together.

I would like to give a very special thank you to all those who have done so much to show this book in its true colours – Jonathan Root, Daniel Sandler, Simon Titterington, Anna Hickman of Simpson Piccadilly, Lilleywhite's, Charles E. Foote & Co, Adrian Mann, the Worshipful Company of Glovers and the Museum of London, the two Peters at the men's period department of Berman and Nathan, Herbert Johnson Ladies Department, Tiger Tiger, Rachel Rackow at Premier who modelled Kensington Dandy, Ali Evans at Select who modelled Harvest Home, Caroline Michel who modelled Tzigane, Freddie Baveystock who modelled Heraldry, Julia Warner, Terry Quigley, Martha Yamashiro, Ray of Travelwise, Jane Carr, Karen Bromley, Sarah Beal, Alexander Stilwell, Liz Calder, Julian Holland who designed the book, my editor David Reynolds, and my inspiring travelling companion Peter Hopkins, who has been wonderful all over the world.

Photography of Belvedere, Cottage Garden Cardigan and Sweater, Chow Chow, Kensington Dandy, Heraldry, Izmir, Parsley, Whirling Dervish, Turkish Kelim, Pennsylvania Dutch, Tzigane, Christmas Cracker, Gingham, Harvest Home, Paisley Stripe, Chivalry and Lantern Festival by **Jonathan Root**.

Hair and makeup for the same designs by **Daniel Sandler** at Lynne Franks.

Women's clothes, hats and accessories for the same designs, and for Tweedie Sweater and Cardigan, Persian Garden, Trebizond and Lucrezia from Simpson, Piccadilly.

Earrings and jewellery for Belvedere, Cottage Garden, Chow Chow, Kensington Dandy, Heraldry, Izmir, Parsley, Whirling Dervish, Turkish Kelim, Pennsylvania Dutch, Tzigane, Gingham, Harvest Home, Paisley Stripe, Chivalry and Lantern Festival by Adrian Mann.

Flowers for Harvest Home, Kensington Dandy, Cottage Garden Sweater and Chivalry by Heals.

Toy Yorkshire terrier for Cottage Garden Cardigan from Tiger Tiger, London. Boots and belt for Transylvania and shoes for Lucrezia by Charles Jourdan. Fabric poppies for Tzigane from Herbert Johnson Ladies Department. Teacup and saucer for Blue Willow by Wedgwood.

Photography of Tweedie Sweater and Cardigan, Persian Garden, Trebizond, Lucrezia and Kaori O'Connor by **Jaçek Kropinski**. Photography of Flora, Blue Willow, Sweetheart Sampler and Transylvania by **Neil Kirk**.

Jonathan Root was assisted by Simon Titterington.

Lyrics from Noel Coward's song *Mrs Worthington* reproduced by permission of the Noel Coward Estate and Chappell Music Limited.